An Economist's Miscellany

From the Groves of Academe to the
Slopes of Raisina Hill

Expanded Edition

KAUSHIK BASU

OXFORD
UNIVERSITY PRESS

OXFORD
UNIVERSITY PRESS

Oxford University Press is a department of the University of Oxford.
It furthers the University's objective of excellence in research, scholarship,
and education by publishing worldwide. Oxford is a registered trademark of
Oxford University Press in the UK and in certain other countries.

Published in India by
Oxford University Press
22 Workspace, 2nd Floor, 1/22 Asaf Ali Road, New Delhi 110 002, India

© Oxford University Press 2020

The moral rights of the author have been asserted.

First Edition published in 2011
Expanded Edition published in 2020

ISBN-13 (print edition): 978-0-19-012089-4
ISBN-10 (print edition): 0-19-012089-4

ISBN-13 (eBook): 978-0-19-099010-7
ISBN-10 (eBook): 0-19-099010-4

Typeset in Bembo Std 11/13.7
by The Graphics Solution, New Delhi 110 092
Printed in India by Replika Press Pvt. Ltd

To the memory of my mother, Usha Basu (1919–2010)

Contents

Prologue

I HAVE, OVER THE YEARS, TRIED MY hand at various kinds of writing, and this book puts a selection of these, warts and all, on display. What binds these chapters together is the fact that their writing has been a source of untrammelled joy to the author. Writing research papers can be a source of satisfaction, but of a very different kind. Often the effort has to be sustained over long stretches of time and there are dark periods of toil and disappointment. The writings collected in this book are different in the sense of the immediacy of the joy their crafting provided.

For the title of this book I have chosen a variant of the British mathematician John Edensor Littlewood's celebrated book, *A Mathematician's Miscellany*. Littlewood was a famous mathematician, among whose achievements stood out the fact that he, along with G.H. Hardy, taught mathematics to a mathematical genius—Srinivasa Ramanujam. *Miscellany*, his book of diversion from his regular work, became a celebrated monograph. Preposterous though it may seem to take cue from such a famous book, I could not think of a more appropriate title. Some of the puzzles and paradoxes that Littlewood discussed in that book became famous in their own right. I cannot claim to be presenting anything quite as profound in this book. But it is also a book of *miscellany*, for it includes a play, two translations of Bengali short stories, and the description of a board game. On the other hand, it is an *economist's* miscellany, since, for all the diversions, a majority of the essays are on or connected to the world of economics. This must suffice by way of explanation of my choice of the title.

From a life devoted to research, lecturing, and some popular journalism, on 8 December 2009, with excitement and trepidation, I joined the Indian government's Ministry of Finance as an adviser. I decided it was time to call it a day for journalism since there was a potential conflict of interest. I wrote two 'closing' columns and put that to rest. The book begins with these closing columns and the rest is, essentially, a collection of what I wrote and published before I joined the government.

Two years ago a publisher of children's books asked me to write a short essay on why I read and what I read, saying that they were asking a number of 'intellectuals' to write in order to encourage children to take up reading. I balked at the invitation since I do not belong to that category. At the same time I felt I had to write, since the cause was a worthy one. Notwithstanding the fact that I do not consider myself an intellectual at all, I thought deluding children into believing I am and inspiring them to read more would be a lie that utilitarian philosophers would approve of. So I said yes to the publisher.

The details of my reading life I gave them were however true,[1] namely, that I began reading to get the better of the nerds in my school. I was talking of the boys with thick spectacles who came first or second or third in my class in Kolkata (formerly Calcutta). I was quite bad at studies, even though I too wore spectacles and of a thickness to match the finest minds. As a consequence, there were many students ahead of me. It was to counter their showing off about world affairs, Indian history, and the names of China's top 20 Communist leaders, that I began reading. Technically, I could

---

[1] See my essay 'Why I Read, What I Read', in *Why I Love to Read*, New Delhi: Scholastic, 2009.

learn these things by asking others but then those asked would know that I did not know. Reading was the only way to appear innately knowledgeable.

It was a hopeless battle; I do not think I ever managed to get the respect of the top students, let alone master the names of China's top 20 Communist leaders. But in the process I discovered my own natural reading interests. I was never a glutton for the printed word as some intellectuals are, but soon there were authors and genres of writings that I found myself obsessed with. Conan Doyle I read all, P.G. Wodehouse I devoured; and I read Tagore, Bankim, and Sarat Chandra in Bengali. A friend of a cousin of mine told me about the writings of Bertrand Russell. This was an eye-opener for me. That even the most sacred opinions—such as those concerning religion, afterlife, and the institution of marriage—could be questioned, reasoned about, and rejected if honest reasoning led one to do so, was a revelation. My parents, while traditional, were never orthodox. If reason got in the way of some received doctrine, my parents never silenced me. I was lucky in this.

Reading would soon become essential fodder for my own interest in writing. I enjoyed reading philosophy, world politics, plays, and poetry. I certainly read more plays than I watch. Since I spend a lot of time thinking and writing, time is always in short supply, so I pick and choose a lot. Philosophy has to be deductive, poetry romantic, plays and fiction humorous, and politics intriguing, if they are to catch my attention.

All these interests are on display in this book. The essays are, with a few exceptions, short and varied. But I like to believe that at least some of them will take longer to read and absorb than may appear on a mere page count; and I hope that they will give the reader thoughts to ponder over. Harold Pinter once wrote a very short poem. It went as follows:

'I saw Len Hutton in his prime.
Another time, another time.'

No doubt somewhat concerned about its brevity, he sent it off to his friend, the playwright, Simon Gray, and phoned him after a few days to ask if he had received the poem. Much to his delight, Gray replied that he had received it, but had not finished reading it.

I hope that my short book of short chapters will give readers not just the pleasure of reading but also some grist for thought and to ponder over.

In putting this book together I have been helped by Alaka Basu, Supriyo De, and Shweta, who read through the manuscript and offered several comments. I would like to thank them for their help. As I mentioned earlier, most of the writing for this book was done before I joined the government in December 2009. Early in December 2010 my editor from Oxford University Press, Nitasha Devasar, phoned me to put gentle pressure to deliver the manuscript before the end of that month. I said yes but was worried. Though I needed only a few days to complete the manuscript, the mounting pressure of work in the Ministry of Finance, especially with the Union Budget around the corner had me worried if I would get to meet the deadline. The lucky break came on 9 December, in the form of shingles. It was painful but the few days of respite it gave me from routine office work was what I needed to complete this book.

My mother, Usha Basu, passed away on 7 October 2010, while this was a work in progress. Coincidentally, a few days before that I decided to include in this collection, a page of a diary entry that I had written on her turning 90. My mother was a great source of inspiration to me. She had an unquestioning belief in my being the force of good on earth. Since that belief would be intact no matter what I did, at one level it placed no restraints on me. But it also did. I dedicate this book to her memory.

Kaushik Basu

25 December 2010

Introduction to the Expanded Edition

My book, *An Economist's Miscellany*, was a collection of popular essays that I wrote in the nooks and crannies of my academic life, till the end of 2009. 8 December of that year marks a watershed in my professional life. That was the day I joined the Indian government as chief economic adviser and remained in that post till 2012. During those years, I wrote little beyond the memos and circulars on policy matters concerning India and most of those were without a byline. This expanded edition supplements those early writings in the first edition with essays and op-eds that I published after the nearly three years in government.

Leaving the groves of academe and research for the slopes of Raisina Hill and the world of policymaking and politics in 2009 was a transformative experience for me. Barring the two opening essays which I wrote immediately on joining the Indian government as chief economic adviser, all the other essays in the original edition of *An Economist's Miscellany* consist of my earlier writings. In my new job, I decided to stop writing for newspapers and magazines for reasons of potential conflict of interest, and that self-enforced embargo remained in place for the years that I held office in the magnificent North Block on Raisina Hill. I resumed some writing during my four years in the World Bank in Washington, D.C., but much of these were blogs on the Bank's website. I resumed regular writing for the media only after leaving the Bank in October 2016.

When the proposal came two years later from my editors at Oxford University Press (OUP) to publish an expanded edition of the earlier book, I wondered if there would be enough new material. But as I took stock of my writings over the last six years, I discovered, much to my surprise, that I had written more than I had realized. I had clearly been making up for the lost time when I served in the government. There was a lot that I could choose from for this second edition and that explains the nearly 150 new pages which this edition has.

The question that I had to ask myself was not whether there was enough material but whether there would be value added to doing a new edition. What convinced me that there may some value is the shift of focus that occurred with my experience of the real world of policymaking. This expanded edition captures, hopefully, this dual perspective of the world: one from the ivory tower of academe and the other from the policymaker's perch.

I have always had a keen interest in the world around me but in a somewhat unusual way, as an observer of everyday life. When I travel to distant lands, which I have been lucky enough to do in ample measure, my interest is not just in the museums and mausoleums but equally in observing the ebb and flow of everyday life in different societies. Crowded bazaars, ramshackle by-lanes, and conversations with ordinary people are as transfixing for me as palaces and manicured gardens. In my earlier essays, there is a lot of writing from this observer's perch.

What changed and presumably coloured my later writing is that my years of policymaking were an engagement with the world not just as an observer but as an active participant, with the idea of making a difference. I do not want to pass judgement on which one is the more noble enterprise but these two perspectives, I hope, add a dimension to the expanded edition that may be of some interest to the readers.

In a recent essay, reviewing the book, *Markets, Governance, and Institutions, in the Process of Economic Development* (2017), edited by Ajit Mishra and Tridip Ray, my former student and now a well-known social activist, Jean Drèze takes me to task about my original motivation for doing economics,[1] which has a bearing on the above paragraph.

Jean writes that some forty years ago, I said in a lecture how I do 'economic theory for its own sake, without any illusion that it helped to improve the world we live in' (p. 1). He goes on to observe, 'I have a feeling that Kaushik has changed his mind on this.... [He] ended up dabbling quite a bit in economic policy, and even holding positions that necessarily involve changing the world we live in.'

I do not recall if I said what he attributes to me but I can believe I said it because that is what I believed in. And as far as changing my mind goes, I have to disappoint Jean. I have not. Let me explain.

I am not saying whether it is good or bad but, I have to admit, when I did research on economics, I did it for its own sake. I know there are more noble economists who came to the profession to change the world for the better but I am not one of them. I found the seeming chaos of the world all around us, the puzzles of the economy, and the philosophical paradoxes they throw up for us so fascinating that I wanted to understand them, unearth their mystery, and explain them to others. It was an aesthetic pursuit, like music, art, or Euclidean geometry. I did what I did it because I could not help it. And, I have to admit, I did this 'without any illusion that it helped to improve the world we live in'. There are just two observations I would make by way of self-defence.

First, I tried to make up for this in 2009, when I was invited, quite out of the blue, by the Indian prime minister, Dr Manmohan Singh, to be chief economic adviser to his government. I recounted in my book, *An Economist in the Real World* (2015) that as I mulled over the decision to join government, I told myself that since my life

---

[1] See Jean Drèze, 'Ajit Mishra and Tridip Ray (eds): Markets, Governance, and Institutions in the Process of Economic Development', *Indian Economic Review* 53, nos 1–2 (2019): 1–4.

till then was one of pure indulgence—that in the joys of deductive reasoning and solving puzzles, if I were to take myself away from research, I would do so with only one purpose, that of serving the public good. I tried my best to live by that for the seven years in policymaking.

I was once told that most people spend 80 per cent of each day being selfish and 20 per cent on altruistic concerns. If that is so, I do not feel too bad because I have done much the same, though in a slightly different way. I spent the first 34 years of my working life being totally selfish, and the next seven years trying to be totally unselfish. That makes for roughly the same percentage.

Second, it is arguable that some of the most useful discoveries are by-products of research done as an end in itself. In other words, at least in the domain of science and ideas, to aim to do good may not be the best way to do good.

Just as this book straddles the world of enquiry and the world of decision-making, it also straddles two contrasting geographies—India and the US, the countries where I have lived the longest.

I was among very few students from India in the West, who, immediately on completing their studies abroad, chose to return to India. It is difficult to explain the choice because it was not really a conscious one. It was an instinctive decision. I never considered an alternative. I had gone to England to study, and returned after the studies were over. In retrospect I feel lucky I did this. As an economist with an interest in development, living in India was like being in a laboratory, where I could observe and analyse round the clock. It is true, I never did empirical research, the way that is defined. But I did use street corner conversations, observations in bazaars, and watching the ebb and flow of life in India to ask developmental questions which I then tried to answer. I had never studied development economics formally. It was my reading alongside the Indian experience that helped me learn the discipline.

Fortunately, I managed to publish a lot of my research during my years in India, which gave me mobility later. I also learned a lot about the eccentricities of the publishing process during my Indian years. An interesting story was my paper, 'Technological Stagnation,

Tenurial Laws and Adverse Selection,' which came out in *American Economic Review* in 1989.

Having written the paper sitting in India and unsure of where I could publish it, I thought of relatively non-competitive journals, and chose *Manchester School*, which had once published Arthur Lewis's classic paper on the dual economy but no longer had that stature. Believing it would be easy to get my paper in there, I submitted my paper to the journal. After several months I heard back from the editor, with two referee reports, both negative, one of them dismissing my paper as flawed. The editor rejected my paper.

I believe serious journals try not to be biased about what address a paper comes from, but bias does creep in. It is not deliberate but the product of the belief that what is happening in your neck of the woods is the important work. So if you are based in a top school and working on problems that your colleagues are working on, the editors assume that you are working on important problems. But if you have formulated the research question on your own and it is not an area in which the big schools are involved, the chances are that the editors and the referees will feel this is not important work. It is an unconscious bias. I consoled myself that that is what happened with my paper, but nevertheless, I felt dejected and tossed the paper and the reports into my drawer at the Delhi School of Economics, treating that as burial for good.

Several months passed and I wondered if we were right in treating the journals as rationally ranked as we do. To most people it would seem that a paper rejected by *Manchester School* would not stand a chance of making it to *American Economic Review*. It suddenly struck me this was my chance to test whether this attribution of rational decision-making on the part of journals was valid. So I pulled the paper out of the drawer and dashed it off to the *American Economic Review*. A few months later, I heard back from the journal. My paper had been accepted. The editor, Hal Varian, wrote, saying that one referee liked the paper and another asked for it to be rejected, but he had decided to overrule the later. I remain grateful to Hal for this rare case of overruling a referee, and that, too, for an unknown author, from not Boston, Cambridge, Ithaca, or the Bay area, but

Mayur Vihar, Phase I, Delhi. When sending the revised version for publication, I had to resist the urge to thank the referees of *Manchester School*, for this would never have happened but for them.

At a fundamental level, everything in life is luck, since we are products of our environment and genetic make-up, neither of which we choose. I suspect many people subliminally know this but prefer not to remind others or themselves of it because it is a useful myth, the way God, according to Voltaire, is a useful myth, judging by the quote widely attributed to him: 'There is no God, but don't tell my servants that.'

It was a series of lucky breaks that opened doors for me to read, write, lecture, and travel. This book is not one of research and analysis, but of life around these, of collateral encounters, of visiting cities and regions that in their own way had an enriching effect on me.

There are also several essays on morality because this is important to me and it is so downplayed in economics. By morality I do not mean the following of a sacred text or adherence to a religious code, but basic human values: of kindness and compassion, of integrity and humility—traits that are hardwired into most of us (though some are exceptionally skilled at suppressing them). These morals are compatible with being religious and also with atheism. A religious person's good behaviour undertaken to ensure a berth in heaven is not morality but good cost–benefit analysis. The morality I am talking about is best associated with the Enlightenment thinkers. They are essential building blocks for society's success and even survival.

It is for an interesting reason that they are neglected in mainstream economics. The discovery of the invisible hand of the market, going back to Adam Smith's work in 1776, refined later by Leon Walras in the late nineteenth century, and completed in the mid-twentieth century by Kenneth Arrow and Gerard Debreu, demonstrated that individual selfishness can, given certain attendant conditions, lead to social optimality. This was such a surprising discovery that it absorbed the attention of the profession. For some of the less thinking members of the profession, the many attendant conditions that come out so clearly from Arrow's and Debreu's work were forgotten; selfishness was treated as sufficient. In recent years, there is a growing recognition that morals play as important a role as individual drive. They are the nuts and bolts of society. Interspersed through these light essays, there are some of these serious themes woven in, in the hope of persuasion.

These essays were not meant to be deep commentaries on economics but, nevertheless, I hope that through their rendering of pure description and occasional reflection, they will help us make sense of the world and provoke some readers to think of ways to better human lives and remove some of the misery and deprivation that we see around us.

Since I wrote the original version of *An Economist's Miscellany* invoking a mathematician's idiosyncratic collection, J.E. Littlewood's *A Mathematician's Miscellany*, this may be an occasion to invoke a philosopher logician, W.V. Quine, and his eccentric collection of essays, *Quiddities: An Intermittently Philosophical Dictionary*. In the preface to this delightful book, Quine pointed out that his book has a few philosophical essays 'but lowlier themes occupy more than half the book and afforded me more than half the fun'. Something similar is true of my present book. There are several essays on economics and economic problems of our contemporary world, some on values and morals, but, I have to admit that lowlier themes occupy more than half the book, and Quine was right—writing this was a source of great joy and fun, and in publishing these essays all I can wish is that the reader gets at least some of the pleasure reading it that the writer got writing it.

Kaushik Basu
New York
20 March 2019

part one

Making Introductions

Entering North Block*

The Last Column, The First Week

THIS WAS MY FIRST WEEK IN office as Chief Economic Adviser and this will be my last column. As I enter my new life, there will clearly have to be many adjustments, and the loss of my column and the accompanying sense of wistfulness is just one.

The changes were apparent the very first day I arrived in my office in the North Block within the imposing ramparts of Lutyens' New Delhi. As I got out of my Ambassador car with my weather-beaten briefcase and cheap laptop, two persons emerged from nowhere and whisked these out of my hand. My first instinct was to run after them and recover my belongings. My usual experience, for instance, when going somewhere with my wife, is to have heavy

---

* The first section 'The Last Column, The First Week' was originally published as 'Differential Calculus', in *Hindustan Times*, 18 December 2009. The second section 'Life in the Heart of Indian Government' was originally published in *BBC News Online*, 6 January 2010.

things *given* to me, not *taken* from me. The only times I have had things taken from me have been in mugging incidents, such as the one in Venice.

Relieved of my bags, I walked jauntily into the high-ceilinged building. As I approached my office and reached out to push open the huge wooden door, my man Friday did it for me. In these five days, I have not once touched the office door when getting in. It is like those airport doors with sensors, which open up automatically when people approach them.

The hardest learning that I am expected to go through is not about these mechanical and, in some ways, trivial matters, but concerns speech. The problem stems from the fact that I speak clearly. The art of political speech is apparently to say things which sound meaningful but are impossible to pin down. No one can say that what you said is wrong because no one can say what you said.

I now realize that I had, prophetically, created a character like this in my sole literary venture—the play 'Crossings at Benaras Junction', which appeared in the *Little Magazine* in 2005.[1] There is a sham travel agency that organizes tours for foreigners. The travel guide, Lachhu, is a street-smart ignoramus. No one can ever accuse Lachhu of giving wrong information because he has mastered the art of indecipherable speech. When a group of travellers from Europe asks Lachhu about the history of Benaras, Lachhu is on the mat, but recovers quickly: 'Benaras is valdest city. ... Wayne the tame cum the river Ganga the people catlest the centium dreem. ...' The foreigners nod unsurely and Lachhu's confidence picks up: 'Gem kalidusten gest come. Ve de mandareen kartejenna ven ten lethen is Agra, Jaipur, ... and the Benaras city.'

Since I mentioned the Venice incident, let me complete the story, because it is one achievement I am proud of. Also, it illustrates the art of translating theory (in this case, game theory) into practice, something that I will have to do in my new job.

---

[1] It has been reprinted in this volume (see Chapter 10).

My wife and I had bought ice-cream from a road-side stall just outside St. Marks Square. The best time for a pickpocket to strike (I realized later) is when both hands are occupied juggling cones. And indeed, within minutes of buying ice-cream, I realized my wallet was gone. It had money, credit cards, and travel documents. Alaka wanted to rush to the nearest police station. I felt that would be useful service to Venice but of no use to us, and I was not feeling charitable. I told her that there were two possibilities. Either the thief had run into the milling crowds in the main square or was still in the small cluster of people buying ice-cream. If it was the former, the wallet was lost; if the latter, there was some hope. Just then a young couple walked away from the group licking ice-cream. There was some probability—they fitted the age profile of pick-pockets—that they could be the culprits; so we began tailing them. If they were guilty, they would soon check if we were still behind them, I reasoned to myself. Soon they paused to look into a shop window and casually turned back.

So we also turned back. I told Alaka I was now almost certain that they had taken it. Alaka did not believe me but, being intrepid in these matters, promptly walked up to them and asked if they had seen anybody fishy near the ice-cream vendor since we had lost our wallet there. To this the man turned his pocket inside out and said, 'Check my pocket if you think I have taken it.' I told Alaka, in Bengali, that that response clearly confirmed his guilt. And I got aggressive and insisted that he allow me to check his back-pack. He agreed and said that, since we were in the middle of the street, we should move to a side. As we did so, his girlfriend moved away. The readiness with which he opened his bag made me signal to Alaka not to let the girlfriend out of sight. Alaka was clearly now persuaded for she literally held the girl physically.

As the man rummaged in his bag, I threatened to call the police. The game, he realized, was up. He asked me to speak softly and called his girlfriend. The wallet emerged from her back-pack.

Late that night my wife and I walked to the same vendor to have another round of ice-cream to make sure that we did not get scarred for life with a phobia of street-corner ice-cream.

Life in the Heart of Indian Government

I T IS LESS THAN A MONTH since I relocated to Delhi to be Chief Economic Adviser to the government, in the Ministry of Finance. The offer came out of the blue and I agonized over it. As a researcher, I did economics for the love of aesthetics, not for relevance. In defence, I will simply say that that is the only way to do good research. The primary motivation that drives a researcher is a creative urge, the urge to unearth beauty and order, be it in nature, society, or the chaos of the market.

If I moved from the ivory tower to the world of policy and politics, I would not only be working in a setting totally alien to me—the daunting world of the Indian bureaucracy—but I would also have to reorient my objective, for one thing was clear to me: if I did make this major move, it would be to get something worthwhile done for society, to give my absolute best towards creating a better India.

This is an intimidating objective where failure is more likely than success. The only consolation was what a colleague at Cornell laughingly told me, 'If you fail, you can come back and write a sizzler on Indian politics and policy.' I dithered for a day or two and took the plunge.

In early December I moved to my high-ceilinged, Raj-era office in Lutyens' Delhi, the North Block. I had landed in the belly of the beast that I had studied for so long from outside through the analyst's neutral lenses.

The first week was harrowing. My in-tray reached for the ceiling till someone pointed out that on my right was an out-tray. Questions concerning the economy came at rapid fire from parliament and from policymakers. I was asked, for example, if allowing futures trading in food created inflationary pressure on the spot market price of food. This is the kind of question on which I would love to spend some months thinking and reading and then write a paper. Here I had 24 hours to respond.

For all the bewilderment of the first week, there was one pleasant surprise. I did not expect the level of professionalism and commitment to work that I encountered in my ministry. It is entirely possible that this is a recent phenomenon and special to Delhi, but the level of individual industry that I have seen in my first few weeks is entirely on a par with or even higher than the best private sector firms. In addition, the top brass combines this professionalism with an unexpected unassuming air. This augurs well for the Indian economy.

Let me clarify, I have not changed my mind about the slowness of our bureaucracy. There is enough hard data to show that we take too long to clear the permits needed to start a new business, we take too much time to close a business that has gone bankrupt, and our procedures for enforcing contracts are too cumbersome. I believe that to streamline these and make them faster will be like starting fast trains between cities, building better ports, and providing ample electricity. It can have a magical effect, energizing the entire economy of India.

What my first few weeks of the view from within has convinced me is that the problem lies with the system and not with the individuals who comprise it. It is like ace drivers caught in a traffic jam; a huge waste of a valuable resource.

We have to re-examine the structures of decision-making in our bureaucracy so that permits are given quickly for new enterprises to start and bankrupt ones to close, food grains are released promptly when prices begin to rise, justice is dispensed quickly when somebody is wronged, and visas are given (or not given) as promptly as possible.

A part of the problem arises because of flaws in the way we see the role of the state. The state has to be an enabler of enterprise, not a substitute for it. India is far too big and complex for the government to be able to directly provide food to all, education to all, and employment for all. The government should instead create an enabling atmosphere that allows ordinary individuals to provide these vital goods and services to one another. This, in turn, means that the government's default option should be to permit rather than prevent. If we manage to effect a restructuring along these lines, with so much talent in the government, this will give another boost to India's growth.

As I begin in my new job and try to do my share, I will of course miss my Cornell life. I moved to the US in 1994 with apprehension. Once I discovered the American university, I could not but appreciate its openness, its fierce regard for individual freedom and voice, and its multiculturalism. On the latter, though, India, with its pluralism, also does very well. The babble of varied accents and styles that I encounter even within the hallways of North Block is very reassuring.

POSTSCRIPT   It is time to bid adieu to my column. Let me close with a story that sums up the joys and vexations of multicultural life. A newly arrived Indian couple driving through La Jolla get into an argument about how to pronounce the name of the town. When they stop at a restaurant for lunch, the wife asks the waiter: 'My husband and I realize that neither of us knows how to pronounce the name of this place. How does one pronounce it?' The waiter, an immigrant from China, says: 'Don't worry. In my one year here I have heard many people mispronounce it. But it is easy. First you say buh, then guh, and then you say kingggg.'

two

Ambiguity, Equivocation, and Economics*

U NTIL A FEW WEEKS AGO THERE was no agreement among experts on whether or not a recession was imminent. Then last week, America's National Bureau of Economic Research— widely viewed as the final arbiter on recessions—declared that the recession is here; but, not just that, it started in December 2007. So a recession, it seems, is not only unpredictable, but also cannot always be recognized when it is there. Clearly, this is not the high point of the economics profession.

The fact that this financial crisis came upon us with so little forewarning has led to a lot of criticism of economics as a discipline. Some of the criticism is valid, but not all. First, it needs to be appreciated that in economics a prediction itself can alter the object of the prediction. Hence, for certain kinds of economic phenomena, forecasting may be a logical impossibility. Consider predicting a fall in stock prices one month in advance. If anyone can master the art of doing this, then, as soon as the person makes this forecast, people will sell their shares and prices will come down immediately. So no

* Originally published in *Outlook*, 29 December 2008.

one can have a reputation for predicting share price declines well in advance.

Second, in these troubling times, the demand is for economists who do not dillydally but make clear statements, who do not waver about the causes of the crisis but are unequivocal. This, however, is the wrong lesson.

I am currently reading Jean-Jacques Rousseau's autobiography, *Confessions*. Poor fellow. When at last, in his late forties, he makes it as a man of letters, music composer, trenchant critic of eighteenth-century European mores, and, above all, the grand philosopher, his bladder gives way. Page after page he laments about poor 'urine retention' and how he cannot accept invitations from kings and dukes for fear that he may have to run, mid-conversation, to the loo. He sees the best doctors of France and Geneva. The medical diagnoses that follow and are described in some detail remind me of the pronouncements on the current crisis by finance experts. Notwithstanding the primitive knowledge of human anatomy, Rousseau's doctors prescribed with confidence treatments that had no scientific basis.

The correct stance in such situations is to recognize that we do not understand. So for economists, now is the time to be sceptical and to question. Fortunately, scepticism is the mainspring of knowledge. It may not be entirely a coincidence that at the same time that contributions to knowledge in ancient Greece peaked, the philosophy of scepticism was also at its height. Pyrrho of Ellis (*c.* 300 BC), the 'apostle of disillusionment', lectured on the value of equivocation. Pyrrho's disciple, Timon, wrote about the essential ambiguity of nature. Later, in *c.* 200 AD, Sextus Empiricus penned a series of books challenging traditional knowledge. This is clear from the titles of his many books—*Against Dogmatists*, *Against the Physicists*, *Against the Ethicists*, *Against the Professors*. He wrote more, but you get the point.

In economics, the big open question is the connection between financial assets and the real economy. If one million rupee notes owned by a businessperson burn down, what will happen to the total amount of apples, homes, and haircuts in the economy? Not only do we not have an answer to this, we do not even have a methodology for answering this question. Till we get to grips with this, the link between financial crises and recessions will remain ambiguous.

In this age of quick claims and hasty recognitions, our urge is for quick assertions. However, 'social phenomena' are inherently ambiguous. To ignore this is to court failure.

POSTSCRIPT   Tenuous though its links may be with science and scholarship, and feeble though it may be in humour, let me end with the best account of ambiguity that I have heard. It consists of a husband's remark and how one may interpret it. After a lady was declared dead and was being carried out of the house in a coffin, the pall-bearers bumped into a wall, whereupon, they heard a groan. The coffin was promptly set down and, lo and behold, the lady had not died. She was taken out and nursed back to health. Ten years passed, and then she died. Her corpse was placed in a coffin; and, as the pall-bearers carried it out, they heard her husband's anxious voice, 'Mind the wall.'

part two

Academic Transgressions

three

Policy
Foreign and Domestic*

China's Power and Corbett's Gun

UNITED STATES PRESIDENT BARACK OBAMA'S JUST-concluded trip to China has caused much consternation among America's conservative media. They view this as capitulation on the part of the US. Whereas, in 1998, Bill Clinton in a public discussion with Jiang Zemin talked about China's poor human rights record, the Dalai Lama, and the Tiananmen Square episode, and, in 2002, George Bush also pressed China on similar issues, this visit of an American president was distinctly different. President Obama deferred indefinitely a meeting with the Dalai Lama in Washington to mollify the Chinese. In Beijing, he assured his audience that 'we recognize that Tibet is part of the People's Republic of China'

* The first section, 'China's Power and Corbett's Gun', was first published in *Hindustan Times*, 21 November 2009. The second section, 'The ABC of 123', was first published in *Hindustan Times*, 15 September 2010. The third section, 'India Globalizing', is a revised version of a lecture given at the conference on 'Managing Globalization: Lessons from China and India', Singapore, 4–6

and only then added that 'the United States supports the early resumption of dialogue between the Chinese government and the representatives of the Dalai Lama'.

Nevertheless, this did not help very much. The US did not manage to bring up matters of human rights, nor the subject of China's currency, the renminbi, being kept undervalued to promote China's exports, though both these are major concerns of the US and other industrialized nations. Unlike the Russians, who, under pressure from the US, finally made an open statement that they were willing to impose sanctions against Iran to thwart its nuclear programme, Hu Jintao made no effort to toe the American line on Iran and, in fact, stressed how China held a different view on this matter of foreign policy. Finally, almost as if to drive the point home, the very day after Obama's departure, China put Zhou Yongjun, a long-time US resident and leader of the Tiananmen Square protestors, on trial.

The simple fact of the matter is, as an article in the *New York Times* wistfully put it, 'This is no longer the United States–China relationship of old but an encounter between a weakened giant and a comer with a bit of its own swagger.'

The conservative media and numerous right-wing bloggers in the US are upset at Obama's bending over backwards to make peace with China. Their mistake is the failure to see that this has little to do with Obama. For years, in fact decades, the US has bought more goods from China than it has sold. This has led to a mounting American debt and explains China's staggering foreign exchange reserve of over $2,000 billion. To get a sense of how large this is, one simply needs to know that the second highest reserve-holder, Japan, has less than

April 2005, to celebrate the founding of the Lee Kuan Yew School of Public Policy, at the National University of Singapore. The author would like to thank Omkar Goswami and Jairam Ramesh for comments and conversation. This was originally published in David A. Kelly, Ramkishen S. Rajan, and Gillian Goh (eds), *Managing Globalization: Lessons from China and India*, Singapore: World Scientific Publishing, 2007. The fourth section, 'A Higher Opportunity', was first published as 'Economic Graffiti: A Higher Opportunity' in *Indian Express*, 15 September 2017. The fifth section, 'The Ethics of Reducing Inequality', was first published in the Project Syndicate website on 29 March 2018.

half this amount. If China off-loads a substantial amount of these dollar reserves, it can bring the dollar crashing down, with devastating consequences for the American economy. Of course, such an action will hurt China since the value of its own reserves will fall, but the hurt will be nowhere near what the US will have to contend with.

Seeing how China has taken a tough stand against the world's largest and most powerful industrial nations on matters of not just its internal economic and political policies, but foreign policy and international politics too, and got away with it, some commentators in India have lamented India's weakness and argued that India should also take a similar tough stand.

This is, however, exactly the wrong lesson to take away. China has power not because it is asserting itself but it is able to assert itself because it has power. And its power and influence have little to do with how it conducts itself today but everything to do with the slow, almost imperceptible, accumulation of economic strength achieved over several decades.

What this reminds me of is a Jim Corbett story that I read years ago. It was such a long time ago that I am not quite sure how much of it is Corbett and how much my imagination. But whatever its origins, it illustrates the point well. Jim Corbett was out in the hills of Kumaon in search of a dangerous man-eater. I do not know if Robin was with him, but he certainly had his gun, cocked in the direction from where he had heard a sound, when he suddenly realized that the tiger was glaring at him from a different direction, and dangerously close. If he tried to quickly turn his gun, the cat would jump at him before he could pull the trigger. So Corbett froze, and then began turning his gun slowly, imperceptibly so. The tiger, thinking that nothing was happening, stayed still in its crouch. After an interminable 15 minutes, Corbett's muzzle was pointing straight at the tiger and its game was up.

China perfected the art of Corbett's gun. It strengthened its economy and built up global credit with doggedness and over a long stretch of time. The process was on from the time of Nixon, through the Reagan years, Clinton, and the Bushes. The changes were so steady that the US was lulled into believing that it was living in an unchanging world. But the world did change and Obama came to power in this altered world.

I am not sure that aiming for global power is the best of ambitions, but if that be the ambition, then the right lesson is not to simply act tough and talk tough but be prepared to work hard, steadily and relentlessly, on the economy, or, in other words, to follow Corbett's manoeuvre.

The ABC of 123

HAVING SPENT MUCH TIME THE LAST few weeks studying the '123 agreement' for nuclear cooperation between India and the US, I now believe that it will be a grave mistake for India to turn down the agreement.

India's crude oil and petroleum imports guzzle up one-third of the country's entire export earnings, thereby elbowing out the purchase of many other vital products. Our coal reserves are expected to run out in a few decades. Environment-friendly energy sources, such as the sun and wind, are potentially important but we do not yet have the technology for large-scale production. Under the circumstances, it is imperative for India to plan on energy alternatives that will not destroy our environment. Nuclear energy fits that description; but our ability to produce this has been seriously hobbled since 1974, when India first tested a nuclear device and the US and other countries ceased selling us technology and fuel for nuclear power generation.

The reason why 123 is important is because it will break this impasse, allow us to produce our own energy, and free India, in the long run, from the crippling need to rely on imported oil and petroleum. On many policy matters, I find the Indian Left to be a valuable voice against the popular grain. But I am disappointed by the Left's objections to the nuclear agreement. It has raised basically two objections—that this will take away from us the right to test another nuclear weapon and it will compel India to align its foreign policy with that of the US.

There has been a lot of debate on both these counts. Some have argued that there will not be any US reprisal against India if India tests another bomb and US President Bush assured us that a section of the agreement, which talks of the need to contain Iran, is not binding but 'advisory'. These arguments have been countered by observing that the US signed the 123 agreement in its own interest (it is even named after section 123 of the US Atomic Energy Act, 1954), and that its Hyde Act ensures punitive action will be taken should India test another nuclear bomb.

These are valid observations, but they do not constitute an argument against the agreement. For that, the only relevant question is: will these matters be made worse by virtue of this agreement? And the answer is no. If India tests a nuclear weapon or takes a foreign policy line which is at variance from the American one, it is likely that there will be a negative US response. But this will be true whether or not we have the nuclear agreement. It is also likely that the US will take back the equipment and fuel that we would have received as part of this deal. But if that happens, India will simply be back to where she was without this agreement. So the agreement cannot hurt.

There are two further points to be kept in mind. The first concerns the Nuclear Suppliers Group (NSG). The NSG, consisting of 45 nations, was set up in response to India's 1974 nuclear test to prevent the export of nuclear material to nations, like India, that have not signed the Treaty on the Non-Proliferation of Nuclear Weapons (NPT). Once 123 is signed, the US will persuade these nations to remove the embargo. This will then create such huge vested trading interests for these nations that, if at a later date India's relation with the US sours, it will be unlikely that the tap can be switched off again.

Second, the apprehension that India will be pushed around shows a lack of self-confidence. This may have been true 15 years ago, but no longer. India is today a large and growing economic force in the world. We are in a position to hold our own line in foreign policy whether or not we have an agreement with the US. And for that reason, it will be foolish not to have it.

India Globalizing

WRITING IN THE *Financial Times* OF 23 February 2005, about China and India, Martin Wolf observed, 'The economic rise of Asia's giants is, therefore, the most important story of our age. It heralds the end, in the not too distant a future, of as much as five centuries of domination by the Europeans and their colonial offshoots.' Optimistic predictions about China and, more recently, India, have begun appearing with a certain regularity in the media. Ted Fishman wrote in the *New York Times Magazine* (4 July 2004: 27), 'If any country is going to supplant the U.S. in the world marketplace, China is it.' In an interview to the *IMF Survey* (21 February 2005: 40), Wanda Tseng, mission chief for India in the International Monetary Fund (IMF), said, 'India is one of the fastest growing economies in the world and is certainly looking to continue growing strongly.' Stephen Cohen in his influential book, *India: Emerging Power*, writes, 'India has long been counted among the have-nots. The situation is rapidly changing, which is what will make India such an interesting "great power" for the next dozen years.' In Standard and Poor's *CreditWeek* (5 January 2005: 12), Joydeep Mukherji characterizes China and India as 'global success stories in reducing poverty and moving towards a prosperous market economy' and notes that 'since China initiated economic reform in 1978, its national income has more than quadrupled; since India began liberalizing its economy in 1991, its per capita income has almost doubled'. In the inaugural address to this conference,[1] Mr Lee Kuan Yew, in a speech crammed with statistics and deft analysis, predicted that India will be propelled into the 'front ranks' of the global economy, and went on to say that 'China and India will shake the world. ... In some industries, [these countries] have already leapfrogged the rest of Asia.'

[1] Conference on 'Managing Globalization: Lessons from China and India', Singapore, 4–6 April 2005, to celebrate the founding of the Lee Kuan Yew School of Public Policy, at the National University of Singapore.

Several Asian economies have grown at record-breaking speeds for the last four decades, but there was no talk of a gestalt change in the world economic order, in the manner suggested by Martin Wolf or Lee Kuan Yew, as long as the two largest nations of Asia remained stagnant. But, starting with China in the early 1980s and India in the early 1990s, this seems to have changed, certainly in the perceptions of the media. There is an increasing chorus of assertions that the global order is going to alter course, with a cluster of eight or nine Asian countries taking the lead. But before we take this 'most important story of our age' as reality, we must check how well it is grounded in facts. Is it really true or one of those 'truths' created by repetition?

Irked by the tedious habit of double and treble checking facts in US journalism, the British magazine, *Private Eye*, had once asserted that it relied, instead, on the 'legendary British journalistic staple' that some facts are simply 'too good to check' (quoted from Lyall 2001). It is important for us not to fall into this staple of treating some 'facts' as too newsworthy to check. My first objective is to critically scrutinize this 'big story' of our times. The Chinese economy is by now more firmly on the path of rapid growth, and so the interesting question is about India. With India's population comprising some one-sixth of the world, this is an important question in itself, but it acquires an even greater significance because, if the Indian (or the Chinese) economy stagnates, this will in itself vastly diminish the overall prospect of Asia and, indeed, the world.

I will begin by taking a close look at India's recent performance. It will be argued—to take away any unnecessary suspense from the matter—that the optimism is justified, though in ways that may not always be right. Moreover, it needs to be tempered by an awareness of the pitfalls. Much of the talk of the rise of India refers to its geo-strategic position, its defence capability, and its recent good *economic* performance. The data that have emerged over the last few years show that it is the economy that is the dominant feature of the rise of India. This—though still precarious—has happened more rapidly and in more ways than generally appreciated.

A large part of this essay will dwell on the policy options available to India and how these choices have to be made with care if the apple cart is not to be toppled. A sustained GDP (gross domestic product) growth rate of 8 per cent is feasible for India. And, given that China has already grown by approximately 10 per cent per annum over the last two decades and shows no sign of slowing, the global economic landscape is indeed likely to change over the next three or four decades like never before.

There are of course many possible missteps. A war can put an end not just to growth but also people. Political instability can cause any of these countries to spiral downwards. And in economic life, as in life, there is always the unforeseen. A century ago, most observers were sure that Argentina would be a great economic power and many were sceptical about the US. In the early years, after World War II, the Asian economies, with the exception of Japan, were presumed to be basket cases. Korea, Singapore, Hong Kong, Taiwan, and Malaysia turned these predictions on their head. The risk cannot be discounted that the current optimistic predictions about China and India will once again be turned on their head.

We must therefore tread with caution, trying to evaluate the policy options with as much objectivity as possible. In a globalized world, many of the policy choices involve intricate inter-country coordination and so we must discuss these as well. The rapid growth of such large countries brings with it responsibilities not just within the boundary of each nation but also for the global economy and polity. And lots of open questions remain about how these responsibilities will be shouldered.

Globalization can cut two ways with countries. It will be argued here that, in the case of India, globalization has been a boon. India has made critical use of it—maybe more so than even China—to restructure its economy and leverage growth. But globalization can also cause large segments of the population to be marginalized. This is not only politically destabilizing, it is morally unacceptable. So in crafting the next generation of reforms, one has to keep in mind the importance of policies for better distribution of income and for countering some of the negative fallouts of globalization.

The Triggers

In his book on Singapore's trajectory from poverty to a developed state, Lee Kuan Yew spoke of India's unfulfilled potential. 'India is a nation of unfulfilled greatness,' he wrote (Lee 2000: 412); but he also noted that changes were afoot that could launch the economy. He wrote about when Manmohan Singh, the then finance minister, and P. Chidambaram, the commerce minister, visited Singapore in the early 1990s. 'Both ministers were clear on how to improve India's economic growth and knew what had to be done' and that 'the impetus to the Indian economy came from Manmohan Singh, [Prime Minister Narasimha Rao's] Finance Minister' (ibid.: 409).

This kind of mixed feeling about the Indian economy was pervasive in the 1990s. What happened over the last 10 or 12 years was beyond anyone's expectations and led to the dramatic optimistic turn in global opinion that I discussed in the last section. Actually, India's growth performance had improved from the late 1970s but there was no indication that this would sustain, let alone rise to the point where it raised hopes of India lifting itself out of poverty. But the growth continued and picked up steam; and from 1994 the GDP growth rate broke the 7 per cent mark for three consecutive years and over the last decade averaged over 6 per cent per annum. India's foreign exchange balance, which hovered at a precariously low level for decades, began to rise from the early 1990s. India's savings rate that had hovered around 12 per cent in the late 1960s had risen to 23 per cent by the late 1970s. But none of these much-repeated facts is reason enough to merit the optimism of India becoming a major economic power. The reasons for optimism lie in facts that exist beyond these broad aggregates.

First, not only has India's growth been very high over the last decade, more importantly, this has been the best decade in terms of two *social* indicators. It has been a decade of faster growth in literacy than witnessed in any previous decade since India's independence more than half a century ago. And this last decade is also the one in which poverty seems finally to be on the wane. This is not to gloss over the undisputed fact of worsening inequality, but I will return to this topic later.

Second, for the first time—and this has happened only in the last two or three years, and could not have been predicted even five or six years ago—Indian firms have made a small but sure-footed appearance on the global scene. The impetus for this came from many sources. Initially, there were the software companies, Infosys, Wipro, and others, which burst onto the global scene as major success stories and had a large advertisement effect for India Inc., in general.[2] These companies were known for their quality products and also for 'clean business'—two particularly scarce resources in Indian business. India's large foreign exchange reserves played a role in the internationalization of Indian companies. In the Forbes list of best under-$1 billion companies, there were 10 Indian companies in 2001, 13 in 2002, and 18 in 2003.

Third, there has been a windfall in India's outsourcing business, related, somewhat surprisingly, to the US presidential race. Early in his election campaign, candidate John Kerry had criticized US companies that outsourced back-office work to developing countries. He later back-tracked on this, realizing that it was neither good economics nor commendable ethics to propagate protectionism against poor nations. But once this subject made its appearance in the media, it refused to go away. A host of writers and commentators on US television, such as Lou Dobbs on CNN, went out of their way to vilify American companies that outsourced jobs for greed of profit.

This was a clarion call for a host of small American companies that had the greed of profit but did not know of this great opportunity. Company managers employing as few as five or six secretaries realized that, barring the two or three persons they needed on call, they could have the rest of their secretarial staff located in poor English-speaking countries and make huge profits. For the Third World, the advertisement effect of the repeat attacks on outsourcing was an unexpected boon. Since advertising on US television is so

---

[2] For accounts of what spurred this sector, see Narayana Murthy (2004), Singh (2004), and Basu (2004a).

expensive, they would never have done it on their own. Several countries have gained and India, which already had an organizational structure in place and a ready supply of English-speaking workers, has done exceedingly well. All statistical indicators show that India has had a sharp rise in outsourcing work over the last year; and, more interestingly, there is now a sudden rise in cubby-hole operations, with three or four persons sitting in a room, glued to computers, and working for American and European companies.

Fourth, and this has been barely noticed, there is new synergy between India and China. This has no doubt been aided by China's joining of the World Trade Organization (WTO) and the removal of quantity restrictions on imports; but also by the greater maturity of the Indian economy. Trade between India and China has been growing very rapidly over the last three years, the Himalayas not being as big a hindrance to modern trade as they were historically.[3] In 2003, the total trade between China and India was of the value of $7.6 billion; now, two years later, it is expected to cross $17 billion. It has been felt in India that this whopping increase is of some strategic value. Since it is in the interest of the US to maintain better economic and political balance by bolstering its trade and concomitant political ties with India and China individually, and since the ties with China are already at a high, the main focus will be on India.

Finally, these strong economic developments come with a fortuitous political change. No matter what moral position one takes on this, the fact is, with the rise of global terror, US political interests have come into alignment with India's. As Thomas Simons, ex-US Ambassador to Pakistan, had noted, the Soviets left Afghanistan in February 1989 and insurgency in Kashmir rose from the summer of that year. This was no coincidence. Some of the same fundamentalist forces that were engaging the Soviets were clearly settling into a new job.

This is today a common problem for the US and India. And, combined with the fact that India and the US share similar political systems, this makes India a natural strategic partner for the US.

---

[3] Though, even historically, Indo-Chinese interaction was greater than is popularly supposed (Sen 2004).

Moreover, especially with Condoleeza Rice as Secretary of State, the US is likely to embark on a policy of trying to use India as a balancing force against China's inevitable rise to world power, a source of considerable apprehension for the US.

The Strait of Malacca, through which more than 60,000 ships pass each year, is a vital artery for Western trade with Asia and, for that very reason, a potential flash-point in a future US–China conflict. The Indian navy has been a growing presence in the strait. This is clearly happening with US approval, since the Indian flotilla keeps an eye on terrorist activity and, at the same time, allays the risk of the region coming under exclusive Chinese control. Even for China, it is better to have a third-country presence in the South China Sea than a face off with the US, one on one.

For India to nurture these economic and political advantages will involve a pragmatic assessment of its self-interest but also, I like to believe, a commitment to certain values. It will entail cooperation with China and the US, but also the strength to retain moral independence in matters of global politics and internal economic policy. This may require giving up some short-term gains, but would command greater respect in the long run.

Unless India makes a major blunder or gets inadvertently drawn into some costly war or generates so much inequality as to cause political instability, the growth should continue. And to aim for a sustained growth rate of 8 per cent and a rapid decline in poverty is entirely within the realm of the feasible.

The Foundations

But I have moved on too fast. To understand what the major factors were behind the quickening growth rate of India and the recent changing structure of the Indian economy, it is necessary to go back a few decades. It is important also to keep in mind that the causes of as large a phenomenon as a country's overall growth will invariably be diverse. Geography, culture, leadership, and the global situation, all play their roles and the absence of one critical factor can stall an otherwise booming economy. Even so, one can try to locate the salient factors behind an economy's buoyancy. In trying to answer this, it is, however, important to determine when the growth spurt first began. In the case of India, there are two possible candidates—the late 1970s and the early 1990s.

A cursory look at growth rate data and graphs (see Table 3.1 and Figure 3.1) does not reveal very much. The reason is that India's

TABLE **3.1**   GROWTH RATE AND GROSS DOMESTIC SAVINGS
RATE IN INDIA, 1950–2001

(per cent)

	Rate of Gross Domestic Saving	Annual Growth Rate of GDP at Factor Cost		Rate of Gross Domestic Saving	Annual Growth Rate of GDP at Factor Cost
1950–1	8.9	–	1976–7	19.4	1.2
1951–2	9.3	2.3	1977–8	19.8	7.5
1952–3	8.3	2.8	1978–9	21.5	5.5
1953–4	7.9	6.1	1979–80	20.1	–5.2
1954–5	9.4	4.2	1980–1	18.9	7.2
1955–6	12.6	2.6	1981–2	18.6	6
1956–7	12.2	5.7	1982–3	18.3	3.1
1957–8	10.4	–1.2	1983–4	17.6	7.7
1958–9	9.5	7.6	1984–5	18.8	4.3
1959–60	11.2	2.2	1985–6	19.5	4.5
1960–1	11.6	7.1	1986–7	18.9	4.3
1961–2	11.7	3.1	1987–8	20.6	3.8
1962–3	12.7	2.1	1988–9	20.9	10.5
1963–4	12.3	5.1	1989–90	22	6.7
1964–5	11.9	7.6	1991–1	23.1	5.6
1965–6	14	–3.7	1991–2	22	1.3
1966–7	14	1	1992–3	21.8	5.1
1967–8	11.9	8.1	1993–4	22.5	5.9
1968–9	12.2	2.6	1994–5	24.8	7.3
1969–70	14.3	6.5	1995–6	25.1	7.3
1970–1	14.6	5	1996–7	23.2	7.8
1971–2	15.1	1	1997–8	23.5	4.8
1972–3	14.6	–0.3	1998–9	22	6.6
1973–4	16.8	4.6	1999–2000	22.3	6.4
1974–5	16	1.2	2000–1	–	5.2
1975–6	17.2	9			

Source: *Handbook of Statistics on Indian Economy,* Reserve Bank of India, 2001.

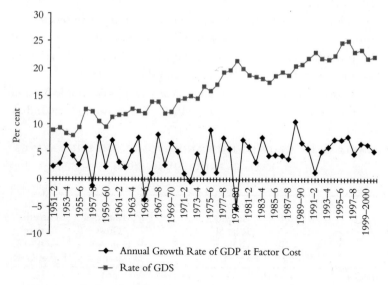

FIGURE **3.1**   GROSS DOMESTIC SAVING AND GROWTH
RATE IN INDIA, 1950–2001

Source: Table 3.1.

growth rate *peaks* have remained more or less unchanged. Careful examination of the data reveals, however, that the downturns of the economy have become less severe over the years—and that is really the crux of India's recent better performance. In fact, since 1980, independent India has not had any year with a negative growth rate, while, before that, there were four such episodes.

A clever way of seeing this is to construct a moving average. If in each year we plot the average growth rate of the previous 10 years, we get the graph shown in the *Economic Survey 2003–04* of the Ministry of Finance, reproduced as Figure 3.2. Once one does this averaging of the growth rates, the changes begin to show quite clearly. The graph begins to move up in the early 1980s. Another way of looking at this is to examine the average growth rate for each plan period—typically five years. This is shown in Table 3.2. It is immediately clear that there is a break from the late 1970s. Indian economists find it uncomfortable to talk of the emergency years, 1975–7, when Indira Gandhi took

TABLE 3.2   ANNUAL AVERAGE GROWTH RATE IN INDIA
ACROSS PLAN PERIODS

		GNP at Factor Cost, 1993–4 Prices (per cent)
First Plan	1951–6	3.7
Second Plan	1956–61	4.2
Third Plan	1961–6	2.8
Fourth Plan	1969–74	3.4
Fifth Plan	1974–9	5.0
Sixth Plan	1980–5	5.5
Seventh Plan	1985–90	5.8
Eighth Plan	1992–7	6.8
Ninth Plan	1997–2002	5.6
Average	1951–2002	4.4

Sources: *National Accounts Statistics 2001*, Ministry of Statistics, Government of India; and *Economic Survey*, 2003–04, Ministry of Finance, Government of India.

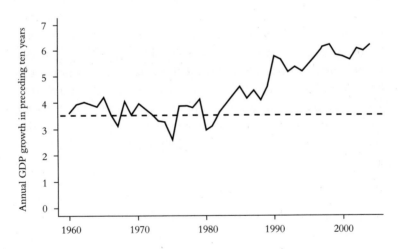

FIGURE 3.2   MOVING AVERAGE OF GROWTH RATE

Source: *Economic Survey, 2003–04,* Ministry of Finance, Government of India.

dictatorial control of the country. But there is no denying that, despite the trauma, or maybe because of it, the emergency years mark a break in India's performance. The economy grew by an astonishing 9 per cent in 1975–6[4] and the Fifth Plan, 1974–9, was the first five-year plan period during which the per capita income of the economy grew by over 5 per cent. It would never fall below that subsequently. Hence, the late 1970s break is undeniable.

The next break occurs in the early 1990s, as is evident from Figure 3.2 and Table 3.2; and there has been much discussion about which of these two was the serious break from the past, representing some underlying change rather than a temporary and superficial shift (Basu 2000, 2004a; Rodrik and Subramanian 2004). I believe that there was *some* genuine change in the late 1970s and early 1980s, but the serious take off of the Indian economy occurred in the early 1990s. A part of the higher growth in the 1980s was made possible by heavy government borrowing, a large fiscal deficit, and also a substantial international debt. The crisis in the early 1990s, while triggered by the Gulf War, was inevitable sooner or later.

Moreover, much of what was achieved in the early 1980s was an outcome of a small coterie of entrepreneurs, close to the government, breaking out of the bureaucratic stranglehold that was India. This did give a boost to growth but could be detrimental for the economy and polity in the long run with the risk of sliding into crony capitalism, a risk that is by no means zero even now. The only fundamental change in the late 1970s and the early 1980s was that India's savings and investment rates had risen over the previous decade like in no decade before that (and, for that matter, since) (see Table 3.1; also Majumdar 1997).

The sustainable change occurred—I would argue—with the reforms of the early 1990s. These were reforms that, with the removal of industrial licensing, lowering of tariff rates, and greater freedom to the state governments to pursue global investment, for the first time, attempted allowing freer competition and greater

[4] This was outperformed only once in independent India's history, in 1988–9.

play of anonymous market incentives. For a newly growing economy there is always the risk of anonymity breaking down and a few industrial houses gaining control of the market, thereby causing long-run harm to the economy. And India is in no way immune to this. But from the 1990s, there was hope of genuine competitive markets to come into play. And indeed the 1990s have seen faster growth than any previous period (Ahluwalia 2002).

The growth would have been even faster but for the slowdown after 1997. But this slowdown, it is arguable, was beyond the country's control. From July 1997, Thailand went into its biggest crisis and this spread from one country to another with alacrity, engulfing most Asian economies and subsequently carrying over to other parts of the world. India, which had very little global exposure at that time—its capital account convertibility was minimal and trade as a fraction of gross national product (GNP) was small—did not get hit directly by a flight of capital or collapse of the rupee, but nevertheless had to cope with the cooling down of the global economy. As a consequence, its growth rate fell.

With the Asian crisis behind us, India has bounced back once again, marking a (per capita income) growth rate of 8.5 per cent in 2003–4 and 6.9 per cent in 2004–5. That the changes in the 1990s are deeper is also suggested by changes in social indicators like the literacy rate and the incidence of poverty. As mentioned earlier, Indian literacy rose rapidly, from 52 per cent to 65 per cent, during 1991–2001. Poverty, as measured by the percentage of people living below the poverty line, also declined in the late 1990s. By some estimates, the decline was sufficiently large that not only did the percentage fall but the absolute number of people below the poverty line declined as well (Deaton 2001; Deaton and Drèze 2002). Even though there may be some controversy about the absolute numbers (Sen and Himanshu 2004),[5] the decline in the head-count ratio of poverty now seems certain.

[5] The controversy was caused by the decision of the National Sample Survey (NSS) of India to change the reference period of consumption for most items from 30 days to 7 days. To make this transition smooth, it was decided

If the early 1990s mark the take-off of the Indian economy, what are the main causes? I would argue that the most important causes are related to India's international sector. It was a crisis in India's international sector that started the reforms and it is the international sector that has been the engine of growth. The aggregate economy of India has benefited enormously from globalization and there is still scope for huge gains in the future.

In June 1991, India came close to defaulting on its international debt commitments, with the balance of payments deficit running high, foreign exchange balance precariously low (enough for 13 days of normal imports), and fiscal deficit high. This prompted major reforms in 1991 and, more so, in 1992. Import tariffs, which had climbed sky high, were brought down; convertibility on the current account was increased; industrial licensing removed; and a variety of incentives to attract foreign capital both as foreign direct investment and as portfolio investment were instituted. These changes, coming on top of the higher savings rate (then hovering at around 23 per cent) that had been achieved by the early 1980s, led to a robust boost to the economy.

If one dissects the overall growth, it becomes clear that the biggest effect has been in the international sector. India's foreign exchange balance grew steadily and is now at a comfortable level of over $130 billion (see Table 3.3 and Figure 3.3). The information technology (IT) sector had its celebrated take off in this decade (Narayana Murthy 2004; Singh 2004). India has gained enormously from globalization. If one looks at where the output from the IT sector is going, one will find that 60 per cent of it is being exported. Once this sector made a global name for itself, this had a promotional effect for India as a whole and soon there were other sectors such as

---

that in the 55th round of the NSS, data would be collected for consumption in both 'the last 30 days' and 'the last 7 days'. The remarkable consistency between these two sets of data made it clear that one of those questions may have 'contaminated' the other, thereby providing an ideal brew for controversy and confusion. However, while on poverty there is controversy, regarding inequality there is almost total consensus that, no matter how one looks at it—across regions or across individuals—there has been a steady increase.

Kaushik Basu

TABLE 3.3   FOREIGN EXCHANGE RESERVES

Year	Foreign Exchange Reserves, $million	Aggregate Export of Goods and Services, $million	Short-term Debt, as % of Forex Reserves	Debt–Service Ratio
1977	5,824			
1990	5,834	18,477	129	35
1994	25,186	26,855	14	26
1998	32,490	34,298	16	18
2002	75,428	52,512	10	14
2005	130,000	68,000		

Sources: *Economic Survey* (various years), Ministry of Finance, Government of India; and press releases of the Ministry of Commerce.

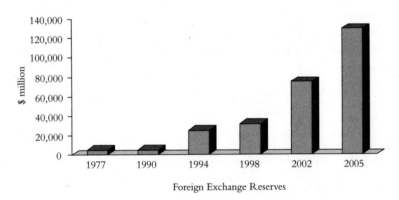

Foreign Exchange Reserves

FIGURE 3.3   FOREIGN EXCHANGE RESERVES

bio-technology and even steel that were beginning to do well. And now with quotas having been terminated, under the Multi-Fibre Agreement, textile exports of India are expected to go up from the current annual value of $14 billion to $50 billion by 2010.

The Next Round of Reforms

Despite all the good portents, much remains to be done. The country continues to be crushingly poor. Even though poverty has fallen, inequality is on the rise and can reach destabilizing levels. India needs to push on several policy fronts to make a big dent on poverty and for the bottom quintile of the population to feel the prosperity. Turning from this general pronouncement to details, I would emphasize five essential policy thrusts for the next round.

First, governments worry about big things, like money supply, the balance of trade, and budgetary deficits. These are of course important but, often, an economy fails not because of these but because of the malfunction of what I have elsewhere[6] called 'the nuts and bolts' of the economy. A number of studies have shown that India trails behind other countries when it comes to the enforcement of contracts, the effort spent by citizens on overcoming bureaucratic hurdles, and the time taken to start a business and, more so, to close one. We now have hard statistics to evaluate where India stands on these matters of nuts and bolts. These are summarized in Table 3.4. If you want to start a business in India, it will take you on average

TABLE 3.4   NUTS AND BOLTS OF THE ECONOMY, 2003

	No. of Procedures to Start Business	Time to Start Business (Days)	Cost to Register Business (% of Per Capita Income)	No. of Procedures to Enforce Contract	Time to Enforce Contracts (Days)	Time to Resolve Insolvency of Firms (Months)	Index of Labour Regulation Most Flexible (0)— Most Rigid (100)
India	10	88	50	11	365	136	51
China	11	46	14	20	180	31	47
Hong Kong	5	11	2	17	180	12	27
Malaysia	8	31	27	22	270	26	25
US	5	4	1	17	365	36	22
Singapore	7	8	1	23	50	8	20

Source: *World Development Indicators*, World Bank, 2004.

[6] In the BBC News Online column, available at http://news.bbc.co.uk/1/hi/world/south_asia/3819315.stm (accessed on 18 February 2011).

Kaushik Basu

88 days to get the requisite clearance. In China this takes 46 days, in Malaysia 31, and in Singapore and the US an astonishing 8 days and 4 days, respectively. If your business runs into the problem of someone violating a contract, in India it will take you one year to solve the problem, in China 180 days, and in Singapore 50 days.[7] But even if you can enter and have contracts enforced, the real catch in India is in getting out of a business. To resolve an insolvency case takes 8 months in Singapore, 26 months in Malaysia, and 136 months in India.

To me, these are the crucial ingredients of an economy's success. If the state can provide these functions efficaciously, the market can take care of much of the rest. To achieve this needs widespread reform of governance. Many mainstream economists believe that all the government has to do is be scarce. It would be nice if life were as simple. In reality, government just has to perform certain functions if an economy is to prosper. One can see this somewhat from Table 3.4. There is very little difference in the *number* of government procedures that one has to go through to start a business or to have a contract enforced. In fact, in India the number of procedures for enforcing a contract is much smaller than in Singapore, US, or Malaysia. So the problem is not resolved by government removing the procedures and regulations—a modern economy cannot do without these. There is no getting away from the fact that the government of a modern economy has to have lots of regulations and procedures; it just has to learn to get these jobs done quickly and efficiently.

One specific facility that government needs to provide urgently is that of patenting inventions. Establishing property rights on one's ideas is not a very generous thing to do, but when the industrial world is doing so, one does not have much choice in the matter. According to the latest comparable statistics available (World Bank 2005), the number of patents filed by Indians in India in 2002 was 220. Of course, this will be less than in industrialized nations. What

---

[7] In litigious US, it seems to take as long as in India, though I have some scepticism about this figure.

is surprising is how big the gap is. The figure for the US for the same year is 198,339 and for Japan it is 371,495. And it is not as if there is not enough scientific work going on in India. By Third World standards, India does fairly well on this. In 2001, the number of scientific and technical journal articles published in India was 11,076. The figures for the US and Japan are, respectively, 200,870 and 57,420.

In the US, every university and large institute provides facilities for filing patent protection on ideas. India needs, as do most Third World countries, to move towards this. And this is a task that cannot be left entirely to the market; government has to shoulder much of the responsibility.

Second, there will have to be important labour market reforms. A legacy of India's Industrial Disputes Act, 1947,[8] is that it is exceedingly difficult to lay off or retrench workers. This law was enacted in the belief that it would help employment. But of course a potential employer who knows that he will not be able to retrench his workers may decide not to employ workers in the first place. During a recent visit to some textile factories outside Delhi, the chief executive officer (CEO) of Orientcrafts—a major supplier of fashion garments to American department stores—told me that, since in the fashion industry demand has huge seasonalities and in India it is difficult to lay off workers during the lean season, he simply employs, all year round, the number of workers needed during the lean season.

But the problem now goes beyond labour laws. These laws have spawned a culture of job guarantee, irrespective of performance, which has—and this is my main concern—hurt labour by keeping labour demand low. While the laws do need reform (see Basu 2006a, for discussion), much that happens in the labour market depends on more amorphous factors, like norms and polity. So there will have to be a broad thrust on this front. And it has to begin by educating the trade unions that these changes are needed not for

[8] Interestingly, this Act became effective in April—that is, before India's independence.

other sectors of the economy but for reasons of the welfare of the workers themselves.

The liberalization of labour laws should be introduced in tandem with the implementation of a basic social security and welfare system. It is possible for India to have a minimal social welfare system which will provide a floor for workers who find themselves temporarily out of work. I return to the topic of direct welfare interventions later.

Third, infrastructure continues to be a bottleneck for further progress. Poor roads, poor ports, interrupted electricity supply, and inadequate airport facilities are strangling opportunities in many sectors, especially in those where the timing of sales is important, such as garments and apparel. From a factory in India to a department store in New York, a garment takes on average 32 days. It takes half this time from several East Asian countries. Bureaucracy is a big factor in this but also, the Indian ports being outdated and small, large ships do not come here. So, garments have to travel by feeder vessels to be transferred to mother vessels in other ports, before they can set out on their long journey to Europe and the US.

Government has to spend money on making a big thrust on infrastructure in several dimensions. Investment in infrastructure can boost private sector employment in a big way and this is the best way to create jobs without causing fiscal strain. But, of course, the investment itself will require money. Where will this come from? Government should use a combination of borrowed money and some of its foreign exchange reserves, but after making sure that the projects are viable (Mukhopadhyay 2004).

Some analysts, including some IMF economists, have cautioned government not to do so for reasons of fiscal prudence. The concern—namely, that we must not make the mistake of treating forex reserves of the government as free money—is correct but the conclusion wrong. Suppose Mr X earns $100 in New York and on returning to Delhi, changes it to rupees. India's forex reserves would have risen by $100. If now government spends this, then, given that X will also be spending his $100-equivalent in rupees, we will end up spending $200 worth of money as a consequence of having earned $100. Hence, this will amount to a rise in our fiscal deficit.

But, if this money is spent not on consumption (like paying wages or subsidizing products), but on investment, then the pressure on the deficit is not necessarily bad. In fact, *at this juncture of the Indian economy*, that is what I would recommend—the lid has to be firm on the *revenue* deficit, not the entire deficit. It is like a person who has Rs 1,000 but decides to start a new factory by spending Rs 2,000. Of course, he will run up a deficit. Whether this is a good idea or not depends critically on how much faith we have in his ability to run the factory.

With all investments, there is what may be called 'the risk of Gander'. In 1938, the world's largest airport was Gander International. It was an essential refuelling stop for planes crossing the Atlantic. The local government calculated that as air traffic grew, the demand for Gander International would inevitably rise and invested heavily in enlarging the airport. But planes became fuel efficient in ways that could not have been anticipated, and Gander is today one of the most underutilized airports.

About this kind of risk—that comes with sudden technology changes or unexpected political shifts—there is nothing we can do. The only mistake would be to allow the fear of this to paralyse us into doing nothing. Since India is on the upswing, it is worth the risk of expanding our infrastructure. Of course, this should be done judiciously and with our eyes open. In using some of its dollar reserves, India will be exposing itself to the risk of a liquidity crisis. On the other hand, using dollars has the advantage that this will not immediately cause a rise in demand for Indian goods (which could cause inflation). The trick is to use the right combination of borrowed rupees and dollar reserves.

The aforementioned policy will also have the desirable byproduct of raising India's investment rate (total investment as a percentage of national income). India may never reach China's investment rate of over 40 per cent, but it is time to break the 30 per cent barrier. India's investment rate has not had any secular rise since the late

1970s, when it reached 20 per cent, and in fact had a slight decline in the late 1990s. And this is the fourth policy thrust that India needs—to boost its stagnant savings rate (see Table 3.1). A part of this is caused by the large revenue deficit of the government. It is time to think of policy interventions to correct this.

Fifth, the country needs to plan a variety of more imaginative direct interventions to improve the standard of living of the poorer sections. This involves properly targeted government interventions to combat illiteracy, morbidity, and inequality. Spending on education, health, and social security will cost money. But if we add up the huge subsidies that are given in indirect ways to the rich and the powerful (just consider how well a city is maintained where the rich live), we will find little excuse to skimp on the poor. Moreover, the total revenue (from taxes and other sources) collected by the Indian government is 13 per cent of the national income. This is much below the potential. The figure for most Scandinavian nations is around 40 per cent, for Singapore 25 per cent, and the US 21 per cent. If government works on correcting this as it raises its spending on the poor, it can keep budgetary pressures under control. It is of course important to design interventions that will not damage market efficiency too much and will result in positive net gains. The scope for action here is immense. It is primarily a matter of resolve on the part of government.

The problem of inequality is somewhat different from that of poverty. There is more that government can and should do but, at the same time, there is no getting away from the fact that there are severe limits to how much can be done about inequality by a single country in today's globalized world (Basu 2004b). Inequality needs *global* policy coordination. I have elaborated on this in Basu (2006b). The essential idea is this. With globalization, one segment of the labour market that is acquiring greater international mobility is the professional and technically qualified workers. Hence, top-end salaries in Third World nations are being driven up. Unless there is some global coordination in keeping the spread of incomes within limits, a single country's attempt to compress the variance in incomes too much will cause flights of professional labour and capital. This could in turn impede growth and, beyond a point, even increase poverty. When a single country tries to combat inequality, this consequence of unilateral policy action has to be kept in mind.

In Basu (2006b) I have tried to develop the principle that inequality should be controlled as long as it does not make poverty worse. My expectation is that this constraint will bind quite quickly in developing countries unless there is coordination of equity policies across nations. The trouble is that, while we currently have international organizations for coordinating trade policies (WTO), labour policies (International Labour Organization [ILO]), and many others, there is no institution or organization for coordinating equity policies across nations. There is clearly need for some global institution building in this area.

A Higher Opportunity

A LONGSTANDING PROPOSITION IN ECONOMICS, under the label of 'industrial policy', emphasizes the importance of the government choosing special sectors to focus on and incentivize. The expectation is that this will create enough spill-overs to drive up overall growth. Industrial policy has had its share of demurrers, arguing that the state should not get into picking winners and losers; but the fact is that it has been used to great effect by Britain, Germany, and other nations during the Industrial Revolution and by China in recent times.

Without entering that debate, I want to point to two areas where the Indian government should put in special effort: medical tourism and higher education. India made huge strides in the former in the early 1990s, but this sector seems to be running out of steam, with other emerging nations taking the lead. We need more effort here. The other sector where the prospect is big is a global hub for higher education. In both these sectors, much can be achieved, without the government having to do the heavy-lifting. Given my own expertise, I focus here on the second.

From ancient Greece to nineteenth-century Britain and twentieth-century US, there is evidence that when nations do well in higher education and research, they do well in economic development. For historical reasons, India has a huge strength here. First, while India's colonial history did plenty of harm, it conferred one advantage. When leaving India, luckily the English could not take away their language. English is the world's most important language and India's strength in it is a natural advantage today. Second, thanks to the far-sightedness of India's founding fathers and, in particular, Jawaharlal Nehru, India took major steps in nurturing higher education and scientific temperament, setting up the IITs, the IIMs, and promoting some fine universities.

One can see the advantage this history has conferred from indirect data. America has a large Study Abroad programme under which its students take a break from their home universities and go to other countries for education. In 2014–15, 313,415 students went abroad under this scheme. The biggest destination is the UK—12.2 per cent of the students went there—followed by Italy (10.8 per cent) and Spain (9 per cent). What is surprising is India does not do too badly on this. It is the 14th most popular destination (1.4 per cent).

If we can build on these strengths and create room for private universities and institutes to flourish, India can become a destination for students from around the world. This would not be a charitable act. The aim should be to provide high-quality education and charge international students the full fee for this (though I would recommend subsidies for students from poor countries).

Private firms that invest in this sector will need some flexibility on how much they charge and what salaries they pay. In the US, universities compete to attract the best professors and so salaries vary vastly. I wish the world were not like this but it is and, to succeed, India has to give this freedom to the private universities. Some of these universities, it is likely, will start up partnerships with universities in the US, UK, and elsewhere, and that should be welcomed.

In the US today, in many good universities, annual tuition fees are above $60,000. If Indian universities are given the freedom, they could charge, say, $20,000, provide comparable education and still make a profit. For a four-year education, this means a saving of over $160,000 to the student. It is likely that students would come to India not just from developing nations but also rich countries. The big advantage of this is that the government does not have to do much beyond creating an enabling environment. The return on this investment will be enormous.

Often, our biggest plans flounder not because of big mistakes, but because the nuts and bolts are not in place. The government has to pay attention to the little matters. For example, students should be able to get visas for their two-, three-, or four-year study at one go. No one will want to come here, however good the education, if he or she is at the mercy of the bureaucrat in the visa office every six months. There are nowadays retrogressive groups trying to take India backwards in the name of Hindutva. They will have to be restrained from shaping curricula if our institutes of higher learning are to flourish.

There is enough enterprise in India and enough profit potential in this sector that private universities will crop up and do the actual delivery once the government provides this basic ethos. As Ratan Tata wrote in the *Oxford Companion to Economics in India*, if the right policies are in place, India can 'leverage the country's scientific and engineering talent pool to create value'.

Of course, regulation will be needed but the main aim of the regulation must not be to control salaries, curricula, and speech on campus, but to ensure that students are not cheated. Several of India's private teaching institutes mislead students by giving them false information about their placement record and tuition costs. Some of them let students in for a small fee and then raise charges midway through the education. We will need intelligent, lean regulation to deter such behaviour.

In this new setting, the quality of universities will vary, with only a handful being of top international standards. That is unavoidable. If we try to have 800 universities (as of February 2017, India had 789) of uniform standard, they can only be uniformly mediocre.

It is true that the private universities are likely to cater to education in the commercially more lucrative disciplines, whereas a nation's advance also depends on literature, poetry, and pure mathematics, which have little immediate commercial value. The advantage of the nation becoming a global hub for education is that this can yield so much income that the government can then take the responsibility of providing these other kinds of education to its own citizens. The government should also take the responsibility to ensure that all Indians get education, taking account of the fact that many are so poor that they will have to be provided education for free.

But even with these caveats, the investment-to-return ratio for the government in the education sector can be disproportionate. Few other sectors can match it.

The Ethics of Reducing Inequality

AROUND THE WORLD, THE EFFECTS OF alarmingly high economic inequality are spilling over into politics and society. Economic insecurity is a driving force behind violent conflicts in the Middle East and the rise of fascist elements in some European countries, not least Hungary and Poland. Even in older democracies such as the US, economic marginalization has led to a strengthening of chauvinist and supremacist identities and other social problems such as the opioid epidemic.

These trends have been ongoing for some time. But, according to Branko Milanovic of the City University of New York, a big shift occurred between 1988 and 2008. During this period of 'high globalization', the two segments of the world making gains were the wealthiest 1 per cent in rich and poor countries and the middle class in a few Asian countries—namely China, India, Indonesia, Thailand, and Vietnam. Meanwhile, the World Bank has shown that 766 million people—around 10 per cent of the global population—were still living below the extreme-poverty threshold of $1.90 per day as of 2013.

Much has been written about the policies needed to rectify this dismal picture. And yet, powerful voices in both rich and developing countries—and, tragically, even among the misinformed poor—claim that current income disparities are fair because they are a result of free markets. Convincing them to support remedial interventions, then, will require a deeper look at the underlying logic and morality of inequality.

I was thinking about this as I read Chris Hughes' marvellous book *Fair Shot: Rethinking Inequality and How We Earn.* Hughes co-founded Facebook with Mark Zuckerberg and is now staggeringly wealthy at the ripe age of 34. His book gives a moving account of growing up in small-town North Carolina, trying awkwardly to fit in with the 'white, wealthy kids', eventually coming out as gay, and doing well enough in school to gain admission to Harvard University.

Hughes ended up rooming with Zuckerberg, which was sheer luck. Indeed, a large part of his book deals with the role of luck in determining individual success. Though Hughes' father taught him that realizing the 'American dream' is a matter of pulling oneself up by one's bootstraps, Hughes eventually reached the opposite conclusion. 'My success at Facebook,' he writes, 'taught me that seemingly small events like who you choose to room with in college can have an outsized impact on the rest of your life.'

Hughes' solution to the problem of inequality is to tax the rich in order to provide a guaranteed minimum income to the lower and middle classes. It is heartening that at least some of America's wealthiest individuals are honest enough to recognize the unfairness of the system, even though they have done well by it.

To understand the logic and morality of inequality, it is worth digging further into what Hughes says about luck. It is not just that one part of his wealth is due to luck; rather, *all* of it is. Luck determined that Hughes would be smart enough to get into Harvard and then meet Zuckerberg once there. Likewise, it was luck that Zuckerberg had learned Atari BASIC programming from his father when he was a child.

Some try to counter this by pointing out that hard work also matters. But that is beside the point. After all, whether or not one has a strong work ethic is itself due to luck, because it depends on one's genetic make-up, environment, and upbringing. Thus, the primacy of luck as a determinant of wealth means that there is no *moral* justification for economic inequality.

At this point, many well-intentioned radicals will conclude that we must therefore have total equality. But the 'therefore' is invalid. Ensuring fairness and equity are important, to be sure, but so is eradicating poverty and improving opportunities for the middle class. Under current conditions, pushing for absolute equality could erode the incentive to work, leading to widespread economic breakdown. We have already seen this happen with many well-meaning social experiments in the past.

We will have to strike a balance. Today's unacceptably high inequality demands interventions to improve education and health, as well as redistributive taxation of the kind that Hughes recommends; but it also requires us to tolerate some income disparities to keep people and economies working.

Hughes' proposal for a minimum guaranteed income is a step in the right direction, but it would be a mistake to view it as the panacea. For the sake of argument, assume that the poorest half of the population cannot afford some vaccine that would ensure them basic good health. One might think that giving everyone a minimum guaranteed income would correct this injustice.

But now assume that there is only enough of some critical resource to produce vaccines for half the population. In this scenario, it would not matter how much money you give to the poorest half of the population: the price of the drug would keep rising to the point where only the wealthiest half the population could afford it. Under conditions of scarcity, the only way to ensure a fair outcome would be to award the vaccines through a lottery.

The effectiveness of a guaranteed income, then, depends on the underlying general equilibrium of the economy. The vaccine scenario is just one example of the kind of complications that can arise. For Hughes' scheme to work, we will have to identify many more possible contingencies, and then design a system to pre-empt them.

References

Ahluwalia, Montek S. (2002), 'Economic Reforms in India since 1991: Has Gradualism Worked?', *Journal of Economic Perspectives*, 16(3): 67–88.

Banerjee, Abhijit and Thomas Piketty (2003), 'Top Indian Incomes, 1956–2000', mimeo, MIT.

Basu, Kaushik (2000), 'Whither India? The Prospect of Prosperity', in R. Thapar (ed.), *India: Another Millenium?* New Delhi: Penguin Books.

_____ (2004a), 'The Indian Economy: Up to 1991 and Since', in Kaushik Basu (ed.), *India's Emerging Economy: Problems and Prospects in the 1990s and Beyond*. Cambridge, MA: The MIT Press.

_____ (2004b), 'Globalization and Development: A Re-examination of Development Policy', in Akira Kohsaka (ed.), *New Development Strategies: Beyond the Washington Consensus*. New York: Palgrave Macmillan.

_____ (2006a), 'Labor Laws and Labor Welfare in the Context of the Indian Economy', in Ravi Kanbur and Alain de Janvry (eds), *Poverty, Inequality and Development: Essays in Honor of Erik Thorbecke*. Norwell, Massachusetts: Kluwer.

_____ (2006b), 'Globalization, Poverty and Inequality: What is the Relationship? What can be Done?', *World Development*, 43(5): 53–62.

Cohen, Stephen (2001), *India: Emerging Power*. Washington, DC: Brookings Institution.

Deaton, Angus (2001), 'Adjusted Indian Poverty Estimates for 1999–2000', mimeo, Princeton Research Program in Development Studies.

Deaton, Angus and Jean Drèze (2002), 'Poverty and Inequality in India: A Reexamination', *Economic and Political Weekly*, 7 September, 37(36): 3729–48.

Lee Kuan Yew (2000), *From Third World to First: The Singapore Story, 1965–2000*. New York: Harper Collins.

Lyall, Sarah (2001), 'Recipe for Roasting the Sacred Cow, Tastelessly', *New York Times*, 12 November.

Majumdar, Mukul (1997), 'The East Asian Miracle and India', Asiatic Society, Calcutta.

Mukhopadhyay, Partha (2004), 'Force-Funding of Infrastructure: Off-budget and Off-Key', *Economic and Political Weekly*, 2 October, 39(40): 4396–8.

Narayana Murthy, N.R. (2004), 'The Impact of Economic Reforms on Industry in India: A Case Study of the Software Industry', in Kaushik Basu (ed.), *India's Emerging Economy: Problems and Prospects in the 1990s and Beyond*. Cambridge, MA: The MIT Press.

Rodrik, Dani and Arvind Subramanian (2004), 'From Hindu Growth to Productivity Surge', NBER Working Paper. Available at www.nber. org/paper/w10376 (accessed on 18 February 2011).

Sen, Abhijit and Himanshu (2004), 'Poverty and Inequality in India, I and II', *Economic and Political Weekly*, 18 September and 25 September, 39(38–9): 4247–63, 4361–75.

Sen, Amartya (2004), 'Passage to China,' *New York Review of Books*, 2 December, 51(9): 61–5.

Singh, Nirvikar (2004), 'Information Technology and India's Economic Development', in Kaushik Basu (ed.), *India's Emerging Economy: Problems and Prospects in the 1990s and Beyond*. Cambridge, MA: The MIT Press.

World Bank (2005), *World Development Indicators 2005*. Washington, DC: World Bank.

four

On the Road*

A Traveller's Guide

I HAVE LITTLE SYMPATHY FOR THE lament I hear from my leisure-class friends in Delhi about how life is hard in the age of inflation. For this class of people, this simply means that they now have to spend more to keep up appearances. Nevertheless, to address them all at one go, I devote this section to some elementary economics of keeping up with, without spending like the Joneses.

We all know that annoying feeling when boarding a flight from the front. It entails walking down the aisle under the disdainful glare of business class passengers spreading themselves out in their ample seats. Here is the technique for avoiding this. As soon as you enter the business class cabin, start peering at the seat numbers, pause, squint, compare with the ticket in your hand, and move slowly forward. Every few steps, keep repeating the same. It will be presumed by the

---

* 'A Traveller's Guide' was first published in *Hindustan Times*, 22 June 2008. 'India's Wild East' was first published in *BBC News Online*, 13 February 2008. 'Among the Zapotecs' was first published in *Hindustan Times*, 28 August 2009. 'Economics and Zen in Munich' was first published in *Hindustan*

dimwits in expensive suits that you are in the same cabin as them, hesitating only because you have still to find your seat. This way you will get the respect of all business class passengers, except those in the last row, who will of course notice you sliding into the next cabin.

You have travelled to wherever you have, and those busybodies keep sending you messages from their shiny Blackberries or iPhones. These devices have several advantages but the biggest one can be got for no expense at all. Every time you send an email, after signing off, type in by hand:'This message is sent from my Blackberry.'Alternatively, you can put this into the 'signature' of your email; that will save you from having to type it each time. Your reputation as an owner of a Blackberry will spread far and wide, with your bank balance unaltered.

The twenty-first century Indian is nothing if not peripatetic. Suppose you have arrived at some distant land, famed for its culture and history. Say you are in Italy; and of course you have to see the famous museums—the Uffizi in Florence and the Cathedral at the Piazza del Duomo in Siena. To really learn about the sculptures, the

Times, 8 December 2007. 'Namaste: Welcome to Israel' was first published as 'Shalom Namaste: Travels through a Fractured Land', in *The Times of India*, 17 February 2007. 'Praying in the Foothills of Mount Fuji' was first published in *Hindustan Times*, 30 September 2007. A slightly edited version of 'The Maharaja Disappoints' was first published as 'Brand India's Image Issue', in *BBC News Online* on 25 December 2006. 'Taking Off: Airports and Economics' was first published as 'Time to Take Off', in *The Times of India*, 11 July 2007. 'Fragments from an Africa Diary: Johannesburg, Pretoria, and Diepsloot' was first published in the World Bank blog on 28 March 2013. 'Samoa Diary' was first published in the World Bank blog on 6 September 2013. 'Bhutan: Development Economics in the Himalayas' was first published in the World Bank blog on 12 January 2015. 'Postcard from Malaysia: Through the Smog, Gently' was first published in the World Bank blog as 'Through the Smog, Gently: Postcard from Malaysia' on 1 July 2013. 'A Hinduism More Tolerant' was first published as 'Economic Graffiti: A Hinduism More Tolerant' in *Indian Express*, 22 June 2018. 'In Good Faith: A Journey, an Education' was first published in *Indian Express*, 20 August 2018. 'An Evening in Florence' was first published as 'Economic Graffiti: An Evening in Florence' in *Indian Express*, 19 October 2018. 'The Turin Miracle' was first published as 'Economic Graffiti: The Turin Miracle' in *Indian Express*, 28 December 2017. 'Does God Exist? There Are Several Possible Hypotheses' was first published in *Indian Express*, 7 March 2019.

frescoes, and the history behind the stones, you need a guide; but guides can be expensive. Fortunately, if you show a little ingenuity, you need not pay at all. On entering, stare at the first few exhibits and hang around. Basically you are waiting for a Scandinavian tour group to arrive. They always come with an English-speaking guide. As soon as you see one such group, start moving with it.

A standard 'good' is something that if one person has it, another does not. The apple I consume is one such good. In the language of economics, a 'public good' is the polar opposite of that. When one person consumes it, others get to consume it for free. When a rich person installs a machine to remove the soot being spewed out by a factory chimney, he gets to enjoy the clean air but so do others. Hence, most environmental goods are public goods.

Of course, you are not supposed to eavesdrop on someone else's guide, but a guide's speech to a large group is a 'public good'. All you need is to be a bit brazen. If you feel uncomfortable because the guide is staring accusingly at you, there is a more advanced technique that can be used in extreme conditions. With most big Scandinavian groups there will be an adopted South Asian kid. Stand very close to the kid. From the body language of the adults it will be obvious that the kid is part of their group and the guide will take you to be the uncle from rural India visiting his niece.

In these places of high culture there is always the scholar tourist who stands endlessly in front of each fresco with the fat book that describes each artwork in the museum, while you breeze past with your thin catalogue of *All Museums of Europe*. Do not develop an inferiority complex vis-à-vis such tourists. Remind yourself that one year later you will both be on par. He will not remember what he saw in such detail and you will not remember what you barely saw.

India's Wild East

TUCKED AWAY BETWEEN CHINA, MYANMAR, AND Bangladesh, and linked to the rest of India by a sliver of north

Bengal that arches over Bangladesh, India's north-east is a region of amazing grace—charming people, ancient cultures, and bountiful nature. As any shrewd observer of the world would deduce from this, it is a region of contested claims, strife, and anarchy. The eight states of the north-east comprise a region of diversity—multiple religions, dialects, and tribes, each with its distinctive culture and history.

In Mizoram there are the Bnei Menashe, who claim to be Jews, descendants of the ancient tribe of Menasseh. Then there are groups from as near as Bihar, such as the adivasis (original inhabitants) who came to work in the Assam tea gardens and stayed on. Their claim to special rights, granted to 'original inhabitants', is contested by the local people, who argue that they have lost that status by their move, for they are not original to Assam.

Some of these contests acquire a farcical dimension, such as when China welcomed but refused to give visas to some delegates from Arunachal Pradesh on the ground that it considered parts of that state to be China; and India insisted that China must insist on visas.

Of all the states of this region, the most troubled is Manipur. I flew into Imphal, Manipur's capital, by a short Indigo flight from Guwahati on the morning of 8 January.

Ryszard Kapuscinski is known to be the great travel writer of our times, but he was more than that. He was a philosopher, an astute and compassionate observer of the human condition. When Kapuscinski journeyed to remote lands, he carried with him the greatest travel book of antiquity, Herodotus' *Histories*. Out of this experience came his own classic book, *Travels with Herodotus*. I am doing what Kapuscinski did, but at one remove; I am travelling with his book.

I arrive in Imphal with a blinding headache and flop down in bed in my artlessly large room in Hotel Nirmala. I try to read, but fall asleep. When I wake up, the winter sun is streaming in through my open windows. From my balcony I can see the chaos of Thangal Bazar—tarless streets, unkempt roof-tops, half-cemented buildings, the anarchy of low-hanging electric wires criss-crossing in different directions and tapped from below by small shops with rusty tin roofs. The flashes of colour come from the women in their stunning *phaneks*—sarong-like wrap-arounds—and shawls, all of whom seem to be endowed with an effortless grace.

There are few signs of the famous Indian economic boom here. This is a region of a collapsing economy, huge unemployment, and interrupted power supply. I was assured that at most times it was safe to touch those exposed wires.

At night I go for dinner to the home of an old Manipuri friend. It is a picturesque 300-year-old house, with a quaint courtyard, mysterious stairways, muslin curtains, and melodious wooden floors. To get there, one has to drive over a rock-strewn and dug-up road. It has been under repair for four years. When we reach the house, there is a power outage and we sit by lanterns and candles. On the way back, there is not a soul on the streets—life is too insecure for that—and my hotel has pulled down shutters from the ceiling and bolted them to the floor with padlocks.

The people of the north-east have high human capital— Mizoram's literacy rate is second only to Kerala's, a history that goes back 2,000 years. Ratan Thiyam's Manipuri theatre is famous internationally. An 11-year-old boy, Honey Kenao, plays the tabla like a grandmaster. He is a prodigy; we will without doubt see more of him. At various institutes and universities where I speak, the discussion is lively and engaged.

But beneath this, the region is simmering. Insurgent groups routinely extort money from bureaucrats, shopkeepers, and professors. Kidnappings are frequent. Trucks on highways are often stopped by competing local powers and either have their cargo confiscated or are allowed to pass after paying a 'tax'. Hardly any new industry worth its name is moving into the region.

There are three immediate actions that the Indian government needs to take. First, law and order. It has to clamp down on extortion and make it clear that the collection of taxes and exertion of force are prerogatives of government. As Max Weber had reminded us, the state must have a 'monopoly of violence'—meaning, if anybody has the right to use force, it is the state. Second, it has to invest in infrastructure—roads, railways, financial services, and electricity.

And third, it has to increase cultural and intellectual interaction between the region and the rest of India.

If we do not act soon, there is every possibility that the region will erupt into internecine warfare of a kind not seen in India before. That will be extremely unfortunate for a region that has so much potential.

Among the Zapotecs

ARRIVING IN MEXICO FROM NEW YORK, the balmy weather, the fragrance of vaguely familiar tropical flowers, and the shades of brown into which I, as an Indian, effortlessly blend, make for a heady atmosphere. To get to Oaxaca one has to change planes in Mexico City. As the door of the airport train shuts, an Indian gentleman enters dishevelled, assured by a lady outside that this is indeed the train to terminal 1. He mistakes me for a Mexican, ignores me, and asks the American across the aisle, 'Does this train go to terminal 1?' A few minutes tick away; he turns to me and enunciates each word: 'Do you speak English?' Then, lowering his voice to be out of earshot of the American: 'Is this train going to terminal 1?' Before we reach our destination, he has polled the entire compartment. Not for nothing are we Indians known to be cautious people.

But I am now headed to spend three days with the other Indians—the Zapotecs of Teotitlan de Valle. This small town, an hour from Oaxaca, was once the heart of Zapotec civilization. The Zapotecs, it is believed, kept the warlike Aztecs off their backs by giving them their elegantly woven rugs. The Zapotecs may not have reached the heights of conquest and glory as some other Mesoamerican groups, but their culture has the quality of resilience and continues to flourish as it did in 500 BC when Monte Alban, nearby, became a major city with its astronomical observatories and sports arena.

Land here comes cheap; so, while my hosts, Ana Bertha, her husband, Orlando Lopez, his brother Roberto, and their stately mother, Marsalina, are undoubtedly poor, they have land—a large rectangular area, enclosed by a high boundary wall, the height a reminder of the region's periodic insurgency. Inside the compound, three corners are occupied by the Lopezes, their daughters, Daniela, Ana Christina, and Niala, and some of their relatives. The rest is space where goats, donkeys, and bulls live, alongside the roosters and turkeys. During the day the animals roam free amidst the conifers and the cactus, pomegranate, and lime trees that grow in abundance.

Orlando, whose quiet dignity reminds me of the late actor Sanjeev Kumar, spends the day on the roadside in Oaxaca, selling the rugs that they weave. Roberto grazes cattle over large tracts of bush lands and undulating hills. When they are both back at night, the family gathers for dinner—tortillas and corn soup. Perhaps because in the evening we were talking about the local drink, the Mescal, at our first dinner, I refer to Marsalina as 'Mescalina'. This is like addressing the senior lady of a Scottish household as 'Whiskia'. The brothers suppress laughter, Ana Bertha bursts out laughing, and, finally, to my relief, a faint smile flickers across Marsalina's face.

As night settles over Teotitlan, the hills that hem the town fade into darkness; and we chat, as Orlando weaves rugs, and Marsalina and Ana Bertha comb raw cotton and twirl the combed cotton into threads.

Eager to see all the activities of the household, I wake up at 5 am, a good 30 minutes before Santiago Nasar did on that fateful dawn of his foretold death in a magical Central American town. I do not wake to the bellows of the bishop's boat but the braying of donkeys. I want to go with Marsalina to the mill where she gets corn ground for making tortillas, but she has already left.

During the day we walk the children to the Benito Juarez Primary School. Daniela's teacher is absent; so she accompanies us to the municipal market, where local people buy and sell village crafts and food—string cheese, yoghurt, pork rinds. In one corner of the market is an open stall, which is among the few places that sell coffee. I sit there, amidst sombrero-wearing men, for a 'bowl' of coffee, and Daniela, while shyly protesting that she is full, sits next to me to have hot chocolate and cookies.

The morning of my departure I stroll alone, without my translator, in the market, drinking hot chocolate and watching the course of everyday life. To the Zapotecs, I must be as strange a sight as they are to me. They pause to look at me, and those who recognize me from the previous day, break into a welcoming smile.

Sitting in this strange market place, with the morning sun casting shadows on the dew-laden grass, not too far from some ruins that go back 2,000 years, in a town as far away as possible from my familiar worlds, hearing a babble of Zapotec, which is like no language I have heard before, a sudden feeling of belonging comes over me. Despite the differences in language, attire, and other attributes, it is impossible not to feel that I have with these people commonnesses which are deeper than the differences. The little cares, sadnesses, and joys that I shared with them over the previous two days make me feel that, at a deep level, I understand them as they do me, that we share a humanity and history that is common, and that 30, 40, maybe, 50 thousand years of separation do not alter the fact that we have millions of years of shared history and, in all likelihood, thousands of common ancestors.

Economics and Zen in Munich

IN THIS AGE OF COMMERCE AND technology, is the world becoming too mechanical? Some months ago I published an article in *BBC Online*, called 'Time to Give SAARC a Facelift'. A few days later I found my article linked to a webpage on 'Facelift Surgery'. There it sat amidst links to 'abdominoplasty', 'liposuction surgery', and 'weight loss filters'. Clearly, this was the work of robotic intelligence; it would not have happened with the human touch.

Art and commerce are, at one level, poles apart. Yet there is something diminished in a society that tries to compensate for one with the other. Thomas Carlyle's lament in nineteenth-century Britain that, thanks to the rise of economics (he called it the 'dismal science'), the arts were being doomed, may have been mistimed. But it would not be out of place in today's India. While celebrating Lakshmi, there is a genuine risk that we will ignore the non-commercial flanks of society—art, music, good cinema, and mathematics.

Last month, after four days of economics in Munich, I found myself alone and with two free days. I took the subway to the beautiful Marienplatz, and from there walked to the art galleries— Pinakothek der Moderne and Lenbachhaus. Early twentieth-century German art was one of the most astonishing human achievements. Expressionism, Die Brucke, the Blaue Reiter all found homes in Germany. The Blaue Reiter movement was in fact located in Munich, with Wassily Kandinsky, his partner (and in my view the more talented) Gabriele Munter, Franz Marc, and Jawlensky experimenting with new art forms and colours.

It struck me that, in the long run, there was something symbiotic about the rise of the economy and the arts. The latter involves innovation and the love of excellence; and, in different ways, these are also the ingredients of sustained economic progress. In our headlong rush to commerce, if we ignore the arts and aesthetics, this is of course civilizationally bad, but, in the long run, may be bad for commerce itself.

In the nineteenth century, the Bavarian monarchy wanted Munich and its surroundings to be not just a great industrial centre but the world capital of music. The arts in the region developed because of royal patronage. It is arguable that Rousseau would never have written *The Social Contract* if it were not for the generosity of the Duke of Luxembourg.

In the modern world we do not rely on the eccentric patronage of kings and the nobility, but on our universities and institutions to provide a home for all kinds of innovators. In India, while the schools of management and engineering are doing well, the university system is floundering. Literature, the arts, mathematics, and abstract science have little immediate commercial value. So, left to the whims of the market, they tend to wilt. But in the course of time, they play a fundamental role in making people creative, and so they deserve government support and encouragement.

POSTSCRIPT   On the flight out of Munich, I am drawn into another unusual pairing with economics—that with religion. I am seated next to a German scholar. On hearing that I am a professor and before I can tell him that I do not take my profession too seriously, he sallies into a treatise on economics and religion, halting English notwithstanding. After a while I have stopped listening, when, to my dismay, I find him asking me, 'Is Zen Hindu?' Not knowing how and when we have moved to the intricacies of eastern religions, I begin by stammering. But gladdened by the role reversal, I speak in a monologue for, maybe, 10 minutes, giving no breaks, which could grant him a toehold.

Since everything I know about Zen can be said in half a minute, I am very impressed by the last nine-and-a-half minutes of my speech. He is a polite person and listens to me patiently. But even as he nods courteously to a meaningless discourse on Mahayana Buddhism, he looks puzzled. It is almost as if he was expecting a shorter answer to the question. The puzzle is solved when, after much more conversation, breakfast, and coffee, he asks me, 'Is Zen the only Indian who has won the Nobel Prize in economics?'

Namaste: Welcome to Israel

As I snaked my way to the immigration desk at Israel's Ben-Gurion airport, I reached for my visa, return ticket, and the letters inviting me to lecture at Hebrew University and the School of Economics in Tel Aviv. I had been warned that the airport officials could be inquisitorial; so I prepared myself to overwhelm them. It was, therefore, a pleasant surprise when the immigration officer—a genial, dark-complexioned lady—looked my Indian passport over and said, 'Namaste, aap pehle bar Israel aa rahen hain?' She explained that she was a Jew from Bombay, who migrated to Israel 34 years ago. She asked me a dozen questions about India, showing an interest in me that went well beyond the call of duty and was evidently inspired by nostalgia.

Within minutes I am out of the airport and in a taxi on Highway 443 to Jerusalem. I travel past a signboard that has the momentousness of history written all over it. 'Ramallah', it says, for a road veering off north.

Jerusalem, with its limestone houses, cypress trees, and winding bylanes, is a city that has witnessed it all. It is the land of Jesus Christ, of war and carnage, of claims and counter-claims. You can be there on a brief visit—in my case, five days—but the city mesmerizes and inveigles you in ways no other city can. There is in fact a medical term, 'the Jerusalem syndrome', for a temporary mental confusion and emotional high that visitors to Jerusalem have been known to suffer.

In the old quarter, standing on Via Dolorosa, one can sense the ethos of the time when Jesus carried the cross along the cobbled path, collapsing under its weight and having his brow wiped by Veronica. The old walled city, where the Muslim quarter rubs shoulders with the Jewish area, which in turn abuts into the Christian quarter, is a potpourri of ancient cultures and religions. Accompanied by a young post-doc at Hebrew University, I visit the Wailing Wall, the Dome of the Rock, and the Holy Sepulchre, stopping at a small but famous humus restaurant, Lina, for brunch.

On another afternoon, with my friend, the economist Yossi Zeira, I explore Mea Shearim—the Ultra Orthodox area. Talking about economic theory, common friends, and world politics, we walk past modest homes that look like the chawls of Mumbai and down streets with men in robes and streimels, women in mysterious black clothes, and little children made cuter by their traditional attire. Mea Shearim gives way to a quiet, colonial road on which stands the Ethiopian Church.

In Jerusalem, on my last evening, another economist friend and I walk in the beautiful Nahalat Shiva area, smoking nargile, drinking wine, hearing about the history of Jerusalem, and, finally, eating in a restaurant called Barood. Yes, gun powder.

As night descends and music spills out of the cafes and bars, I realize how Jerusalem is, simultaneously, romantic and sad. The city with its almond blossoms and rakefet flowers blooming in the cracks of stones is beautiful. The women—Jews, Arabs, and the dark-eyed Ethiopians—are reason enough to turn your head. There are tales of times gone by etched on virtually every stone. But all this is also enveloped in a sadness special to Jerusalem. There is insecurity everywhere—one has to have a pat down before one sits down in a café or enters a museum. The minorities, like the Arabs I spoke to in restaurants and taxis, feel marginalized and second-class in a hostile land. Standing on the slopes of Mount Scopus in Hebrew University, one can see the partitions in the distance. A cluster of white, gleaming houses belong to Jewish settlers, and next to that, the worn-out homes and streets, where one can see people going about their quotidian lives are all Palestinian homes, under the Palestinian Authority.

This is a country of check-posts and barriers and it is easy to despair, and the government's misguidedly aggressive policies do not help. But fortunately, this is also a land of a vibrant press and remarkable voices—voices that are morally resonant, ringing out across racial and religious boundaries and pleading our common humanity. I am thinking of the columns of Gideon Levi and Amira Hass, and of the songs of Dana International (who, incidentally, has tried to blur not just the boundary between the races, but also the sexes).

On my last evening, I take a taxi from Beit Hakerem to my hotel in Mount Scopus. My taxi driver, a young, happy-go-lucky man, asks me where I have come from. Though I have travelled from the US, exploiting the question's ambiguity, I opt for the more exotic 'India'.

'I love India,' he says, and adds what sounds like part question, part exclamation, 'The land of Madhaba Gandhi!'

'Yes,' I reply, seeing no reason to quibble over minor details.

'Is he still the Prime Minister?'

'No. He is not.'

'But Madhaba Gandhi was a great man,' he says, disappointed at this turn of events. 'So who is the Prime Minister now?'

'Manmohan Singh.'

'Ching? Is he Chinese?'

I assure him the 1962 war had not gone that badly for India. I don't think he follows me but he smiles warmly and says 'namaste', which leaves me wondering what he thinks the word means.

Praying in the Foothills of Mount Fuji

SOME TIME AGO, I SPENT A few days in Hakone, a spectacular hill resort, a few hours' drive from Tokyo. The rolling countryside was covered with lush rhododendron bushes and every now and then when the clouds cleared, behind the pink and mauve of the flowers we would see Mount Fuji rising heavenwards like an immaculate work of art.

I think it is culturally ingrained in us Indians to overeat when we get free good food, the way camels do with water. So the very first night at the conference banquet, I gorged on endless amounts of sushi and marinated fish; and by 2 am that night, in the solitary confines of my hotel room, I was sick.

I had had food poisoning only once, the first week of taking up my first job in Delhi, after eating at the University Coffee House's famed 'mutton dosa'. In the new unfamiliar environ, in the middle of the night, my wife had run to our neighbour, Chauhan, who, it was rumoured, was a doctor. Rushing in helpfully, adjusting his dressing-gown, Chauhan asked me if I felt like vomiting; and, when I said yes, he thought for a while and said gravely, 'That means you have nausea.'

Whatever one makes of his deductive skills, the injection that he took out from a tiffin box that he had judiciously brought along with him and gave me a shot with, cured me in 30 minutes flat.

Alas, where would I find the talented Dr Chauhan 20 years later and thousands of miles away from Delhi? The only person I knew here was the president of the Japanese Economic Association. But I was loath to wake him up at that unearthly hour; and, for all I knew, he was also battling the forces of marinated fish at that time.

Maybe it was because of the closeness of the ethereal Mt Fuji, it suddenly struck me—why not try praying? As a kid I was devout and prayed regularly, making my mother and older relatives proud of me. I lost my faith in my early teens, as soon as I reached the age of reason. The misery and suffering of human beings that I could see all around me just did not square up with the existence of a powerful and merciful God. If he was powerful, he had to be short on kindness to permit so much pain on earth. And in case he was kind, it had to be he did not have the power to act on his kindness. I did not feel any angst as some thinkers, like Bertrand Russell, had done when they threw off their childhood faith. I just felt that it would be dishonest of me to believe in what I saw no evidence of. And I have to give tribute to the tolerance of old-fashioned Hinduism that my very religious relatives showed no intolerance towards me for my personal beliefs and some, I am sure, prayed extra hard on my behalf.

Anyway, that miserable night, toying with the choice between waking up the president of the Japanese Economic Association and dying quietly in the foothills of Mt Fuji, the case seemed compelling to give prayer a shot. So feeling somewhat self-conscious, I knelt down on my bed, folded my hands, and said, 'God, take pity on me and please make me well. In case you feel upset that I have come to you only in the time of dire need, look at it in another way. Unlike other people, who call on you day and night with little rhyme or reason, I never do. The last time I prayed must have been several years ago. So now you have to do me this one favour.'

And I lay down quietly. Fifteen minutes later, I was absolutely fine.

From this incident we can make one of two deductions. Either God does not exist and what happened that night was pure coincidence. Or God exists and loves me for my lack of faith and for not troubling him with daily prayers.

The Maharaja Disappoints

INDIA MAY BE SHINING, BUT AIR INDIA is not. I last flew the Maharaja more than a decade ago and I was curious to see how the country's premier international carrier was now faring. So when last month I had to make a quick trip to India, I decided to fly Air India.

When I enter the cabin, a technician is on my seat, trying to repair the hand-held TV remote attached to the seat handle. When I tell him that I do not plan to watch TV, he is relieved and exits quickly, leaving the remote dangling. The seat covers, lined with velcro, are peeling off in several places. In the bathroom, there are fittings held in place by brown tape. The soap dispenser refuses to dispense soap. There is a bar of soap wrapped in cellophane, but the cellophane turns out to be industrial strength. I end up squashing the soap in the skirmish to take it out.

After we are ready for take-off, our pilot—American, judging by the accent—tells us he has just been informed by ground control that, thanks to a queue, we will have to wait for over an hour for take-off. This hazard of our over-crowded skies, of course, has nothing to do with the airline. After 90 minutes, with people in various positions of repose, our plane rumbles on to the tarmac. But there is no further reminder to put seatbacks in upright position. Next to me is a lady, snoring in a near-horizontal position. As we take off, the cabin looks like one of those modern dance scenes, with passengers in acrobatic postures being gently heaved up into the sky.

Across the aisle, seat 17B has a peculiarity that, inexplicably, no other seat has—a narrow, tray-like structure fitted to the handle, jutting out into the aisle some four inches. Soon after take-off, the passenger in that seat, a small, bespectacled gentleman, discovers this mysterious contraption. He must be a scientist for he examines it with the concentration of Faraday observing electromagnetic waves or Sir Mortimer Wheeler puzzling over a just-discovered Mohenjodaro relic.

With the unerring instinct of a scientist, who, on discovering a puzzle and before investing too much time solving it, checks out if it has already been solved, he asks a passing stewardess what the tray is for. She, clearly no Marie Curie, has noticed this for the first time and blurts out, 'Sir, this is a tray.'

'Thank you, thank you,' says the impeccably polite scientist, adding hesitantly, '...but, I was wondering why only my seat is having this excellent facility?' The pretty stewardess, undisturbed by this anomaly of nature, giggles and says, 'So that you can keep your glass or bowl on it.'

'Naturally,' says Faraday, deciding to abandon the quest for knowledge.

Two hours before the end of the flight, well after the main meal is over, the same smiling attendant distributes the inflight menu cards.

On my return journey from Delhi, the sound system in my cabin is not working. The safety announcement is a melange of gurgling sounds interspersed with alarming words like 'oxygen' and 'life-jacket'. If you think you will follow the instructions by looking at the TV monitor, you face another disappointment. The screen is like a cartoon show with blurred, distended faces, putting on oxygen masks, which are pixel-jumbled, like when on the news channel they need to show streakers being taken away by the police.

Undeterred, the November issue of the inflight magazine, *Namaskaar*, proudly informs the traveller: 'Air India has been unanimously voted the "Best South Asian Airline" by readers of TTG Asia, TTG China, TTGmice and TTG-BTmice China.' (I feel resentful of my school teachers for not having taught me what TTG stood for.) 'The airline was presented the prestigious award at the glittering 17th annual travel awards ceremony by TTG Asia Media in Pattaya.'

India has been spending money on advertising brand India to the world. That is fine but the biggest advertisement for a country is its actual products that are visible all over the world. It is unfortunate that Air India puts on such a disappointing show. India is clearly capable of better, as is evident from our domestic airlines. The Jet Airways flights that I take between Delhi, Hyderabad, and Kolkata have a quality as good as or better than the best anywhere in the world.

Given the strategic importance of Air India, what should be done? Privatization should be a priority, though that in itself may not be enough. America's domestic airline industry is fully privatized and with minimal regulatory controls, but it is in dreadful shape— with abysmal punctuality record and poor service quality. Clearly, privatization has to be combined with intelligent regulation.

But above all, it is the love of excellence at the top that is crucial. That is what has made our IT and pharmaceutical industries what they are and it is apathy of the top administration that has made Air India what it is. We need to hold the top management of Air India responsible for not just a poorly run airline but, more importantly, also for providing negative advertisement for India.

Taking Off: Airports and Economics

SOME OF THE ECCENTRICITIES OF INDIAN airports are charming. Take the modern tea-dispensing machines, where, thanks to Indian ingenuity, the automaticity is totally dispensed with. The other day, as I tried to insert coins into one such machine at Delhi airport, a middle-aged lady intercepted, took the coins from my hand, dismantled the front panel of the machine with the dexterity of a magician, tucked the coins in, took a plastic cup out of the automatic cup dispenser, placed it under the tap and turned some knobs, which brought forth the magic potion.

The charm, however, paled during the Indian flight to Kolkata, when the passengers were informed of a 'short circuit' in the aircraft's music system. The music could neither be switched off nor kept on continuously. So we would hear the strains of 'Mera joota hai Japani', then total silence for some seconds, then 'lal topi russi, phir bhi', again silence.... For the first 15 minutes it was amusing; by the end of the two hours it was maddening.

Even worse were the four hours (originally supposed to be one) I recently spent at the Air India terminal of Mumbai airport, waiting for a flight to Delhi. What showed on the flights display board did not match what was being announced, which did not match the ground reality. Further, the announcement system was being used not just to inform travellers, but also to send messages to the CISF (Central Industrial Security Force) staff: 'CISF staff please open gate 18', was announced several times with increasing firmness.

A stall called 'Celebrations' advertised tea for Rs 20, but a sleepy custodian told us to go to another stall, 'Georgia', where we were informed that the machine had broken down. The Air India staff was totally unhelpful. The only kindness was from the life-size cut-out of a smiling stewardess doing namaste. The whole scene was a far cry from the stories of booming India; it was like a surreal recreation of a failed state.

India's state-run airlines and the nearly 100 airports are an embarrassment. Our top officials and bureaucrats should occasionally travel incognito to check out the state these are in.

Some may argue that it is only a tiny fraction of India that travels by air. So if our government's aim is to serve the poor and the disadvantaged (and I believe that should be the government's aim), then surely airports should be low down in the nation's list of priorities.

This reasoning is flawed. The economy is a sufficiently complex organism that some sectors which appear far removed from the object of policy are actually critical. Aviation is one such sector. It is an infrastructure that enables an economy to function better and creates the potential to help all segments, including those who never travel by air. Further, because this is such a visible sector, its significance is even greater. It can have a large 'advertisement effect' for the nation and encourage trade and foreign investment.

It is because of these larger concerns that I have been looking at the plans for Delhi's newly privatized airport. I have spent time talking to the GMR group that has the primary responsibility of setting up and running Delhi's privatized airport, and examining the blueprints. The plans and the first steps at execution are extremely good; there is reason to expect that, in another three or four years, Delhi airport will take a mega-leap into the twenty-first century, with large benefits for the entire economy.

I do not believe that privatization is the panacea to all problems. There are examples of superbly run public-sector concerns in Europe and East Asia; but the fact remains that our public-sector airline companies and airport authority have done a miserable job. Some of the statistics speak for themselves. Till recently, the airport's housekeeping staff had an absenteeism rate of over 35 per cent, which makes our primary-school teachers in state schools look like models of diligence. Teachers absent themselves from work 25 per cent of their working days.

Then take the duty free shop. The Airport Authority had given it to the India Tourism Development Corporation (ITDC) for Rs 20 crore a year. Now GMR has given it to Alpha Futures and is expected to earn revenues of over Rs 100 crore. Earlier, the airport used to earn around Rs 3 crore per annum from advertising. This figure is now expected to reach Rs 40 crore.

These are additional incomes virtually out of thin air—earned simply by looking for the highest bidder, and getting the staff to be energetic and efficient. A part of the privatization deal is that government is going to earn 45.9 per cent of gross sales. And all signs are that this share will exceed what the government earned when it had the whole airport to itself.

The chief executives of GMR were concerned that, since many of the functions of the airport, such as the customs and the road transport to and from the airport, will remain with the government, a large part of the success of the airport will depend on how these services are delivered. I was impressed by this awareness of complementarities and do believe that a lot depends on this. But, if the main functioning of the airport is improved, that itself should have a salutary effect on the complementary state sector. The possibility that Delhi will be running an airport that is as large and

Kaushik Basu

comparably efficient as Singapore's Changi International, in the not too distant a future, seems a reality.

Fragments from an Africa Diary: Johannesburg, Pretoria, and Diepsloot

I NEVER THOUGHT I WOULD DESCEND to being the kind of person who read budget speeches for pleasure. I was, therefore, alarmed when, on settling into my seat for the long haul from Washington to Johannesburg via Dakar, I found myself reaching out to Finance Minister Pravin Gordhan's budget speech that he had just delivered to the South African Parliament. Worse, I soon found myself reading it with pleasure. The pleasure came from two sources: the fluency and the eminent sensibility of the speech, and comfort from the realization that the problems we contend with, wherever we are located in the world today, are fundamentally similar. South Africa is wrestling with keeping its fiscal deficit under control, its flagging growth rate up, and yawning inequities in check. Musing about these problems I dozed off. When I woke up the cabin was dark. Curious about who was going to Africa, I looked around. Of the passengers in my cabin, 20 per cent were black, 70 per cent were white, and 90 per cent were watching *The Best Exotic Marigold Hotel.*

When I step out of the airplane at Johannesburg's O.R. Tambo International Airport, the air is bracing, the sky clear, as only the African sky can be, and the warmth and smiles of the people switch on in my head the opening lines of Rabindranath Tagore's famous poem in Bengali, simply called *Africa.* Its magisterial lines keep replaying silently in my head. Tagore wrote it in 1936, one year after Mussolini's invasion of Ethiopia: a poet's protest against the savagery of the powerful.

There are officials from the World Bank's Pretoria office to receive us. There is Asad; there is Sandeep. Jacob will be the person in charge of driving me around for the next two days. He is the font of wisdom. Every time we are stuck on a question, be it one pertaining to street directions, South African politics, or history, we would just have to lean over and ask Jacob. A charming woman comes and shakes hands with me; I am told she is my security officer and will be with me during my stay here.

As we drive to my hotel in Pretoria, cruising down well-maintained boulevards, past magnificent homes, at a street crossing, two luxury cars have come to a halt and a well-dressed man, presumably an occupant of one of the cars, is pinned down on the road by another man, probably from the other car. It is a disturbing scene. I ask Jacob what is happening. 'They are having a fight,' says Jacob matter-of-factly, making it impossible for me to pursue the investigation any further.

There are few countries in the world that carry as big a burden of history as South Africa. The brutality of apartheid weighs down not only the pages of the nation's history books but contemporary policy debates and documents. South Africa is a nation that combines the First World and the Third, with little in between to mediate. In virtually all statistics, the long history of apartheid casts its shadows. Unemployment among whites is at a manageable level; unemployment among blacks would make the worst performing in the Eurozone crisis look good. The story is similar for health indicators, poverty head counts, and per capita income. South Africa today has an impressive body of people at the helm of policy but the challenges are equally impressive. History can be a difficult adversary. Coloured people do not have to leave the precincts of the main cities before dusk as they once had to under apartheid law, but thanks to poverty and housing costs, many of them still do. They return to their townships, where land is cheap and housing affordable. In fact, the percentage of blacks living in townships has gone up in the last ten years from 30 to 37.

I was in South Africa primarily to attend a conference on township economics and I had insisted that the one free day I had before the conference began I would get to spend in a township.

So the next morning, Celestin, who had travelled with me from Washington; Asad and Sandeep from the local World Bank office; my security officer and a special armed security person (again a woman) for going into the township; two visitors from Brazil, Anaclaudia and Eduarda, who are experts on the problems of the favelas; Xiaobo who is an expert on China's village enterprise and a former student of mine from Cornell whom I am meeting after many years; some local people; and I head out to Diepsloot, a township located half way between Pretoria and Joburg and home to around 200,000 people.

One enters Diepsloot via a modern shopping mall, which could have been in Jakarta, New Delhi, or Washington. The manager of the mall, Mzo, is a charming person; he takes us around proudly showing how well the mall is run. But as soon as one enters the interior of this sprawling township, the scene changes sharply. Diepsloot was created *ex nihilo*, in 1994, as a residency for displaced people and low-skilled workers. Over time, through lack of work, the low skill has, for many, sloped off into no skill. The terrain is rugged—iron and asbestos, roads that are potholed and undrained. Even the poor homes are protected with barbed wires and the artless cubism of grills.

We walk into homes, knock on arbitrary doors, talk to street vendors and local business persons. I am assured that there would be no way to do this after dark when people bolt their doors and the streets wear a deserted look and crime is rampant. As often happens in crime infested areas, there is something lovely about the people at an individual level and the disarming honesty of the residents take me by surprise. A cheerful young man from Mpulanga runs a local eatery—an open stove and some ramshackle chairs and tables. He explains to me that he has no right—ownership or tenancy—to the land and ramshackle structure where he runs his 'restaurant'. And he is harassed by the police for that reason.

A vegetable vendor, Christina, says that at all times she is ready to run with her wares when the police come, because she has no rights to the shop and the space on which the shop stands. A very striking hardware shop-owner—a woman of great dignity, who came from Natal with one suitcase and now runs an impressive two-room store—when queried if she can be asked to leave the land since she has no titles to it, tells me without a moment's hesitation: 'That can happen tomorrow.'

With such an acute property rights problem, it is easy to see that only those with an extraordinary appetite for risk would set up business here. Not surprisingly, entrepreneurship is spare and sparse. Few people from Diepsloot go to nearby cities, like Joburg and Pretoria, to work because transport is meagre and costly. Those who do, end up spending on average 20 per cent of their income on transport. Since so few people go to work, it is not worthwhile setting up a more efficient transportation business. And since there is no efficient transport, not too many people get to work. It is really a Catch 22 situation. Late in the afternoon, we eat lunch at a restaurant called Mome's, run by an amicable person, Maxwell, on the edge of Diepsloot. A councillor from the township (one of two), Mr Rodgers, and some local business people, join us for lunch. We discuss the economics of townships. The pressing policy needs are not difficult to fathom. The property on which people live and run business operations has to come with tradeable rights. The right can be that of ownership or tenancy but they must be transparent and people must have the freedom to sell those rights and move on when they need to. I cannot help recalling a paper I wrote with Patrick Emerson (published in 2000 in *Economic Journal*), where we demonstrated the power of well-specified property and tenancy laws. Second, the state needs to step in to provide minimal infrastructure, which includes the soft infrastructure of law and order.

The following day is spent cooped up in a conference room. The World Bank has done extremely impressive work collecting data on Diepsloot and analysing the challenges the township faces. We have a lot of discussion on that not only with researchers but local administrators, mayors of different towns, and several senior politicians, including the finance minister of South Africa. We discuss South Africa's problem, the Brazilian model of dealing with urban slums, and China's hyper-specialized small towns and villages. One town in China, we are told, produces 40 per cent of all the ties sold in the world; another town a majority of buttons in the world.

Later that evening, and before and after the conference, I get to talk to a host of leading policymakers of South Africa. A lot of conversation invariably turns to BRICS since South Africa was then preparing for the BRICS summit. We discuss the proposed BRICS bank. Before I came to the World Bank, I had been working on the BRICS bank blue print, and several individuals are interested in hearing from me about the scope for such a multilateral bank. But, and this is a sign of our globalizing world, the greatest interest is in Europe. When will the Eurozone crisis end? Will the edges of the zone splinter off? And if that happens, what will be the consequence for emerging economies, such as South Africa, India, Brazil, China, and Indonesia? I tell them what I have maintained for a while now—that times will be hard for the Eurozone till at least the beginning of 2015, since there is a large repayment wall that will loom up upon banks at that time.

Talking to policymakers in Pretoria, Joburg, and Cape Town, and earlier in many other fora, I realized why there is so much distrust of public statements. Responsible policymakers are supposed to calm markets by assuring people that the crisis that just occurred—in Greece, Cyprus, or wherever—is an isolated event and will not spill over to larger economies. That being so, when leaders tell people that the crisis that just occurred is an isolated event and will not spill over to larger economies, no one believes them. The net casualty is that when it is indeed the case that there is no spillover risk, there is no language to convey it. This is the reason, I believe, one must try to speak the truth as much as possible even on touchy and difficult topics. That may occasionally cause the stock markets to wobble a little, but the credibility gain will benefit us sufficiently in the long run for it to be worthwhile. By foregoing a little bit on the next morning's calm, we would have gained on next year's stability.

Two days after the township conference in South Africa, after visiting and speaking at the University of the Witwatersrand and the University of Cape Town and after meeting many more officials, including the head and officers of South African Social Security Agency (SASSA), working on biometric identification of individuals for disbursing social welfare, Celestin and I left on 6 October for Dakar. But that is another story for another day.

Samoa Diary

A DISCOMFITING FEATURE OF GOING TO places off the beaten track is the surprise shown by the natives themselves. I recall traveling to Dushanbe from Moscow by Somon Airways; the flight attendant—a young Tajik woman—on learning that I am an Indian living in Washington, looked puzzled and asked, enunciating each word, 'Why, may I ask you, are you going to Tajikistan?' The slight sense of alarm caused by the query hinting at faulty decision making on my part was heightened by Aristomene Varoudakis, a gifted economist and one of my advisers at the World Bank, pronouncing, ten minutes into the flight: 'So far, so good.' Those words, meant to be comforting, were disquieting in their suggestion that this was a journey in which ten minutes without a mishap deserved a toast.

The same was true as I headed to Samoa. The flight was full of Samoans who could have walked out of a Paul Gauguin frieze, a few surfers, and some missionaries. Jimmy Olazo and I from the World Bank did not fit into any of these categories and faced the inevitable interrogation on why we were going there. Samoa is indeed an unusual country to visit. It is impossibly small, with a population of less than 200,000. Its resources are meagre, consisting of fish, some agricultural products, and spectacular scenery. To an economist, the viability of an economy like this is a conundrum. Where do you get the economies of scale from to produce your cars, hospitals, clothes? How much fish and tourism can you supply to the rest of the world to pay for these? Is it possible to help Samoans organize a steady flow of workers, skilled and unskilled, to other nations and rely on their remittances? How do you provide any insurance against the risks of natural disaster and calamity, a concern that, as I discovered over the next three days, dominated the lives of the Samoans? How do you conduct monetary policy in such an impossibly small nation?

These and other questions overwhelmed me during my brief, 3-day visit. I found answers to some, there were many queries that remained a puzzle, and I developed ideas on strategies that can be used to mitigate risk and help the Samoan economy. I had long meetings with the prime minister, Tuilaepa Aiono Sailele Malielegaoi, the finance minister, Faumuina Tiatia Faaolatane Liuga, the governor of the central bank, Atalina Ainuu Enari (a woman), senior officials of the health ministry—impressively, seven women and one uncomfortable man. Details of all these will go into various official documents and the mandatory Back to Office Report and need not detain us here in the cryptic pages of a blog.

Samoa rekindled in me what I have long admitted being—a closet anthropologist. This happened as I flew in reading Margaret Mead's *Coming of Age in Western Samoa*, which begins with all the evocation of a morning raga:

The life of the day begins at dawn … the shouts of the young men may be heard before dawn from the hillside. Uneasy in the night, populous with ghosts, they shout lustily to one another as they hasten with their work…. As the dawn begins to fall among the soft brown roofs and the slender palm trees stand out against a colourless, gleaming sea, lovers slip home from trysts beneath the palm trees or in the shadow of beached canoes, that the light may find each sleeper in his appointed place. Cocks crow negligently and a shrill voiced bird cries from the breadfruit trees.

I am aware that the accuracy of Mead's Samoan anthropology has been called into question but, nevertheless, these lyrical lines capture the spirit of Samoa. It may be a form of geographic infidelity on my part that the last country I have visited seems the best, a place I could settle down in, like Robert Louise Stevenson did in a sprawling estate just outside Samoa's capital 'city', Apia. Having just left Samoa, that is exactly the way I feel—it is the most beautiful place on earth, with rolling hills, tropical flowers, gentle people ('the people are mellow', in the words of the young owner of the one Indian restaurant in the nation) and no sense of urgency. On the last day, before catching my flight out, I, along with Jimmy, Maeva, and Antonia, attempted to climb the peak where the great writer lies buried. From the slopes of the hill one gets a majestic, panoramic view of this impossible kingdom and a sense of what lured Stevenson.

There are contemporary examples of outsiders settling down here. One morning we go to meet Vanya Taule'Alo a short drive from Apia. Vanya is a remarkable woman who came from New

Zealand in 1976 married a local—I assume that is how she got the Taule'Alo—and made her home in this village. She now spends her time painting and running an art gallery, displaying the handicrafts and arts of local Samoans. Her own art is remarkably original and imaginative and her home, which she opened up to us with a little persuasion, is itself a work of art.

All this cannot blind us to the fact that Samoa has its share of troubles. It is a poor nation, living on the edge of disaster (Cyclone Evan alone, in December 2012, destroyed 16 per cent of the nation's assets), with few luxuries of modern life. Yet, it has magical qualities. There is poverty (with 3 per cent of the population below the 1.25 dollars-a-day poverty line) but there is no squalor. This is so baffling that to someone familiar with poverty in sub-Saharan Africa or South Asia, it is easy to be deluded into thinking there is no poverty here. Indeed, one is confronted with troubling questions about the use of a common poverty metric across nations as varied as Samoa, Senegal, and South Africa. There is a jail and there, are I am told, inmates, but crime in this nation is negligible. I learned later that the police in Samoa, unlike ordinary citizens in the US, are not allowed to carry guns.

There is hierarchy and elitism but I could not help admiring the fact that soon after I left the bustling fish market on Sunday morning having watched the fishermen sell their catch to ordinary folks, including women adorning their hair with tropical flowers like in the Gauguin paintings, and the sun rise, the prime minister was there buying fish for himself and his family. (As a man who was at the market later told me, 'You may not have recognized him because he was wearing a hat.')

At first sight, the Islanders seem overweight. But that is simply a reminder that many of our perceptions are socially conditioned. The natural grace of the people soon obliterates any awareness of this. As the local newspaper, the *Samoa Observer*, noted pithily about the beautiful Miss World contestant from the island, Penina Maree Paeu, she 'defies the beauty pageant stereotypes'.

The Indian restaurant I mentioned above is called Tifaimoana. We were seeing it during our many rounds up and down Apia. So, on the last night, Jimmy and I decided to walk down there from our hotel, Tanoa Tusitala. It was rather late when we set out. The roads were deserted, barring a few stragglers and stray dogs. I was curious to find out who this romantic soul was who had travelled so far to set up a restaurant. Its manager turned out to be a young man from Kalyan, Mumbai. Three years ago, his brother-in-law who has some business in Fiji came here and did a back-of-the-envelope calculation about the financial viability of an Indian restaurant in Samoa. They brought in two cooks from Dehradun, one to run the tandoor and the other everything else. They hired local helping hands and Tifaimoana was founded, and judging by the fingers that were being licked and the slurping sound of the seven or eight late night diners, it was serving what till its founding was a latent Nurksian demand.

I am aware that it is easy for an outsider to be overwhelmed by Samoa's irresistible charm and overlook the many challenges this tiny nation faces. To do so will do injustice to its people. Samoa's big challenge is the environment. This is one place where global warming and the rising sea level are not academic matters. Every citizen of this nation is aware of this. The increased incidence of natural disasters— the tsunami in 2009 and Cyclone Evan in late 2012 are the most recent reminders of this. I travelled extensively and saw the ravages left by these. The place where the tsunami struck is like a picture postcard of Pacific island beauty. The catch is that between the shore and the steep mountains is just a sliver of land. When the tsunami came the people were trapped; scrambling up the hills hurriedly, many failed to beat the waves and the casualty was high.

There is now a lot of ongoing activity led by the World Bank— simple initiatives that can make a life-and-death difference, such as putting in systems of sirens and announcements to inform residents of approaching storms and tsunamis and building paths along the hill slopes so that residents can scramble up to safety. There is also need to move some important buildings like schools to higher areas, since global warming will continue for some more time even if we are able to eventually arrest it. Samoa is not a rich nation and there is desperate need for ongoing support to carry out these tasks as soon as possible. The World Bank is present all over the two main islands of this nation, Savai'I and Upolu, building roads and supporting other infrastructure but the challenges are many and there is need for more global support and engagement.

As my three packed but wondrous days quickly came to an end and I prepared to leave Samoa, I asked an inhabitant of Apia, 'Why is there so little crime and burglary in Samoa?' His answer came pat: 'That is because our homes are completely open, with no walls and no doors. That is why no one dares to go in and steal.' I have to admit that as I walked up the tarmac to the plane waiting to fly us over a vast expanse of the Pacific to Auckland, I tried to dissect the logic of that retort and had to contend myself with the thought that this was a logic that worked only in Samoa, a country after my heart.

Bhutan: Development Economics in the Himalayas

LANDING AT PARO IN BHUTAN INVOLVES making a question mark–shaped manoeuvre while dropping altitude rapidly to avoid making wing contact with the Himalayan mountains surrounding the Paro valley where Thimphu, the capital, is also situated. A fellow passenger informs me that there are only nine pilots in the world who are trained to make this landing. I use up one of my rare prayers to request that it be one of those flying us now. It is, I think, the infrequency of my prayers that makes them so effective; our plane descends smoothly and tiptoes on to the tarmac.

During my four-day visit, I start by meeting with and lecturing to economics students from Bhutan and the neighbouring countries—India, Bangladesh, Sri Lanka, Pakistan, Nepal, and Afghanistan—brought together as part of a programme to build intra-regional intellectual cooperation and understanding, sponsored by the World Bank; I conclude my Bhutan visit by dining with and engaging in a roundtable conversation with policymakers, thought leaders, and corporate heads from around the country. Between those opening and closing events, I have two meetings with the engaging prime minister, Tshering Tobgay, on challenges facing Bhutan and the region; I meet and consult with the finance minister as well as with officials of the Central Monetary Authority; converse with the director of the Centre for Bhutan Studies, Dasho Karma Ura, and engage in a memorable conversation with His Majesty, the fifth king of Bhutan, Jigme Khesar Namgyel Wangchuck.

A highlight of the trip was a visit to two urban infrastructure development projects in the Thimphu suburbs with the mayor of the capital, Kinlay Dorjee, and Genevieve Boyreau, the Bank's resident representative and senior economist. The projects are being supported by the World Bank Group. Amidst all of this, I also manage to walk up, with the World Bank's Joe Qian, to the magical Cheri Monastery and come down after two hours, feeling as though I had spent a week at a meditation camp.

Bhutan is an amazing country, embodying simultaneously tradition and modernity, rarely seen elsewhere. There is a deep-seated heritage of Buddhism and innate simplicity that marks all aspects of life. This is combined with a striving for high environmental standards, organic farming, and an attempt at a smoking ban not just in buildings and parks, but in the nation.

Much of Bhutan's challenge for development stems from these twin traits of deeply held tradition and a drive towards a modern notion of sustainability. This is a nation that has had remarkable success in fighting extreme poverty. The percentage of people living below the poverty line of $1.25 (PPP-adjusted) fell from 47 per cent in 1981 to 3 per cent in 2011. In percentage terms, this is the sharpest fall, a shade faster than China's decline from 84 per cent to 6 per cent over the same period. As reported in the Bank's 'Bhutan Poverty Assessment 2014', growth in the country has been inclusive and Bhutan is a society graced with a high degree of social mobility.

Nevertheless, there are some clouds of concern. After a period of rapid development, including double-digit growth in 2011, the GDP growth rate slowed down 2.1 per cent in 2013 as a result of the global slowdown and domestic macro-structural strains, including a high current account deficit. Moreover, unemployment, while not high by Eurozone standards, has risen, and, in particular, there is a perceptible rise in unemployment among educated youth.

To attend to these challenges while preserving the nation's admirable cultural heritage and environmental commitments is not easy; this came up in virtually every discussion forum and bilateral meeting, as did the topic of regional cooperation among the eight SAARC countries, which is particularly important to Bhutan, since it is a small land-locked nation.

The nation's big business is hydro-electric power generation and export of power to India. Another sector with significant potential is tourism. The country has an interesting tourism policy, which consists of requiring, with minimal exceptions, that each tourist spend at least $250 per day. While the urge to follow a 'high value, low impact' tourism policy is understandable, it is not obvious that the method currently used is optimal. For one, I believe Bhutan can afford to charge more in the peak season and less in the lean season to improve on utilization rates and increase the revenue earned from tourism. Moreover, it can use non-linear pricing, and possibly even alternative auction systems, and increase the revenue it earns from this sector.

I have no precise solutions to offer but I know that by using good analysis and a little operations research, the nation can enhance its earnings from and employment-generation capacity of the tourism sector. I know this from experience because when I worked in India and the government was planning to auction 3G spectrum, our estimate was that this had a value of approximately $7 billion. Luckily, the government decided to use a professionally designed auction instead of selling it at the government-estimated price; the money raised turned out to be over twice the estimate. It is difficult to overemphasize the power of good policy design.

With its success in nurturing human capital and health, Bhutan should also be able to develop its education and information technology and digital data management sectors. These advances could help absorb its educated labour force.

Finally, there is indeed scope for huge developments in inter-regional trade, travel, and tourism. South Asia is one of the least economically integrated regions of the world. Success in advancing inter-regional economic cooperation is of course not within the reach of any single country. Much will depend on collective determination and also the resolve of the big country of the region, India. This should however be treated as a priority for South Asia and maybe little Bhutan can play a neutral role in egging on the big players.

Successful and prominent cities and regions in Asia and, more generally, the Orient are often named as 'such-and-such place of the East'. After four magical days in Bhutan, nestled peacefully in the high mountains, with a warm and friendly citizenry, I have decided that, reversing this tradition, I shall now think of Switzerland as the Bhutan of the West.

Postcard from Malaysia: Through the Smog, Gently

Preamble

My travels in Malaysia begin at the distant eastern edge of the country, in Sabah's capital, Kota Kinabalu, the strange name a reminder of the distance I have travelled from home. Meeting local folks, regional politicians, and masters of local arts and crafts, it quickly becomes evident that this ancient island, Borneo, symbolizes all the mysteries and romance of human movement through history. The people who seem settled here forever arrived one day after travelling great distances, braving the wilds and the seas. They were then the modern people who had come to an ancient land. They would soon be absorbed and become the natives in the eyes of the next wave of arrival and modern-day visitors like us.

Frederico, Vivian, Kup (a senior officer of the Ministry of Finance), and I are received at the airport at Kota Kinabalu by a charming young woman, Intan. She is tall and has a headscarf carefully draped around her head covering her hair. Intan explains she is part Arab, part Chinese, and part Bijau, an ancient tribal people. She smiles and adds that she considers herself Bijau.

Sabah seems a melting pot of cultures and peoples of different kinds. From my hotel window, I can see the ocean and on the edge of it a canopy of irregular blue rooftops. I am told this was originally a bazaar run by Filipino immigrants. Two men sit comfortably on their haunches and chat, thereby revealing that the middle-income status of Sabah is relatively recent. I am most impressed by the complete comfort with which two obviously transsexual students sit among the boys and girls at the art school, Kolej Yayasan Sabah, laughing, chatting, and painting. This is what civilization should be judged by.

The Economy and Its Challenges

Coming into Kuala Lumpur from Borneo, the first thing one notices is the haze. Peninsula Malaysia is shrouded in a haze from burning wood and shouldering peat in Indonesia. When we arrive the 'API haze count'—an index of the intensity—hovers around Italy's sovereign debt-to-GDP ratio. Make what you will of that. This gives rise to a gentle smoky aroma from which there is no escape. I deal with it by persuading my mind someone has spilled a bottle of single-malt Laphroaig whiskey in the vicinity. It works; I enjoy every moment of my visit.

My visit to Malaysia is to witness the country's economic challenges first hand, launch the Malaysia Economic Monitor (MEM), meet Prime Minister Najib Razak in his office in Putrajaya to discuss Malaysia's economic problems, address the prime minister's Economic Council, explore the scope for greater interaction between the World Bank and Malaysia, and meet with policymakers who've had their hand on the tiller, guiding the economy, which is now expected to grow by 5.1 per cent for both 2013 and 2014.

According to the MEM, resilient domestic demand is spurring a recovery from a slow first quarter in 2013. Higher consumer and business spending is expected to boost GDP, and the country's external sector will be a key driver, offsetting the impact of tighter fiscal policies on the domestic economy.

Yet Malaysia's trade is dominated by crude oil, palm oil, natural gas, and rubber, and we all know that putting all of one's eggs in the proverbial commodities basket is not a good idea. With the demand for commodities dampened by weak growth in key export markets such as China and Europe, and an abundance of global supply, Malaysia needs to accelerate structural reforms to ensure that its economy remains diversified and dynamic.

So far Malaysia's sound policy choices have ensured that revenues from resource extraction were reinvested in the economy in the form of machines, buildings, and education. This supported high rates of growth, the benefits of which were shared among the citizenry, raising the average incomes of the bottom 40 per cent of rural households by 7.1 per cent a year over 20 years, while poverty fell quickly.

Given the Bank Group's two new goals of getting extreme poverty down to less than 3 per cent by 2030 and of promoting real income growth of the poorest 40 per cent of each country's population, I am convinced more than ever that we have much to learn from Malaysia. What I did not know earlier is that Malaysia had set itself the goal of focussing on the poorest 40 per cent of its population well before the Bank adopted this as a target.

What is most impressive about Malaysia is its effort to transform its business ethos. Government bureaucrats are repeatedly reminded that their aim is to help citizens and enable entrepreneurs to do business efficiently. One can see palpable manifestations of this in several areas of governance such as during our visit to the Urban Transformation Centre in Malacca. Passports are now issued within two hours of receiving applications.

Malaysia has formidable challenges. It is a multi-cultural, multi-ethnic society and will have to address the tensions and fissures that all such societies have to deal with. It has to continue to diversify and modernize its industry and, above all, build human capital and promote research and innovation.

A Hinduism More Tolerant

KOLKATA IS WHERE I WAS BORN and lived till the age of 17, when I left for college in Delhi. It is a city I visit regularly and where I maintain a home. Maybe because of this familiarity, I never felt the need to write about it.

That changed earlier this month, when on a whim I decided to spend a night in Belur Math, the Ramakrishna Mission (RKM) temple-complex on the western banks of the Ganga, on the edge of the city. Here is the mission's own description of Belur: 'Sprawling over forty acres of land on the western bank of the Hooghly (Ganga) ... a place of pilgrimage for people from all over the world professing different religious faiths. Even people not interested in religion come here for the peace it exudes.'That last sentence meant I would not be unwelcome.

You arrive there ploughing through Kolkata's winding alleyways and over-crowded streets, with lonely men in shirt-sleeves leaning out of windows, and then suddenly it appears, a place of strange serenity, basking on the bank of the old river Ganga, exuding the same sense of timelessness, captured in so many songs, from Bhupen Hazarika's tribute to the Brahmaputra to the Pussycats''Mississippi'.

Swami Vivekananda's own lines penned some 120 years ago, in his little room overlooking the river, captures this well: 'Here I am writing in my room on the Ganga, in the Math. It is so quiet and still! The broad river is dancing in the bright sunshine, only now and then an occasional cargo boat breaking the silence with the splashing of the oars.'

What is remarkable about RKM is its organizational excellence. You see this in the schools, colleges, and hospitals it runs all over India. Despite the thousands of visitors and tourists dropping in every day at Belur, the premises are spotless. Its various activities— from a variety of social work to the chanting of hymns—run with clockwork precision.

I got a sense of that when my wife and I arrived at the Mission's International Guest House early in the evening of 12 June and the check-in clerk cheerfully told us that breakfast would be served at 6:30 a.m. I asked him the standard question in hotels: up to what time would breakfast be served? He looked nonplussed. 'It is at 6:30,' he repeated with an emphasis on the 'at', which said it all.

There was nothing much to do in the evening. We chatted with several of the monks and some of the visitors, and listened to the mystical chanting by the missionaries, set to the strains of dhrupad, in the cavernous main temple, with people sitting in complete silence. By the time we stepped out, it was late, late in the evening, the crowds they were gone; the clocks had ceased their chiming and the deep river ran on.

The International Guest House is just outside the formal premises of the mission. It is on the bend of a narrow lane next to a *pir dargah* where we could see a couple of men conversing late into the night. Clearly, the whole area is under some supervision by the RKM because the lane is quiet and clean with a few bright overhead lights, which defy the darkness of the night. Between the slats of our shuttered window one can see the occasional passer-by—monks in saffron and white, stray workers returning home from the day's toil, and women in traditional white saris with red borders and bindis adorning their foreheads.

The challenge was the next morning. The *mangalarati*, we are told, is not to be missed. It takes place at 4 a.m., sharp, needless to add. The walk down the deserted alley in the darkness of the night, with those quiet overhead street lights, and homes on both sides with shuttered windows could have been a scene in an Eliot poem or a bylane in Cavafy's Alexandria. The mangalarati and the breaking of dawn over the river had a spiritual quality that made my imagination drift back to India's Vedic times. It must have been this blending of everyday life with the mysteries of nature that sparked the deep philosophical musings that make the Vedas so special.

I cannot thank the RKM enough for the warm and cordial welcome it gave us. I needed it not just because in the rough and tumble of everyday life, we spend so little time to meditate about life's unknowns, where we come from, why and where we are headed, but also because I needed to see this face of Hinduism—philosophical, tolerant, and embracing of other religions.

This is so different from what is being propagated in the name of Hinduism by today's right-wing Hindutva groups. Chatting with the young monks and the visitors to the temple, I also felt good to see most of them clamouring to separate themselves from the narrow-minded Hinduism and the hatred of Islam, Christianity, and Judaism being preached by some groups, and the murders and hate being spewed out in the name of protecting the cow. It was good to see ordinary Hindus realizing that they do not want to be part of this culture of hate.

One reason why Vivekananda set up the Mission here was that it is close to Dakshineshwar, a temple built by Rani Rashmoni, who, being low-caste, had difficulty finding a Brahmin priest. She eventually found two renegade brothers. The younger one, Ramakrishna, especially broke all the rules and rituals of religion with alacrity and had a simple message of universal love, which was echoed by his disciple, Swami Vivekananda, in his famous Chicago address, on 11 September 1893: 'I fervently hope that the bell that tolled this morning in honour of this convention may be the death-knell of all fanaticism.'

And for us, it is well-worth remembering what the current president of RKM, quoting Vivekananda's speech, wrote, 'A century has gone by since these words were uttered. At the fag end of this twentieth century, one feels that we are travelling backwards towards the age of barbarism, when might was right and group loyalties alone counted.'

In Good Faith: A Journey, an Education

FROM THE TERRACE OF THE SMALL GUEST HOUSE, with the dawn struggling to break through the mists of a monsoon night, the landscape is desolate. A light wind blows over the vast, largely uninhabited landscape, creating a hush of rustled leaves. Far away, a lake gives off a faint, early morning shimmer. Peering into this landscape, at once mystical and mysterious, one could visualize the moors of Yorkshire at the time of the Bronte sisters. Standing alone on the terrace, gradually seeing the green of the palash trees, the red and blue of the swings in the school yard, and the distant hills of Purulia, where Bengal abuts Jharkhand, my mind fills with hope.

This was the end of a three-day visit, which began on 28 July, when I landed at Ranchi and drove for four hours through Jharkhand and the western fringe of Bengal. I was there to see a village school and an eye hospital run by the NGO, Nanritam. Nanritam was founded in 2002, in memory of Swami Lokeswarananda of the Ramakrishna Mission, by two women. It started work in the Para Block of Purulia District in 2004, with a team of dedicated doctors and social workers, many of whom travel there regularly from Kolkata and the nearby town of Purulia. The original aim was to run an eye hospital and agricultural extension work for poor farmers. That work is still flourishing. The eye hospital with its modern surgical equipment, clean rooms and corridors, and a steady turnover of poor patients, many staying overnight for surgery, could well be a facility in a modern city.

But, given my own interest in education, I spent a disproportionate amount of time at the school set up in 2014 next to the eye hospital—the Filix School. It turns out to be an unexpected experience. The school already has over 400 students and classes run from nursery to grade 6. Most students pay a regular tuition fee but a large number—for this is a poor region—pay nothing. But all wear the same uniform and sit together, learning, laughing, and playing, unaware of their diverse wealth, religion and caste backgrounds.

Living in New York, I had, for some time, been wanting to see how a 3-D printer actually works. Little did I know that my first experience of 3-D printing would occur in Filix School, with a group of wide-eyed sixth-graders jostling to show me how it works. What is rare about the school is the quality of modern education that is being imparted. They learn about their heritage and history, but, importantly from the point of view of career, they learn to speak English, are taught logic, mathematics, and modern science.

Some of the techniques of education used here are from Finland, which has been a leader in school education, and a country that the founders of Nanritam visited with the explicit idea of bringing the best ideas to India.

Both teachers and students seem to enjoy school. As I go from class to class, the students shower me with logic and IQ questions. Some of these are tough enough that I have no idea what the answers are, and so am forced to employ the only strategy for such situations: I pretend that I am pretending that I do not know the answers.

The model of Filix School deserves to be taken to other parts of India. The modernity of this school is exemplary and it is encouraging to see how well the children of these remote areas are embracing it. With the arrival of artificial intelligence and robotics, this kind of education will be critical. It is important for India that we spend time doing science and mathematics, instead of trying to show that we did science and mathematics five thousand years ago.

After the school visit, I take advantage of being in this tribal terrain, where, till a few years ago, it would be impossible to move around because of the risk of Maoist attacks, to visit little villages with evocative names like Chorida and Tamna, and travel through the hills of Ajodhya, an extension of the Chota Nagpur plateau.

The Santals, who inhabit these villages and forests, constitute one of the largest tribes of India. Dark skinned and beautiful, they settled in the Indian subcontinent way before the arrival of the Aryans. Their villages, lined with artisan homes, with hand-painted facades, are a visual treat. Their language belongs to the Austroasiatic group that is used by nearly 120 million people, spread over South Asia, the Khmer region, and southern China. It originally had no script of its own. Raghunath Munda, an innovative Santal leader, developed a script in the early twentieth century, called Ol Chiki, which has now caught on widely.

In the village of Hathimara, in Huda Block, a talented young artist tells us about their art and festivals. The big one is Kali puja, though unlike in traditional Hinduism, they do not have any idols to go with the festival. Talking to these people, it is impossible not to marvel at our own history and wonder where we come from, who our ancestors are, and the connections that all human beings have across vast geographic spaces and continents.

The final morning, I wake up early to see the dawn break and attend the morning prayer, mangal arati, at 5 a.m., at the chapel of Ramakrishna. The chiming of the bells and the chanting of the Sanskrit verses adds to the sense of wonder.

I do not want to mislead my reader. I am a sceptic, with very few beliefs, beyond logical truths. I believe that anything that is not logically impossible is possible. What fascinates me about the mangal arati is not religion but its aura of philosophy. It is a reminder of how little we know and the need for humility. It captures a spirit of Hinduism so different from the cults of hatred being abetted by political groups. Travelling through these villages, talking to ordinary folks, I am heartened to see them distressed too by these cults. And that is what gives me the hope I mentioned at the start.

An Evening in Florence

IT IS THE SIXTH OF OCTOBER and I am changing planes in Lisbon. As we settle into our seats and fasten seat belts, a flight attendant sprays the cabin liberally with some pressurized liquid from a can. The intercom crackles and a voice with a marked Portuguese accent, which makes me for a moment wonder if I am in Goa, tells us that the spraying of this disinfectant is required under the law, and assures the passengers that it will not adversely affect our—and, alas, I cannot make out if the next word is 'health' or 'wealth'. I comfort myself that it is good to know at least one of these two will remain intact.

The reason for the cavalier feeling is that I am headed to one of the most beautiful cities in the world and for a wonderful purpose. I am going to Florence to get an honorary degree or, what sounds better in Latin, laurea honoris causa. To get a degree is nice; to get it without work is bliss. But the real source of joy is Florence. Florence, like Athens, is among the rare cities in the world that can lay unequivocal claim to having served as a cradle of human civilization.

As Bertrand Russell wrote in *History of Western Philosophy*, 'The modern as opposed to the medieval outlook began in Italy, with the movement called Renaissance. Florence was the most civilised city in the world, and the chief source of the Renaissance.' As I spend my free time walking around the city and seeing some of the great works of art and sculpture, it is impossible not to marvel at Florence's achievements from the fourteenth century all the way up to the seventeenth. It was the city of Machiavelli, Dante, and Botticelli. Michelangelo was born there, Galileo was born nearby, in the Duchy of Florence, and Leonardo da Vinci worked there.

But talent alone is not enough to spread art and science through the world, as happened with the Italian Renaissance. Florence was lucky to have a remarkable business house at that time, the Medicis, who used their enormous financial power to nurture the arts, philosophy and science. The most notable was Lorenzo de Medici, who, in the late fifteenth century, became a patron of the scholars, artists and poets, and played a pivotal role in spreading the Renaissance to the rest of the world.

However, it is foolish to confine all of one's attention to museums and galleries when visiting an interesting place. I find the street life and interaction with ordinary people fascinating. Italians are friendly and warm; so it is easy to start up conversations. Walking in the streets with my friend, Mario Biggeri, I meet some interesting people. There was, for instance, a small display of roadside art by a hippie-looking person. The art was stunning; I had never seen anything like that on a roadside. With Mario translating, I learned that his name was Luigi Lanotte, and he came from Puglia. When I commented on his talent, he acknowledged my praise shyly and said that his art was in several galleries and the gallery owners disapproved of his roadside display; but, he explained, he found the galleries too confining and would never abandon street art. Clearly, he was one of those true artists interested in art and could not care less about the marketing.

A walk through the Merkato Centrale with its mixture of roadside vendors, cafes, and stores can be an anthropologist's delight.

I paused to buy a leather belt from a young vendor who seemed to have a flourishing business. He struggled to speak in English and I tried a few Italian words, all to no avail. Then we discovered, we had another common language—Bengali. It turned out that a large fraction of the shops and stalls there were operated by Bangladeshis. They seemed to be happy and doing well and were clearly pleased to chat with me in Bengali, though one of them pointed out that my accent sounded wrong.

Travel is wonderful, for the experience and also for the faux pas. After the ceremony of the degree conferral in an ornate auditorium of the Università degli Studi di Firenze, I went with some faculty members to a café for lunch. The food in Italy and most of continental Europe is excellent. I sometimes wonder if Britain managed to out-manoeuvre other European nations in the race to colonize the world because it spent relatively so little time and energy on good food.

After the meal of a delicious lasagne, it was time to order coffee. When the waiter going around the table taking our orders came to me, I said, 'One cappuccino.' He looked pale and there was a hushed silence. I wondered if, like my Bengali according to the Bangladeshi shop-owner, this time I had mispronounced cappuccino. There was an embarrassed murmur around the room. Then one of the professors leaned over to me kindly and whispered: the waiter is baffled because that is what English ladies drink, and that, too, only before 10 a.m.

My poor taste had been revealed and there was nothing I could do about it.

As the time comes for my departure, I feel a strange sense of optimism. Strange because Italy has been going through a difficult phase, with a surge in right-wing politics, fuelling hatred against refugees fleeing conflict and persecution, and arriving in Europe seeking shelter. Yet, spending a few days in Italy, meeting people not just in the halls of academe, but in the markets and cafes, experiencing their natural warmth and kindness, I cannot help feeling that the future belongs to the people and not the hawks of fringe political groups, who may be having their time in the sun, but not for long.

The Turin Miracle

ABOUT A YEAR AGO I WAS INVITED to give the Luca d'Agliano Lecture in Turin. This annual lecture has established itself as a major event, I was keen to share some new research I have been doing on law and economics, and I had never been to Turin. In short, there was every reason to give this lecture; and in the process I got to spend three blissful days in Turin.

I lectured on law, economics, and corruption control, covering an expanse of material, from Kautilya's writings, c. 300 BCE, to contemporary research. In most emerging economies, from China and India, through much of sub-Saharan Africa, to Brazil and Argentina, corruption seems like an endemic problem. As Kautilya had, maybe too cynically, noted, 'Just as it is impossible not to taste honey on the tip of the tongue, so it is impossible for a government servant not to eat up at least a part of the king's revenue.'

But we know that there are countries, such as Sweden and Britain, that have moved from being high-corruption societies to low, over one or two centuries. There are also economies that have made the transition in even shorter time. This is true of Singapore and Hong Kong, which are today ranked by Transparency International not just above Italy and Greece but above the US, in terms of freedom from corruption. How this transition can be made is a fascinating question and thanks to advances in game theory and the rise of behavioural economics, we have some understanding of this that we did not have earlier.

The many discussions after my lecture over meals in wonderful Turin restaurants were instructive; and, on occasion, amusing. An Italian friend who had gone to Delhi some time back told us about his stay at the India International Centre, and how it was memorable because of the early morning walks he took in 'Modi Gardens'. As I wondered whether to tell him he was confounding historical names with contemporary Indian politics, a suave Italian, who regularly goes to India, leaned over and held forth on the Lodis, and their sixteenth century tombs in the gardens, clarifying that these are not

'Modi Gardens'. The only disturbing part of the discourse was—I cannot be sure of what he meant because he was mixing Italian and English—that it ended with 'not yet'.

Turin is a city of museums and mansions. Most famously, it is the city of the shroud of Turin, the linen cloth in which Jesus Christ was allegedly wrapped after the crucifixion. The jury is still out on whether it is really that cloth since some scientific tests seem to contest the claim.

As always in any city, I enjoy the museums but also watching the rhythm of everyday life in the streets. Luckily, I managed to slip out between meetings and seminars to stroll through the city. Turin is the city where Antonio Gramsci studied and started the weekly magazine, *L'Ordine Nuovo*, and took to political activism, before being arrested and jailed by Mussolini's police; it is the city that Nietzsche lived in and loved, where he had his famous mental breakdown. It is a city with magnificent mansions and, equally, picturesque poor neighbourhoods and ghettoes, enhanced by the many passers-by, with what Auden described as 'soul-bewitching' faces.

My final stop was on my way back to the airport. I toured the Castello di Rivoli, a ninth-century castle atop a hill from where I could see the ancient town of Rivoli, half covered in morning mist. The castle is home to some outstanding contemporary art, elegantly displayed. But the big surprise was the enormous room in the museum displaying art, video and photographs connected to Rabindranath Tagore's play, *The Post Office*. The exhibition was also a tribute to Janusz Korczak, a Jewish writer who staged the play in an orphanage in a Warsaw ghetto, just before he and many of the orphans were sent to a death camp in Treblinka in 1942. It was a sad but moving exhibition that drew the curtain on my three magical days in Turin.

Magical and also miraculous, given that it almost did not happen. A week before I travelled, my US green card had gone missing. After turning our home upside down, to no avail, I joked with my wife that it was time to try prayer, and see if God listens to me. So I sat self-consciously cross-legged and prayed, in gist saying: God, as you well know I do not call on you every day. In fact, I pray once every several years when I am desperate; and today is one of those days, since it will be truly embarrassing for me to cancel this long-planned lecture. I am not sure you exist but, if you do, please appreciate my honesty, and give me my green card. Further, I am not saying that if you do, I will become a believer. Looking around the world, there is so little evidence of your existence that one miracle is unlikely to make me change my mind.

I got up, did my usual late night reading and writing, and went to sleep. Next morning, unmindfully, I opened the same drawer which my wife and I had searched repeatedly. And there it was, in plain sight, the green card. I felt an emotional charge, a mixture of elation and confusion. I tried to reconstruct all the events of the previous few days and could in no way explain what had happened.

So what do I make of it? The most likely interpretation is the green card was always there and neither of us saw it. On the other hand, violations of the laws of induction do not trouble me because of my innate scepticism. I believe whatever is not logically impossible is possible. However, what I experienced was so confounding that the only way I can sum it up is with an equally confounding thought: whether or not God exists, what is certain is he loves me.

Does God Exist? There Are Several Possible Hypotheses

MEETING MY OLD FRIEND, MICHAEL MENEZES, at the beautiful Pali Village Café in Mumbai recently, my mind drifted back to our college days in Delhi and another café.

This was in early 1972, maybe March or April. Our three years in St. Stephen's College were drawing to a close, three magical years of fun and friendship. I did poorly in my final exam but that seemed like a small price to pay for all the joy of not studying. Mike and I decided it was time to do some good and our plan was to match one of our classmates, whose name will remain anonymous, to a very charming student of Miranda House, whose name, alas, I do not remember. So we devised a remarkable entrepreneurial scheme. We wrote a letter to her pretending to be him, professing to be in love with her and pleading her to come to the university Coffee House to meet him. And we wrote a letter to him pretending to be her, professing love and requesting that he come to the Coffee House at the same time.

When that momentous day came, Mike and I headed off to the Coffee House to witness the fruits of our matchmaking. On the way, we had to make a phone call and stepped into one of those phone booths, so ubiquitous those days, where you insert coins to make a call. And there we struck gold, or, more precisely, a 10-rupee note, left behind by someone on the phone counter. There was no one to be seen nearby, and it was too small an amount to go searching for the owner. The thought struck us both that this was an occasion for free coffee. Mike, being a Catholic, wondered if we were about to commit a sin. I assured him of the flexibility of the Hindu gods. Further, somewhere in high school, I had ceased to believe in god. I saw no evidence of god and, in case he was there and had hid the evidence of his existence, he would surely be irritated by the dishonesty of the believers who claimed to see evidence. .

In any case, we decided this was a good test of god's existence. We would see whether or not he punished us for this sin. We walked over to the Coffee House and, soon, as expected, our classmate came in, looking tense. He sat alone in a far corner, an eye on the main entrance. Within minutes she came in, and walked unsurely to his corner. They began chatting. We could not hear the conversation but it was clear that it was running into heavy weather, each claiming the other had asked them to come. Then we saw them both pull out letters from their pockets and thrust them at each other, at which point, Mike and I decided it was time to leave the scene of crime.

As we walked out of the Coffee House, Mike got proof (in his case, a reminder) of god's existence. He reached into his pocket and his wallet was mysteriously missing.

The salad days of college came to an end in June. I packed my bags from my residence in Stephen's Rudra South, bid farewell to my dearest friends, and left for a short vacation in Calcutta and then for the London School of Economics. (Luckily, LSE had given me admission before seeing my final-year performance in St. Stephen's.)

I was delighted when, three years later, Mike, by then a chartered accountant, came to LSE for a master's degree. On a walk one afternoon, we stepped into one of those iconic, red phone-booths of London to make a call. And, yes, an abandoned five pound note was lying, at roughly the same place as the ten rupee note three years ago. There was no one in the vicinity who could be its rightful owner. We gasped at how uncannily similar the situation was. Was god testing us to see if we had learned our lesson? We, on our part, decided we had to check how consistent god was. So we picked up the money and set off to have coffee at Wimpy.

Like Alexander Fleming in his laboratory waiting to see if the bacteria would grow, we sat, drinking our coffee but with our minds transfixed on the experiment. Time ticked away. We finished our coffee, paid for it with our ill-gotten gain and walked out nervously, and back to our hostel. What happened then, was the following: our wallets were not lost.

Given nature's different response to our picking up abandoned notes in Delhi and London, the question remained open: does god exist? There are several possible hypotheses: there is no god, and the loss of the wallet in Delhi was a fluke; there is god but he believes in punishing people for drinking coffee using ill-gotten gains, but only when that is coupled with writing letters in other people's names. However, when Mike revealed later that the experiment was not quite the same because this time, while having coffee, he had clutched on to his wallet, we realized there was a third hypothesis— there is god but he is not that powerful, and in particular, he cannot wrestle wallets out of clenched fists.

The upshot basically is that there is no firm answer. What I would recommend to you, dear reader, is my own philosophy of scepticism.

Live by it and you will make better decisions in life.

five

Persons and Ideas*

Amartya Sen: Re-inventing Himself

FOR SCIENTISTS AND ECONOMISTS, THE NOBEL PRIZE is
often an intellectual death sentence. The honour for some
deep scientific research done (usually) in a person's youth can easily
create a hankering for more. Great scientists, with egos boosted by
the prize, have tried to go back to their early research. But that
is almost always futile. By the time the honour comes, the magic
touch is typically gone.

With his new book, *The Argumentative Indian*, Amartya Sen,
the winner of the 1998 Nobel Prize in economics, has achieved
something that is rare in science and academe—he has re-invented
himself. With this book of magnificent reach and moral vision—

* 'Amartya Sen: Re-inventing Himself' was first published as 'Asserting
a New Vision of India' in *BBC News Online*, 17 December 2005. 'Prasanta
Pattanaik: A Fine Theorist' was first published in *Hindustan Times*, 10 November
2007. 'Engels and the Quest for a Better World' was first published as 'The
First Marxist' in *Hindustan Times*, 23 October 2009. 'Paul Samuelson and
the Foundations of Economics' was first published as 'An Obituary for Paul

spanning history, cultural studies, and political economy—Amartya Sen has illumined a vision of India that echoes the ideas of Ashoka, Akbar, and, most emphatically, Nehru.

This is a vision that emphasizes the multiple and crisscrossing identities of Indians, and the shared global interests of all human beings. Sen points out how Hindu fundamentalism hurts Hinduism and the idea of India, because it is openness and the lack of stridency that has been the hallmark of Hinduism and has given it the resilience that it has shown through its long history. The book documents carefully how Hinduism has been home to a whole range of diverse schools of thought—including some agnostic traditions. In this age of national hubris, wanton violation of basic human rights and religious narrow-mindedness, the message of the book should be of value well beyond India.

Make no mistake. *The Argumentative Indian* is not the kind of work that can earn anybody the Nobel Prize. Its scientific content is too slim for that. Viewed as history, it breaks little new ground and does not surprise us with any new archival discovery. Amartya Sen's early work—for which he won the Nobel Prize—was on welfare economics and the logic of preferences. That work, founded in formal mathematical methods and beautiful chains of deductive reasoning, took the form of using axioms to prove

Samuelson' in *Hindustan Times*, 15 December 2009. 'In Praise of Doubt' was first published as 'Good Policy Entails Right Mix of State and Markets' in *The Times of India*, 15 August 2006. 'Kenneth Arrow: Economist of the Century' was first published as 'Kenneth Arrow: Possibly the Most Important Economist of the Twentieth Century' in *The Wire*, 27 February 2017. 'John Nash: The Shakespeare of Economics' was first published in *Indian Express*, 3 June 2015. 'The Anti-argumentative Indian' was first published as 'Economic Graffiti: The Anti-argumentative Indian: Amartya Sen' in *Indian Express*, 14 December 2018. 'The Problem of Choice' was first published in *Indian Express*, 25 February 2017. 'The Angry Intellectual: Ashok Mitra' was first published as 'Economic Graffiti: The Angry Intellectual' in *Indian Express*, 17 May 2018. 'Stiglitz's Sticky Prices' was first published in the Project Syndicate website on 15 December 2015. 'Manmohan Singh: A Quiet Courage' was first published as 'A Quiet Courage' in *Indian Express*, 25 January 2019.

Kaushik Basu

theorems on how we may aggregate individual preferences into collective choices. There are few works in economics, including his own in recent times, that match the scientific elegance of these early publications of his.

What is remarkable about the new book is that it breaks away so effortlessly from that past. And in terms of practical importance for the world, this may well be the most significant book of his. One important question that arises from this book is the following. If racism, religious intolerance, and sexism are wrong, can nationalism and patriotism, which are so often upheld as noble, be right? An implication (he never says this explicitly) of Sen's argument is that, even though in contemporary society nationalism plays an important role, we should view this as interim and strive towards its ultimate banishment.

Reading Nehru's collected works, I discovered that Nehru was categorical on this. For a prime minister to openly vent his unease about nationalism is an act of extraordinary courage. I quote here from a letter he wrote to the Indian chief ministers on 20 September 1953:

When a country is under foreign domination, nationalism is a strengthening and unifying force. But a stage arrives when it might well have a narrowing influence. Sometimes, as in Europe, it becomes aggressive and chauvinistic and wants to impose itself on other countries and other people. Every people suffer from the strange delusion that they are the elect and better than all others. When they become strong and powerful, they try to impose themselves and their ways on others. In their attempt to do so, sometime or other, they overreach themselves, stumble and fall. (quoted from Gopal and Iyengar 2003: 188)

The philosophical subtext of this letter and of much else that Nehru wrote has a lot in common with Amartya Sen's new book. It is not as though I find myself in agreement with all of Sen's arguments. He takes India to task for developing the nuclear bomb. There is no doubt that the bomb has plenty of negative fall-outs and causes instabilities in the region. But one has to keep in mind the stance of the existing nuclear nations that, having got there, they will (a) not allow anybody else to clamber up;

and, more insidiously, (b) refuse to ever give up nuclear weapons themselves.

I am not naively expecting nuclear nations to give up their weapons overnight but believe that they must declare a plan to do so in the future if they wish others not to develop the weapon. Dividing the world into haves and have-nots and insisting that it will be kept that way forever is simply not sustainable. This is what gives an impetus and even a sense of right to not just India but all poorer nations to challenge the status quo. That right will be lost the day the nuclear nations declare their aim to have a nuclear-free world. Now that India is a nuclear nation, it has a responsibility to strive towards such a future.

Prasanta Pattanaik: A Fine Theorist

WHEN THE LETTER CAME, INVITING ME to a conference at the University of California, Riverside, to honour Prasanta Pattanaik on his retirement, it caught me by surprise. It seemed just the other day in Delhi when we used to talk about Amartya Sen's legendary student, who completed his PhD in record time from the Delhi School of Economics and became full professor at the age of 30, rivalling Sen's own record of underage professorship. That was in the early 1970s.

If most of my readers are unfamiliar with the name of Prasanta Pattanaik, this is because he is an 'economist's economist'. Virtually all his research is in rarefied abstract theory that straddles the narrow space between mathematical logic, moral philosophy, and welfare economics. But within the economics profession he has been hugely successful, with a string of seminal papers, beginning with a note that he wrote in his early twenties and published in the *Economic Journal* in 1967, a year before he completed his PhD. This was followed quickly by papers in leading international journals like the *Review of Economic Studies*, *Journal of Economic Theory*, and a famous article on the mathematical properties of majority voting in *Econometrica* in 1970.

Pattanaik's rise was remarkable. He came from rural Orissa, with none of the surface polish that Indian students from big cities and famous colleges have. His English has a marked Oriya accent. But he has the gift of intelligence and an ability for abstract reasoning that have taken him to the top of the profession. I have co-authored a paper and have co-edited a book (in honour of our common PhD adviser—Amartya Sen) with him, and have direct evidence of his superior mind.

It seemed completely apt that his retirement would be a grand occasion, with speakers from Japan, Europe, and all over the US, and, most importantly, featuring Amartya Sen. It must be because of his special relationship with Pattanaik that he readily accepted the invitation from the University of California. And Professor Sen really rose to the occasion with two magisterial lectures he gave—one on moral philosophy and one on economic theory. It is quite amazing how Amartya Sen continues to grow in stature as a philosopher and public intellectual. I have never seen anyone better able to combine wit and wisdom.

Having followed Amartya Sen's work closely, I know most of his oeuvre and events—scholarly and trivial. But I learned a new story this time. Within a few weeks of being a student in Cambridge, he got tired of the cod dish that was served with unerring regularity in the cafeteria. So when the dish appeared once again, he protested that he did not eat cod. As he moved away with his plate of vegetables, he heard one of the old ladies who served food, berating the other, 'Don't you know, cod is their sacred fish.'

The styles of these two great scholars are a study in contrast. Sen is flamboyant, garrulous, and, by a wide margin, the great philosophical conversationalist. Pattanaik is self-effacing and a person of few words (though he has a quiet sense of humour).

The contrast was evident when Sen arrived on the first evening at the university auditorium for his main lecture. The crowds were large; people had come from several neighbouring towns. As the milling audience poured into the auditorium, Prasanta Pattanaik, Bhaskar Dutta (economist and PhD student of Pattanaik), and I chatted outside the auditorium. A local newspaper reporter came up to Professor Pattanaik and asked, 'Am I right that this big affair is all in your honour?' Bhaskar and I answered for him in the affirmative. She went on to ask many questions and then asked, 'Can I take a photograph of yours?' Pattanaik responded softly that he preferred not to be photographed.

Feeling deflated, she turned to Bhaskar and me and asked whether we minded being photographed. We said we did not; so she clicked. And then asked, 'By the way, who are you?'

Engels and the Quest for a Better World

MARXISM, AS AN ACTUAL SYSTEM OF governance, has reached a cul-de-sac. Yet, maybe because we live in such a troubled world, with collapsing banks, rising unemployment, and bleak global growth, there is a sudden rush of interest in 'other' systems and ideas which would have been given short shrift a decade ago. A book that exemplifies this interest is Tristram Hunt's new biography, *Marx's General: The Revolutionary Life of Friedrich Engels.* This gripping book captures beautifully the romance and passions of nineteenth-century revolutionaries, utopians, and socialists. In the centre of this universe of struggle and hope were Karl Marx and Friedrich Engels. This was a century teeming with people each with his or her idea for a better world—Eugen Duhring; Moses Hess; Marx's daughters, Eleanor and Laura, and their respective husbands, Edward Aveling and Paul Lafargue; Karl Kautsky; Carl Schorlemmer; and many others.

This large cast of characters had, however, only one sponsor, the rich industrialist Friedrich Engels. Generous to a fault, Engels doled out money that he earned in large quantities as a capitalist in Manchester, to many of these activists and to the large Marx clan. Marx's son-in-law, Paul Lafargue, was the author of the book *The Right to be Lazy*; and going by his frequent appeals to uncle Engels for money, he probably lived by the maxim.

For Engels, one of the most difficult periods of his life was the 19 years he spent running a textile and cotton business so that he could provide livelihood for Marx, who was writing his magnum opus, *Das Kapital*, so that one day all capitalist enterprises like the one he ran could be brought to a halt. In his own words, 'One can perfectly well be at one and the same time a stock exchange man and a socialist and therefore detest and despise the class of stock exchange men' (Hunt 2009: 263).

Engels's generosity extended beyond money. Karl Marx, who was stably and happily married, had one romantic lapse with his housemaid, Helene Demuth, which resulted in the birth of Freddy Demuth. Admitting this to his society would have caused Karl great embarrassment. So his eternal friend, Friedrich, quickly stepped in and claimed paternity.

It is impossible to read this book without feeling admiration for Engels, despite his many contradictions. He was intellectually gifted but happy to play second-fiddle to Marx's genius, skilled in business but with little taste for it, passionately concerned about the plight of the poor and grim lives of the working classes but with a naturally cheerful disposition. In many ways, he lived a life surrounded by tragedy. Marx's death would leave him shattered, though he would find consolation in taking on a father-like role to Marx's daughters. Both Laura and Eleanor would, eventually, commit suicide.

All this drama, political and personal, makes this book a fascinating read but, more importantly, the book helps us understand why Marxism, for all its intellectual fire-power, had to fail. Knowledge and science are important in studying society and economy, but, when one is driven by too clear a sense of certainty, there is the risk that knowledge will be replaced by the illusion of knowledge and dogma will dislodge the temper of science. This is what happened. Engels was sure, repeatedly, from 1848 to the time of his death in 1895, that the revolution was round the corner. Each time he was convinced that the 'science of society' that he and, even more, Karl Marx had discovered predicted this. Engels believed that Marx had discovered truths about the trajectory of human society the same way that Darwin had uncovered the evolution of species and great scientists had chalked out the paths of the stars.

While the deep and almost-religious empathy that Marx and Engels had for the suffering of the poor and the dehumanized lives of the workers was moving, their claims to science would never stand up to scrutiny. Even within economics, the marginalist theory that emerged in the late nineteenth century from the pens of Leon Walras, Stanley Jevons, Vilfredo Pareto, and others, would, with all its faults, dominate Marx's paradigm. Neither would succeed in explaining the unfolding of humankind's complicated history, but the new marginalist economics would provide a deductive system with a mathematical structure which, even if it were to be eventually replaced, could be the mainspring of economic science in a way that Marxism could not be.

Marx's analysis never paid enough attention to the structure of individual incentives that could make viable the more utopian system that he, along with Engels, had tried to conceptualize. Not surprisingly, socialism, as conceived of by Marx, has a tendency to mutate, with the government getting captured by powerful groups and lobbies, as happened in the USSR. Jose Saramago was right, when he remarked about the fall of the Soviet Union, that it was not a socialist state that fell but a perverse capitalism.

While Marxism as science has failed, it will be a pity if the idealism and the quest for justice that were the moving forces behind the lives of Engels and Marx are also abandoned. As Hunt (2009: 367) notes at the end of the book, Engels was 'convinced that there was a more dignified place for humanity in the modern age. For him and Marx, the welcome abundance offered by capitalism deserved to be distributed through a more equitable system. For millions of people around the world that hope still holds.'

Paul Samuelson and the Foundations of Economics

PAUL SAMUELSON'S DEATH ON 13 DECEMBER 2009 marks the end of an era for the profession of economics. Born on 15 May 1915 in the small steel town of Gary, Indiana, in the

US, Paul Samuelson straddled the twentieth century like no other economist. Unlike John Maynard Keynes or John Nash, his name is not associated with one or two major breakthroughs. His hallmark was the fact that he straddled the length and breadth of the entire discipline, leaving his imprint on virtually every sub-field of economics, from macroeconomics to micro theory, from international trade, through public economics, to welfare economics. But more important than all this is the fact that he transformed the methodology of economics by providing a rigorous mathematical foundation to the entire discipline. This he achieved in his most famous book, *Foundations of Economic Analysis*—a 600-page monograph crammed with calculus, which he completed in 1937, when he was 22 years old.

Samuelson was enamoured by science, describing it as 'the most exciting game in the universe', but recognized that the creative process is, in the end, the same, be it in music or literature. He wrote about the mystery of 'How Mozart produced his music, Shakespeare his plays, Frost his short poems. ...'

The war delayed the publication of *Foundations*; it came out eventually in 1947. Unlike many other great scientists, whose works were recognized much after they came out or even after their deaths, Samuelson was lucky; his book was recognized immediately as a classic. He became full professor at the Massachusetts Institute of Technology (MIT) at the age of 32. In 1966 he was honoured by MIT, being appointed Institute Professor. And in 1970 he won the Nobel Prize in economics.

Unlike some other great economists of the last hundred years who wrote very few papers, Samuelson was unbelievably prolific, producing over 300 papers, and was also the author of the most widely sold textbook of economics, entitled *Economics*. It has been translated into 40 languages and its total sales have exceeded 4 million copies.

I got to know Paul Samuelson well during 2001–2 when I was a Visiting Professor at MIT. I was lucky to have got an office which was part of a cluster of three offices with a common central area where there were photocopiers and other machines. It is rare to have an office cluster where the majority of the occupants are Nobel laureates. The occupants of the other two offices were Robert Solow and Paul Samuelson. I would pause every now and then at both their offices to chit chat about things.

Paul was into his grey years by then and seemed a bit lonely. His interests were voracious—from the intricacies of science to the lives (and loves) of people. And he liked to chat; and, as is the case with many geniuses, a disproportionate part of what he said centred on him. But Samuelson is an interesting enough topic that I could listen to him if he spoke of nothing else. His encyclopaedic knowledge reminded me of my colleague at the Delhi School of Economics, the late Sukhamoy Chakravarty, though on this particular dimension, Sukhamoy was the more remarkable.

My last proper conversation with him was on 15 May 2002. I was photocopying something in that area outside our offices, when he stopped and said that it was his birthday that very day. The Harvard Club would open some special champagne for him and he asked me if my wife and I would come to the Harvard Club. For an economist, this is the equivalent of Einstein asking a physicist to dinner. One would have to be out of one's mind to say no. My wife and I went to Harvard Club expecting a large gathering at the birthday bash.

It turned out to be a dinner with Paul Samuelson, his charming wife Risha, and the two of us. It was one of the most memorable evenings of my life. We—truth be told, mainly he—talked about art, history, economics, and, of course, economists. Richa is a remarkably warm person and she had clearly spent some very memorable time in India. It turned out we had lots of common Indian friends. She spoke with great fondness of the Indian economist Mrinal Datta Chaudhuri.

Even at that advanced age, the remarkable quality of Paul Samuelson's mind was every bit evident. There are few non-Indians who know about Jyoti Basu, Satyen Bose, *and* Subhas Chandra Bose, and even fewer who know that Bose and Basu are anglicized versions of the same Bengali surname. The first time I had met and introduced myself to Paul, he asked me if I were related to 'the scientist, the Communist or the nationalist freedom fighter'.

When on 14 December 2009 morning in my Delhi residence I opened the newspaper and read about his death, I was overwhelmed by memories of that evening seven years ago. It was indeed the end of an era for the profession of economics.

In Praise of Doubt

OUR LEADERS OFTEN REMIND US HOW it is important to be steadfast in our beliefs and refuse to allow doubts to detract us from the path of our faith. This advice can be a recipe for disaster. The inability to entertain doubts is not just debilitating for the mind but leads to all kinds of fundamentalisms. Even our faith in a great person or book ought to be tempered by having an eye open to the possibility that the person or the book may be wrong. Every human being who believes that he has found the 'book of infallible knowledge' should do the following elementary reasoning. Even if there does exist such a book, the choice of the particular book he reposes his faith in is a choice made by him. So unless he believes that he is infallible, there is no reason for him to treat the book in his hand as infallible.

The philosopher Pyrrho of Elis, *c.* 360–270 BC—yes he did live for 90 years—argued rightly that we must never have unwavering trust in what we perceive since all that we perceive we do through our own senses. He tried to live by his philosophy. Diogenes Laertius, the third century AD writer, famous for writing what was arguably the world's first mug book, wrote a lot on Pyrrho and other early sceptics. Thus, we know that when Anaxarchus of Abdera, also a sceptic, fell into a ditch, Pyrrho went past him with no effort to rescue him. When Anaxarchus was eventually rescued by others and the rescuers blamed Pyrrho for his indifference, the latter made it clear that he was not sure if Anaxarchus would be better off in the ditch or out of it. Anaxarchus himself was extremely impressed by Pyrrho's *sang-froid*. Pyrrho wrote nothing during his long life, for he deemed nothing fit to be immortalized in ink.

The Greeks produced several remarkable sceptics, among them Sextus Empiricus of second century AD, who wrote the definitive treatise on Pyrrhonism. He made the important point that scepticism also has beneficial effects on the practitioner by giving him tranquillity of the soul (though of course no sceptic can be sure of that). Sextus Empiricus was a physician, and I leave it to the reader to decide if he/she would go to him for treatment.

What is interesting is that these early Greeks, including Pyrrho and Anaxarchus, were influenced deeply by Indian mystical thinkers. Both of them travelled with Alexander the Great to India and got to meet Indian sages, some of whom had taken the art of sang-froid even further. One of them told off Anaxarchus for being obsequious to the kings. In the words of Diogenes Laertius (2000: 477), he reproached that 'Anaxarchus [...] would never be able to teach others what is good while he himself danced attendance on kings in their courts.'

We do not have to take the art of scepticism to the length taken by the Indian sages of Alexander's time; nor even to Anaxarchus and Pyrrho. But we must be open to the possibility that all ideas deserve scrutiny and that a time may come when our most hallowed imperatives may have to make way for new ones.

As an economist, I have had occasion to discuss these ideas elsewhere in my writings. I want to here confine myself to some general themes. For over 40 years, we in India strangled market forces and individual enterprise in the belief that government could deliver it all, thereby creating a system where those with greater propensity to corruption were rewarded.

Today, when we hear from the other extremity that it should all be left to the market, we must remember our propensity to extreme views and tenacity to hold on to them despite contrary evidence. We must not err the next 40 years with another flawed ideology.

Good economists the world over recognize that good policy requires a balance between government and markets that has to be crafted with intelligence. Government is needed to redistribute to the poor (the market has no natural propensity for this), provide public goods, and enforce contracts. On the other hand, an economy cannot be run by government alone. Private enterprise has to be encouraged and allowed to flourish.

Consider two recent quotes in the Indian press. '[Foreigners] are not coming here for charity. They will earn profits and create jobs.' 'If the pre-requisite for modernization is privatization, we have to accept it because we want modernization.'

These quotes are not from some right-wing fringe but from two prominent left politicians—Buddhadeb Bhattacharya and Nirupam Sen. The statements do not suggest a love of capitalists (nor do good capitalists care for love, the search for money keeping them nicely busy); they show pragmatism. If you want jobs, if you want an economy to modernize, you need to do certain things. There is no scope for ideology here, as the Chinese recognized more than 20 years ago and we are learning only now.

One fear that all our political parties have is of foreign powers. Is the International Monetary Fund (IMF) infiltrating our polity too much through the sherpas of the ministry of finance? When I was a college student in Delhi in the early 1970s, there was frequent talk of the Central Intelligence Agency (CIA) and the Committee for State Security (KGB) infiltrating our system. Some of these apprehensions were genuine and we must not dismiss them out of hand. But one important thing that we too easily overlook is that every time the IMF hires an Indian and infiltrates India, in a small way India also infiltrates the IMF. And this is exactly what is happening with the US. Its influence in India is on the rise, no doubt; but the influence of Indians is also on the rise in the US. How good or bad this will be in the long run is difficult to tell, but one thing is clear: to play it safe by cutting ourselves off from the industrialized world is likely to be an unmitigated disaster.

Kenneth Arrow: Economist of the Century

IN 2016, I INVITED KENNETH ARROW TO THE World Bank to give a lecture on the history of general equilibrium theory and its contemporary relevance. He gave the lecture with total fluency and obvious relish at the opportunity to engage intellectually with an audience. He was 94 then. He assured me he would write it up as a paper. On the evening of 15 February 2017, I got two emails.

The first from David Arrow, introducing himself as Ken's son, and saying that his father had been ill and hospitalized, but he was back at home and better now, and wanted me to know that he felt very guilty for not having completed the paper. The next email was from Ken Arrow, a brief one, apologizing for the delay and telling me that he planned to complete it within 25 days. Totally touched by his humility in apologizing for not having finished a task at the age of 94, and driven by an assurance from David that it is work that inspires and motivates his father, I phoned Arrow two days later to discuss his paper. He sounded frail but was his usual warm self and as engaged as ever.

Unlike many other economists, I had not known Arrow in person for a very long time, but because of this recent interaction with him, the news of his death on 21 February left me feeling strangely sad. The passing of Kenneth Arrow marks the end of an age for economics. He was among the three or four most important economists of the last century, and in my view, possibly the most.

Ken Arrow's first published paper, 'On the Optimal Use of Winds for Flight Planning', was written when he was 22 years old and had to interrupt his studies at Columbia University to serve in the US Army Air Corps during World War II. He did his MA in mathematics and then switched to economics for his PhD. His PhD dissertation led him to one of the biggest breakthroughs in economics, now known as the Arrow Impossibility Theorem.

A democracy's fundamental task is to aggregate the diverse preferences of the population into some coherent social preference, which could be used to make policy choices. Arrow wrote down some simple normative 'axioms', which any such aggregation process should satisfy. Thus, one axiom says that there must not be an individual such that for all pairs of options, x and y, whenever he prefers x to y, society must choose x over y. This was called the 'non-dictatorship' axiom. Writing down a few such reasonable looking axioms, he stumbled on a stunning theorem, namely that there is no way to satisfy all those axioms. One or the other will be violated no matter how you try to aggregate the preferences of all citizens.

The reason why this is such a fascinating theorem is because it seemingly came out of nowhere; and also because to prove it, you do not need any complicated mathematics, just an ability for sustained reasoning. This gave rise to a new discipline—social choice theory.

His next big breakthrough was in general equilibrium. Ever since Adam Smith's famous book in 1776, economists have talked about the 'invisible hand'—how competitive markets can coordinate the selfish pursuits of individuals to result in socially desirable equilibrium. Would this always be the case and when could we be sure that an equilibrium would actually exist?

This was an enormous research agenda and many economists worked on it in the second half of the twentieth century. But the big break came from the joint research of Ken Arrow and Gérard Debreu, published in *Econometrica* in 1954.

The list goes on. Arrow made original contributions to growth theory, the analysis of discrimination against groups, and healthcare, the latter giving birth to a new discipline—health economics. There was little surprise when Ken Arrow, along with John Hicks, got the Nobel Prize in economics in 1972. He remains the youngest economist to win the Nobel.

It is often claimed and seems a reasonable conjecture that great intellectuals are generally unpleasant human beings. If that is so, then Arrow was a sharp exception. As soon as one got to know him, one could sense his human warmth and natural, unaffected humility. His gentle sense of humour shows up often in his writing.

In his famous book on the impossibility theorem, he explains the ethical principle of treating others the way you would want them to treat you, by quoting an alleged inscription on an English gravestone:

> Here lies Martin Engelbrodde,
> Ha'e mercy on my soul, Lord God,
> As I would do were I lord God,
> And thou wert Martin Engelbrodde.

His humanity is in ample display in his little-known essay, 'A Cautious Case for Socialism', published in 1978. This was not a rigorous paper and he was also not talking of socialism in the sense of state ownership of the means of production. But it was an appeal to our collective responsibility towards one another, the importance of equality and his antipathy to selfishness and discrimination. To quote him: 'Like many others of the time, I was strongly attracted by Gandhi's nonviolent campaigns against British rule. The underlying assumption was the common humanity of ruler and ruled; the appeals to cooperative and altruistic motives seemed to have at least some success as against the simple selfish exercise of power.'

Let me end by quoting Arrow from the same essay, which sums up so wonderfully his own intellectual mindset and generosity towards others, however different from him:

Anyone who knows me [knows] I have always preferred the contemplative to the active life. I prefer the freedom to see matters from several viewpoints, to appreciate ironies, and indeed to change my opinion as I learn something new. To be politically active means to surrender this freedom. I say nothing against activism for others. It is only through the committed that necessary changes come. But each to his own path.

John Nash: The Shakespeare of Economics

ON 23 MAY 2015, AS MY WIFE AND I DROVE BACK to Washington after a weekend in Orange, Virginia, visiting James Madison's home and the birthplace of the American Constitution, our daughter called to give us the news that John Nash and his wife, Alicia, had just been killed in a car accident. It was difficult to fathom. How could a person of such genius, after a life of so much struggle, battling schizophrenia and overcoming it, go in such a banal way?

The news of his death brought back memories of my first meeting with Nash. In 1989, I was a visiting professor at Princeton. By then, Nash's schizophrenia was in remission. He could be seen strolling around the Princeton lawns for hours on end. For the residents of Princeton, this was part of the fixture, and so barely noticed. For me and Jorgen Weibull, also a visiting professor, it felt strange. There we were in classrooms analysing or applying the 'Nash equilibrium' and the 'Nash bargaining solution', and the man after whom these concepts were named was out there, pacing the yard, immersed in his own world.

It was through Jorgen's painstaking efforts that we managed to get Nash to join us for lunch in the university cafeteria. It was exciting to be with a person who was known for his genius, even though he spoke little and, every now and then, seemed to drift off into his own thoughts.

The two vivid memories that stand out for me from that remarkable afternoon were, first, his answer to my question about the origin of his name. He said it came from the Sanskrit *nasika*, meaning nose.

The second was the reaction of Abhijit Banerjee, as he, seeing Jorgen and me, came and joined us at the table, and was introduced to Nash. It was like a young literature student joining friends for lunch and being told that the third person at the table was Shakespeare.

In terms of influence on modern economics and game theory, Nash has few peers. His work provided foundations for analysing both cooperative and non-cooperative interactions among rational agents in economic and political settings.

In addition, he made contributions to various branches of pure mathematics, including differential geometry and isometric embeddability of abstract Riemannian manifolds (whatever that may mean), with implications for not just economics, but computer science and evolutionary biology.

This is remarkable given the brevity of his creative life. His most important papers were written before he was 25, and his creative period was over by the time he was in his late 20s, felled by schizophrenia.

By the age of 30, he had to be confined to a mental hospital. The next 30 years were a battle with paranoia, voices in the head, and delusions.

Nash was born on 13 June 1928, in Bluefield, West Virginia. He was recognized early on as a prodigy; he got his PhD in mathematics from Princeton at the age of 22. His PhD thesis was as short as his productive life—28 pages. One of his most celebrated papers that lays out the conditions under which we can be sure of the existence of a non-cooperative equilibrium in games is just one page and a few lines.

The entire paper was reprinted on a t-shirt designed by graduate students in the economics department at Cornell University in the late 1990s.

Of Nash's many contributions, the one that got maximum play is the 'Nash equilibrium', which is used to understand the behaviour of oligopolistic firms, movements in financial markets, political rivalry and strategizing in conflict, such as during the Cuban Missile Crisis.

The basic idea of a Nash equilibrium is simple. Consider a group of agents, each of whom has to choose an action or strategy. The payoff or utility that each person gets depends not just on that person's choice but on what other agents choose. To take a stark case, you and the oncoming car each can choose which side of the road to drive on.

Your well-being depends on your choice and also the other driver's. A Nash equilibrium is a choice of action on the part of each person such that no one can do better by unilaterally deviating to some other action.

In economics, we know that (under some assumptions) a competitive equilibrium takes society to an optimal outcome. Each individual, acting in his or her self-interest, takes society to an optimum. This was the broad idea that led to the orthodoxy of the invisible hand in economics. The Nash equilibrium gained so much currency because it challenged this central idea by illustrating how perfect individual rationality can lead a group to a collectively bad outcome. We can see this in the area of CO_2 emissions, the provision of public goods, and problems related to the commons.

Here is a simple game theory puzzle for the reader that illustrates this. Two players are told to each choose an integer from 2 to 100. If both choose the same integer, they are told they will get that number in dollars.

Kaushik Basu

But if they choose different numbers, they get the lower of the two numbers with a small adjustment: the person who chose the smaller number gets an additional $2, and the person who chose the higher number has $2 deducted. The question for the reader is this: what choice of numbers by the two players constitutes a Nash equilibrium? This has a unique answer. Try to figure out the answer at leisure.

The next time I met Nash was after he had become a worldwide celebrity. He had won the Nobel Prize, sharing it with John Harsanyi and Reinhard Selten, in 1994, and was the subject of a popular Hollywood film, *A Beautiful Mind*, in which Russell Crowe acted his part. He was part of a conference in Mumbai in January 2003 that brought several prominent economic theorists to town, including Robert Aumann, Roger Myerson, and Amartya Sen. The audience for Nash was large, with some recognizable faces from Bollywood, who may have come expecting to see Crowe. The talk was disappointing, as Nash tried to address some practical policy questions. He was too much of a hedgehog, in the sense of Isaiah Berlin, and so was good at focussing on one thing very deeply, and too unlike the fox to be able to range over many topics, even superficially.

The next day, much to my surprise, as I prepared to give my talk, Nash came and sat in the front row. I was thrilled by his presence— for the full five minutes that he was awake.

The Anti-argumentative Indian: Amartya Sen

AMARTYA SEN IS AN ICONIC WORLD FIGURE. In that treacherous space between economics and philosophy, he may well be the most famous living personality, having published papers in the world's best philosophy journals and the most highly regarded economics journals. When he got the Nobel Prize for economics in 1998, it did not come as a surprise to anyone in the profession. I have a confession though. That year, I was visiting the World

Bank and there was a Nobel lottery among the staff. Having taken a bet on Sen the previous two years and lost, I decided it was time to change my guess. And I lost my money again.

I was fortunate to do my PhD with Amartya Sen. In fact, it was his lectures at the London School of Economics in the mid-1970s in jam-packed auditoriums, with students spilling over on to window sills, that made me change my life-long career plan to be a lawyer.

I first met Sen, fleetingly, in Delhi, when I was a student at St. Stephen's College, and he was a professor at the Delhi School of Economics. But I got to know him properly in London in 1972 when I joined the London School. I did my PhD with him, when he was at the height of his career, working mainly on social choice theory, mathematical logic, and moral philosophy.

There is no surprise, then, that Sen has been a major influence on me, and that I often cite his works in my writings. What has been a shocking experience in the last three or four years is the amount of trolling attacks unleashed on Sen whenever he is cited in popular writings; these come almost entirely from India. The attacks do not have any substance. Clearly, those crafting the attacks, if crafting is the word, do not have the capacity for serious debate. So what they unleash is merely a volley of completely fact-free name calling. Sen, they scream, is an agent of the Congress party, he is a slave of the West, a brainless puppet and they go on, using language so crude that it is not worth repeating.

What is sad for India is not that a few people may want to shout invectives at him, but that the leaders in government have not said anything to counter this crazy chant of abusive trolls.

I am not saying that the trolling should be banned. People should have the freedom to express their opinions no matter how inchoate, but we need leaders, even those who oppose Sen's views, to signal their disapproval of this kind of uncouth character assassination directed at one of the most celebrated intellectuals of our time.

I have known Sen long enough to know not just about his outstanding mind, but that he is totally without prejudice against groups—caste, religion, race. Like Nehru was, he is an atheist, who respects other people's religion; he is totally secular.

Though Sen has openly said that he does not support the present BJP government, he belongs to no party. In fact, the only time he has been a member of any political party, it was that of the left, when he was an undergraduate student in India, at Kolkata's Presidency College.

What is ironic about these politically inspired attacks on Sen is that they come from the very Hindutva groups that are perennially pointing out how Indians do not recognise the contributions of Indians to science, philosophy, and scholarship. What they do not realize is that whether or not that has been true historically, their behaviour provides evidence in favour of their own thesis.

Not for a moment would I say that Sen's ideas must not be challenged, contested, and rejected if one is so persuaded. It is through arguments and contestation that democracy thrives. These troll attacks on Sen are unfortunate because they are attacks on the very matters on which India, despite being a poor country, stood out and commanded respect around the world. It is a tribute to Nehru and his self-confidence that he nurtured scientists, philosophers, and intellectuals, including those who were openly critical of Nehru's politics.

If I take my own field, economics, it is a remarkable fact that there are few nations outside the US and Europe that are so well represented in the frontline as India. In the 1960s and 1970s, the talent that came out of India was quite astonishing. There was, of course, Amartya Sen, but even apart from him it was a string of personalities who started out in India and were doing cutting-edge research in economics. K.N. Raj, Jagdish Bhagwati, Sukhamoy Chakravarty, T.N. Srinivasan, A.L. Nagar, and, if we were to go to a slightly younger cohort, Avinash Dixit and Partha Dasgupta stand out among them.

For a nation's progress, nothing is as important as the nurturing of science, philosophy, literature, and mathematics. Economics is a relatively young science that is now critical for a nation to navigate today's complicated, globalized world. And in assessing the power of ideas, we must realise that ideas must be assessed for their own worth. Doomed are societies in which people, after hearing about

Pythagoras' theorem, want to know Pythagoras' political party affiliation in order to decide whether the theorem is correct.

The Problem of Choice

THERE ARE MANY BOOKS THAT QUALIFY AS GOOD, but it is a rare book that can be described as transformative. Straddling economics, philosophy, and logic, Amartya Sen's *Collective Choice and Social Welfare* is widely recognized as a transformative and seminal work that shaped modern welfare economics.

I still have my dog-eared, read-and-re-read copy of the original 1970 edition, and have long felt it deserves a new edition because, though it is not meant for mass readership, it has the status of a collector's item. Further, the book is organized in an unusual way, alternating between chapters written in ordinary English and meant for all, and technical chapters using mathematical logic and algebra.

The publication of this classic after so many years, in an enlarged edition, is an occasion for celebration. And I am glad it was decided not to touch the original text but to instead add a new introduction (41 pages) and 11 new chapters in the end (204 pages). The new chapters cover topics and research in which Sen has been engaged since 1970, such as the idea of justice, notions of rights, and the relation between democracy, public discourse, and debate.

The central problem of social choice theory is also the central concern of democracy. Given that individuals in any society will hold diverse preferences, ranking policies differently for example, how should society as a whole rank those policies? Given that people may have different preferences concerning whom they want as their political leader, how should society aggregate these diverse preferences and select a leader? While inquiry into these questions goes back over two centuries and engaged colourful characters like the Marquis de Condorcet, the late eighteenth-century French philosopher and mathematician, and Lewis Carroll—yes, the author of *Alice in Wonderland*—the big breakthrough occurred in 1950, when

Kenneth Arrow, a graduate student, proved a stunning theorem that is now called the Arrow Impossibility Theorem (Arrow died on 21 February, days after this review essay was written). He wrote down some simple axioms that any process of aggregation of individual preferences into societal preference ought to satisfy and proved that there is no way of satisfying all these few elementary axioms.

This is one of the most astonishing theorems because it is, in principle, so simple. Its proof does not require any special mathematics or prior theorems. All you need is the ability to reason, but the reasoning is so long and sustained that most people find it hard. I still wonder how Arrow hit upon this theorem in what was then virtually barren terrain.

One of the fascinating stories one learns from Sen's book is his discovery of Arrow's theorem. The year of publication of Arrow's book, 1951, was also when Sen joined Presidency College, Kolkata, as an undergraduate. His classmate Sukhamoy Chakravarty, a voracious reader, 'borrowed Arrow's newly arrived book from a local bookshop with an indulgent owner', and told Sen about the book and this bewildering theorem. This fuelled Sen's emerging interest in democracy and justice and social choice went on to become a life-long interest.

There was no looking back once he began teaching at the Delhi School of Economics in 1963, after finishing his PhD from Cambridge. Sen published a string of papers in top journals and became the leading authority on the interface between moral philosophy and economics.

The Delhi School of the late 1960s described in the book was an astonishing place. It had a number of economists doing cutting-edge research. Sen talks of his 'student from Orissa, Prasanta Pattanaik', and how he 'took my breath away as he showed his ability to solve new analytical problems—however difficult'. Delhi became the world's pre-eminent centre for social choice research. I remember in the early 1970s, soon after I joined the London School of Economics as a graduate student, the celebrated Japanese economist Michio Morishima meeting me in the corridor and asking me if I planned to do my PhD in social choice theory, adding, 'India's subject'.

The late 1960s was also the time when Delhi School's Economics department counted among its faculty Jagdish Bhagwati, Sukhamoy Chakravarty, K.N. Raj, and Manmohan Singh. Outside of the US and Britain, it is difficult to think of too many places that compared with Delhi of that time. This is something to be celebrated.

For that reason, the hate trolling that Sen has received in recent times, especially after his CNN-IBN interview, where, before the last general election, he said, 'As an Indian citizen I do not want Modi as my PM', is particularly sad. It should make Indians proud that their country is a democracy where people can freely express their preferences and disagreement with any leader, be it Narendra Modi or Manmohan Singh. Debating and contesting Sen's ideas would be welcome—I myself have had differences. In fact, a vibrant culture is one where people feel free to dispute any person or any book. But the hate mail and the effort to silence, even though we know it comes from a very small number of people pretending to be many, are regrettable.

On the other hand, Sen has also received an immense amount of appreciation for his contributions to economics and philosophy. I had been told that, since 1998, the year in which Sen got the Nobel Prize, a disproportionate number of babies in India have been named Amartya. Thanks to Google's outstanding search engines, the power of which is illustrated well in the recent film, *Lion*, it is possible to check this claim. So, I went to look at the frequency of the name Amartya among India's younger crop. And indeed, it is true. Not only do we have the Amartya Chatterjees and Amartya Ghoshes, there are also Amartya Singhs and Amartya Patels, and even—and I know I risk making two enemies now—Amartya Modi.

The Angry Intellectual: Ashok Mitra

IT SOUNDS A CLICHÉ, BUT THE DEATH OF ASHOK MITRA, on 1 May 2018, marks the passing of an era. He had been a professor at Kolkata, Lucknow, and Varanasi; a policymaker in

Delhi, Kolkata, and Washington; and a politician, having served for long years as finance minister in the Communist government in West Bengal. He had been a consummate columnist, writing in the *Economic and Political Weekly*, *The Telegraph*, and elsewhere. I do not know if 'obituarist' is a word, but for Ashok Mitra, it deserves to be created. He was the master obituarist. His long life of 90 years gave him the opportunity to write many obituaries, for friends and foes alike. Always a gifted writer, on these occasions he rose to a level of poignancy that has few peers.

These varied activities allow us to describe him in many different ways but, above all, he was the quintessential intellectual. Over the years, I met him in many different locales and settings but the backdrop that captured him best was his book-lined home of the last years of his life, in Kolkata. There he would be in his study, the diminutive man, in his starched white dhoti and kurta, with books covering the walls and shelves and coffee tables, ever ready for an 'adda'—conversation with no well-defined purpose that could range over history, politics, economics, and the genealogy of people. His home summed up a Kolkata of once-upon-a-time. It was the hub of left-wing thinkers. Like at the watering hole of Jean-Paul Sartre and Simone de Beauvoir, friends came from all over the country to debate, discuss, bond, and fall out.

While mentioning Sartre and Simone, one cannot not mention the public spat Ashok Mitra had with Ashok Rudra over these two famed lovers and intellectuals. The debate was about who among the two was the greater mind. It was not clear that its resolution was of any consequence—for India, for the world, or for anyone. In fact, I have to confess I have forgotten who was on which side, but recall they argued with passion and fury as if their lives depended on it. You did not have to be prescient to predict that Ashok Mitra, undoubtedly one of the great intellectuals of our time, would not make for an effective finance minister. He did not.

One of my first encounters with Ashok Mitra was in the late 1970s, when my friend, the economist Pulin Nayak, and I invited Raja Chelliah and Ashok Mitra to give public lectures on centre–state relations in India. It was a jam-packed auditorium. My most vivid memory of the event was just before it began: as I waited with Ashok Mitra outside the lecture theatre, he kept pacing up and down and I could hear him mutter the word 'nervous'. As he went in to speak, I caught the full sentence: 'Delhi's audience makes me nervous.' The reason this is stuck in my head is because when he spoke he gave no evidence of any nerves.

The two most striking traits of Ashok Mitra were his intellectual honesty and compassion for the poor and the dispossessed. The inequities of the world appalled and angered him and led him to believe in the possibility of the Communist project of a classless society.

Despite my admiration for him, I must point out that his emotions sometimes overcame his reason and this led to some important policy mistakes. The ideal of a world in which people work according to their abilities and earn according to their needs is indeed a magnificent conception. Ashok Mitra's mistake was to think that there was an easy way to get there and to hold the world in that equilibrium.

This is the reason why his policies as West Bengal's finance minister did a lot of damage to the economy. For all his idealism and scholarship, the policies he advocated would not and did not take the economy in the direction he wanted it to go. Growth faltered and, more importantly, the state's higher education was damaged beyond measure during his time. English education in schools had a setback. The destruction of these 'elitisms' would have been worthwhile if they led to greater equality or marked a rise in education for the masses. But that did not happen.

Sadly, I got to see little of Ashok Mitra in his last years because of a falling out. When I was Chief Economic Adviser to the Indian government, I had in a paper proposed asymmetric treatment of those involved in cases of bribery. I suggested that in cases where bribery was pure harassment (being used to make citizens pay for things that are their right), bribe giving should be treated as legal; only bribe taking should be punished. Ashok Mitra wrote an angry article in *The Telegraph*, attacking not just my idea but me.

I was not upset because I knew Ashok Mitra well enough to have known that this would infuriate him. My idea sounded immoral and Ashok Mitra would not have the patience or clarity to see it was not. We exchanged some letters, but it was not the same after that. Also, the fact that I was Chief Economic Adviser to the Indian government and, later, worked at the World Bank, did not help.

But then he was also the Chief Economic Adviser to the Indian government (during Indira Gandhi's time) and worked at the World Bank (for longer than I did). I was puzzled. Did he erase these from his memory? Did he carry a distaste for himself for these? I do not have the answers. I draw attention to them only to present a full picture of this complex personality.

Ashok Mitra was a person of great human warmth. He was anguished and angered by the poverty and inequality in the world. The anger at times hindered thinking through what should be done to banish them. And he made mistakes. But with all his contradictions, as an intellectual he was a towering figure, reminiscent of the left-wing French intellectuals of the mid-twentieth century, a person India can truly be proud of. I will deeply miss Ashokda and his writings, especially the obituaries of those who have the misfortune of dying after him.

Stiglitz's Sticky Prices[1]

For a long time, the assumption underlying much of mainstream economics was that the invisible hand worked its magic seamlessly. Prices moved smoothly up as demand outpaced supply and rushed back down when the tables were turned, keeping markets in equilibrium.

To be sure, many observers realized the truth was actually quite different—that prices, and wages and interest rates in particular, were often sticky, and that this sometimes prevented markets from

[1] This commentary is based on an address delivered on 17 October 2015, at a conference at Columbia University honouring Joseph Stiglitz for a half-century of teaching.

clearing. In labour markets, this meant unemployed workers facing prolonged job searches. But the response by others in the field was that what their colleagues described as 'unemployment' did not truly exist; it was voluntary, the result of stubborn workers refusing to accept the going wage.

Among those who recognized the reality of involuntary unemployment were John Maynard Keynes and Arthur Lewis, who incorporated it into his model of dual economies, in which urban wages do not respond to labour-supply gluts and remain above what rural workers earn. Both Keynes and Lewis used the stickiness of prices extensively in their work. But even for them, the concept was only an assumption; they never managed to explain why wages and interest rates so often resisted the pressures of supply and demand.

Columbia University's Joseph Stiglitz, who celebrates 50 years of teaching this year, solved the puzzle. In a series of innovative papers, Stiglitz picked up some elementary facts about the economy that lay strewn about like jigsaw pieces, put them together, and proved why some prices were naturally sticky, thereby creating market inefficiencies and thwarting the functioning of the invisible hand. In Stiglitz's words, the invisible hand 'is invisible at least in part because it is not there'.

Stiglitz set out his argument over a remarkable ten-year period. In 1974, he published a paper on labour turnover that explained why wages are rigid. His analysis has important implications for development economics, and I have used it often. This was followed by other important work, including a paper on credit rationing and interest-rate rigidity (co-written with Andrew Weiss) and another paper on efficiency wages. And then, in 1984, with Carl Shapiro, he published the definitive work on endogenous unemployment.

Other economists' work—for example, George Akerlof's seminal paper on the market for lemons—had laid the foundations for this research on price rigidities. But Stiglitz's papers, published in the 1970s and early 1980s, shifted the mainstream paradigm of the microeconomic theory of markets.

The intuition behind some of Stiglitz's arguments about rigid prices is simple. We know that people often shirk work if there is no penalty for doing so, and that the common penalty in the workplace is the risk of losing one's job. But if one assumes a full-employment equilibrium, as described in textbooks, with the market working without friction, this penalty is ineffective. Threatening workers with the loss of their job will have no effect if they can immediately find another.

The way to create incentives not to shirk is to pay workers above the market wage, making the loss of a job more costly. Of course, if this works for one firm, it will work for others, and so wages will rise, and eventually the supply of labour will exceed demand. In other words, there will be unemployment. And then, even if all firms are paying the same wage, the threat to fire a worker will be effective, because a worker who loses a job will face the risk of remaining unemployed. As a result, the market will reach an equilibrium where unemployment exists, but wages do not drop. This is, in short, the Shapiro–Stiglitz equilibrium.

An excellent survey of this literature can be found in the 1984 paper 'Efficiency Wage Models of Unemployment', by Janet Yellen, now Chair of the US Federal Reserve. (Perhaps some readers can even pick up clues on when the Fed will raise rates!)

As influential as Stiglitz's research has been, this remains an area where much more work can be done. One of my frustrations has been to watch how monetary policy is made in some developing economies, where the authorities all too often copy the rules that industrialized countries follow, without regard to the fact that their efficacy may depend on the context.

Stiglitz's work reminds us of the risk of basing polices on the assumption that interest rates rise and fall smoothly. Instead of relying on rules of thumb about when to raise or lower rates, we need to do some creative, analytical thinking. In emerging economies in particular, there is a strong need for experimental interventions to collect data so that we can move to more scientifically based policymaking.

In the late 1990s, I worked with Stiglitz at the World Bank, where he served as chief economist. At the time, he was engaged in heated debates about International Monetary Fund interventions in East Asia. Indeed, I believe his most important contribution as chief economist of the World Bank was that he changed the IMF. One hopes that his insights continue to have such an impact, as they encourage more analytical policymaking at all levels.

Manmohan Singh: A Quiet Courage

THE RECENT PUBLICATION BY OXFORD UNIVERSITY PRESS of five volumes of writings and speeches by Manmohan Singh, and the release of the film, *The Accidental Prime Minister*, takes my mind back to a conversation, nearly eight years ago, with the accidental prime minister.

On 11 March 2011, I posted an idea on the Ministry of Finance website on controlling one class of corruption—harassment bribery. This refers to cases where a person has to pay a bribe to get something she is entitled to, such as, when, after passing a driving test, she is asked to give cash before she is given the licence, or, after paying all taxes, a businessman is harassed by the tax collector into paying a bribe.

It struck me that one reason harassment bribes were rampant in India was the fact that the Prevention of Corruption Act, 1988, holds both the giver and the taker of bribe equally liable for punishment. This meant that the bribe giver would typically not admit in court to having given a bribe, and this created the comfort zone that encouraged government officials to ask for bribes with alacrity. Amend the law by making bribe-giving legal while heaping the punishment on the bribe-taker, and the incidence of bribery would go down.

That was the idea which got me excited, and, being quite new to government, I wrote it up and posted it on the Ministry's website. Furore broke out of a kind I had never experienced. There were newspaper articles attacking the proposal. There would be supportive articles in some newspapers and magazines and also some endorsement from a few thinking corporate leaders, but those came later.

On Saturday evening, 23 April, just as I thought the controversy was dying down, I got a call from Barkha Dutt, inviting me to appear on her then television show, 'We the People', where, she told me, I could explain my idea and there would be a discussion, which in Indian television jargon means a screaming match.

I was in a dilemma. In my short time in the government, I had discovered that I was comfortable with and even enjoyed participating in these policy 'debates'. However, I knew I had caused the government a lot of grief with the posting of my proposal. A few days earlier, D. Raja, the Communist Party Member of Parliament (for whom I have a lot of respect) had written to the prime minister with a vitriolic complaint about my 'immoral' idea. I had half expected to be asked by the finance minister, Pranab Mukherjee, or the prime minister to take the paper down from the website. To their credit, they made no such request. Hesitating whether I should stir the pot again, I decided to do what I rarely did: ask their advice on whether or not I should appear on Barkha's show.

Mukherjee was away in Vietnam. So I called the prime minister's residence and left a message. Ten minutes later, he called back. This was the first time I was talking to him about my bribery paper, though we had exchanged notes and messages as the controversy brewed.

He quickly got to the point. He had received complaints about my idea and had read the newspaper reports, though he had not read my original paper. He went on to add that he did not agree with me. I tried to defend my idea by suggesting that he was probably misled by the secondary sources. But he was adamant; he disagreed with my proposal. I kept quiet, expecting him to say I should stay off the debate and let the idea die a natural death.

What he said next caught me by surprise. He said that though he disagreed with my idea and it had caused him political difficulty, that did not mean I should not speak about it. The role of an adviser is to bring ideas to the table, even if they are controversial. So I should feel free to appear on TV and explain my idea. The decision, he said, was mine.

This was a remarkable instance of quiet courage. His courage was not that of the schoolyard bully that some people mistakenly think of as courage, not realizing that it takes no courage to silence contrarian voices from a bully pulpit. It is much harder to allow the flourishing of ideas, even ones that contradict yours. Allowing diversity in ideas and people, having universities where students discuss and float new ideas, is what makes a nation strong, and gave India the global stature it has.

From this and several other experiences during my years in the government, it became clear that Manmohan Singh, contrary to what his understated style often seemed to suggest, was a person of immense courage, backed up with clear thinking. This is what enabled him to put new ideas on the table in 1991, marking a turning point for India's economy. This helped create an ethos in which bureaucrats and experts felt included, resulting in well-crafted policies that put India on the global stage.

Some months later, at a G-20 meeting, I recounted this story. There was quick agreement that only in advanced nations are there leaders like this, who have the courage to allow ideas they disagree with to be discussed and disseminated. India stood out as the world's outstanding exception because of the imagination and audacity of Nehru's endorsement of free speech. Several Indian leaders, including Atal Bihari Vajpayee, upheld this tradition, but it can be easily eroded. This is an inheritance we need to cherish and advance: the right to free speech by citizens, a critical media, the flourishing of science and literature and, what is at the root of it all, a quiet courage.

References

Gopal, S. and U. Iyengar (eds) (2003), *The Essential Writings of Jawaharlal Nehru*, Vol. I. New Delhi: Oxford University Press.

Laertius, Diogenes (2000), *Lives of Eminent Philosophers, Volume II*. Cambridge, MA: Harvard University Press.

Hunt, Tristram (2009), *Marx's General: The Revolutionary Life of Friedrich Engels*. New York: Metropolitan Books.

six

Culture and Economics*

Art and Commerce

LAST YEAR I WENT TO THE annual exhibition of paintings at
Delhi's College of Art. Like so much of India, it was a chaotic
affair but, as again with so much of India, the amount of talent on
display was quite remarkable. Most of the works were by students
who had not yet completed their degree, yet one could see the
hallmarks of great art. Being familiar with the contemporary art
scene in India, I was not surprised.

We keep hearing about the big names in Indian art all the time—
Tyeb Mehta, Anjolie Ela Menon, Hussain, Bikash Bhattacharya,

* The first section, 'Art and Commerce', was first published as 'The Art of
the Matter', in *Hindustan Times*, 11 May 2008. The second section, 'Markets
and Aesthetics', was first published as 'Listen to Your Art', in *Hindustan Times*,
9 October 2009. The third section, 'Norms and Prosperity', was first published
as 'The Invisibles', in *Hindustan Times*, 11 September 2009. The fourth section,
'Trust and Development', was first published as 'Placing Our Trust in Trust',
in *Hindustan Times*, 24 May 2008. The final section, 'Where India is Ahead of
China' was first published as 'Economic Graffiti: Where India is ahead of China'
in *Indian Express*, 10 November 2017.

Souza, Atul, and Anju Dodiya—but even behind those headlines, art is flourishing in India like never before. In Delhi, Kolkata, and Mumbai, small art stores and artist enclaves have mushroomed. In Delhi's Hauz Khas Village itself there must be seven or eight art galleries, and on any evening's walk you can reasonably expect to see paintings by the likes of Vaikuntham, Paritosh Sen, Laxma Gaud, Lalu Prasad Shaw, and Paresh Maity. And there are outstanding original painters whose names may not be known beyond the aficionado. Last year, I remember walking into an exhibition in New Delhi, rather opaquely called Kokum Dreams. It was a haunting collection of art by Anoop Kamath, whose name I must confess I had not heard. His were huge canvasses with pale monochrome backgrounds, out of which emerged faces and figures of photographic realism, both sensuous and forlorn, some staring into the distance, some brooding, and some doing a daily chore, suspended in a universe of nothingness.

Being an inveterate art gazer, I feel confident of the extraordinary artistic genius that is coming out of India. In the mid-1980s I remember two artists, who were barely known then—Naina Kanodia and Sanjay Bhattacharya. They have very different styles—Naina's art is a stunning combination of fauvism and the primitive, and Sanjay's work has the quality of a mysterious oriental surrealism. Though their paintings were then cheap, I could not afford them on my Delhi University reader's salary. And now they are stars and of course they are beyond my reach.

Despite all this, Indian art is not doing as well globally as it should. And my belief is that this is not for want of artistic talent but for reasons of commerce. I know there are purists who shirk at the mention of art and commerce in one breath. The recent headlines about how a group of international investors and speculators allegedly exploited several Chinese artists no doubt make us wary of the brew of art and markets. But there can be no denying that good art needs large museums, patronage, and marketing, and the state has the responsibility to provide these, at least initially.

Among the developing nations, the two big commercial successes in art are Mexico and China. Mexico's is an old story. Its art has been famous thanks to not just talent but the exotic and troubled lives of artists like Siqueiros, Diego Rivera, and Frieda Kahlo (though our own Amrita Shergill messed up her life no less than Kahlo).

The new story is that of China. It is true that some of China's contemporary artists—Zhang Xiaogang, He Sen, Zeng Fanzhi—have originality and skill to match the world's greatest painters. Recent auctions have seen some of these artists' works go for over $5 million each—no Indian has fetched a price anywhere near this. But behind this success is a huge amount of investment by the Chinese government in promoting art and setting up stunning new art galleries.

The reason why India is not yet at this level is not because of a dearth of artistic genius, but because of a lack of appropriate institutions and infrastructure. First, we need to stimulate the common person's interest. A trip to Delhi's National Gallery of Modern Art can be quite dispiriting because of the poor quality of display and the paucity of Indian viewers. We need to get our school children interested in art. Our newspaper and magazine editors have as much responsibility for this as our government. Second, we need to invest in infrastructure. We should use our best architects to construct creatively designed museums, so that visitors can see the best of our works in the best of light. This can help propel Indian art on the world scene. When we think of infrastructure, we are right to demand better airports and roads but we must not forget that even the arts, music, and culture need infrastructure and, curiously, once provided with this, they can also yield large commercial dividends that can benefit the whole nation.

Markets and Aesthetics

WHENEVER I HAPPEN TO BE IN Delhi in March, I make it a point to visit the Annual Exhibition of the Delhi College of Art, when paintings and drawings by the students of the college are opened to the public. What one sees takes one's breath away.

As was mentioned in the earlier section, the talent on display is phenomenal. This is true not just of Delhi. One finds the same looking at art by little-known artists in other Indian cities and even towns. One cannot but marvel at the skill and imagination that India's young and unknown artists bring to their work.

What is true, however, is that a vast number of these extraordinarily talented people will ultimately be compelled to abandon their craft to make ends meet. This is even more true for those living in small towns and villages, which do not have even the college exhibitions where one sees the talent on display before it is extinguished. India clearly needs to do more to promote its own culture and the arts.

The reason for this sub-par performance is rooted in mistakes on both the left and the right. The first mistake is to suppose that art has nothing to do with markets and, so, to overlook the fact that for art to flourish, we need a thriving market. The second mistake is the one of supposing that a market thrives only when it is left completely to its own devices. The truth is that markets need nurture by government and institutions. This is true of markets in the US, Japan, and China; this has been true of markets at the time of Adam Smith and is true now.

If we wish the celebration of Indian art (in India and abroad) to reach beyond the few whose works that now regularly make it to London and New York—Syed Haider Raza, Anjolie Ela Menon, Jogen Chowdhury, M.F. Hussain, and one or two others—we need deliberate action on the part of government and our media.

There is a lot that government can do to promote art and art appreciation. One idea, which will need some initial investment but can in the long run pay for itself many times over, is to build in India a Museum of Contemporary Art from Developing Economies. Buying the works of top artists from the US or Britain or France can be prohibitive. Not so for some of the finest artists from Brazil, South Africa, Vietnam, Russia, Sri Lanka, Mexico, and China. Some contemporary Chinese artists, such as Wang Guangyi and Zhang Xiaogang, may command prices like those of the most expensive Western artists but, in general, it is within India's reach to build up a museum that is known globally for having the best collection from the developing world. This would not only increase tourist traffic to India and raise the profile of India in the world, but it could also, in turn, increase interest in Indian art and culture and thereby open new doors for our own poor artists.

Also, once one such a major international gallery comes up, the market for art would pick up on its own and smaller galleries would sprout up in and around this one big effort.

A visit on any random day to Delhi's National Gallery of Modern Art, housed in the magnificent premises of the Jaipur House, can be a dispiriting experience. The art, with the large collections of the works of Amrita Shergill, Abanindranath Tagore, K.G. Subramanyam, and others, is impressive. What disappoints is that so few people visit the museum. On my last visit I felt guilty that the somnolent guards were getting disturbed.

This is where the Indian media comes in. There ought to be more coverage of the arts, music, and even science and mathematics in our newspapers, magazines, radio, and television if we are to have a more learned and productive citizenry.

I am aware that this is a two-way street. The media clearly have an interest in supplying people with what they are interested in. This explains the excellent coverage of what is happening in the life of Megan Fox and J. Lo. This is understandable and one can see why no single newspaper will want to take away that space and turn it over to more educational matters.

The fear of competition can, however, be partly curbed if there is a collective effort on the part of all major newspapers and television channels to devote a small amount of space to nurturing interest in the arts and the sciences. After all, corporations, despite their commitment to profits, do, nowadays, make some concession to 'corporate social responsibility' (CSR). The CSR movement has led companies to agree to take small cuts in profit in order not to pollute the atmosphere and to uphold minimal labour standards even when that is costly. They need to do more; but it is interesting that they do something.

Likewise, we need to promote the idea of what may be called 'media cultural responsibility' (MCR). A commitment to MCR will mean that a newspaper will devote a small amount of space, say 5 per cent to start with, to promote the arts and culture, and interest in science. This will not increase sales and will not, therefore, help with advertisement income, but this small cost, borne by all newspapers, can make a huge difference to the promotion of the arts and sciences in India, and can even speed up development by creating a more enlightened and productive citizenry.

Norms and Prosperity

ONE DISSERVICE TO DEVELOPMENT THAT TRADITIONAL economic theory has done is to place self-interest on a pedestal. One of the key propositions that Adam Smith had developed in his classic book published in 1776 was that if each individual in an economy pursued his or her self-interest— consumers maximizing utility, entrepreneurs maximizing profit— society would automatically achieve optimality, with the 'invisible hand' of the market doing the job. Smith made this claim with lots of provisos, but over time all the caveats fell by the wayside, and the invisible hand doctrine became an alibi for narrow economism and the single-minded pursuit of self-interest.

Fortunately, modern research in economics and psychology is making it clear that our other human qualities, such as altruism, personal integrity, and appropriate social norms and institutions, are vital for economic development.

In India today there is worry about our high growth not being sufficiently inclusive, and leaving segments of the population abysmally poor. Some clues to this lie in our neglect of non-economic factors. Consider the simple act of trying to bring marginalized people into the mainstream of the economy. This is, of course, something that we should aim for; but, if this is done without giving these people basic education, a sense of their fundamental rights, a modicum of understanding of how the modern economy functions, and also some basic health facilities, there is a risk that they will get no benefit by being drawn into the market economy, and may actually lose out.

We have historical research documenting how the Native Americans lost their land to the settlers from Europe. There were battles, but much more important was the use of 'voluntary' contracts, where the natives were simply out-witted or plain deceived. There was, first of all, wanton use of the age-old technique of giving superficially attractive loans and then when the borrowers could not pay back, foreclosing on their property—the sub-prime crisis of the seventeenth century.

The other method was to take advantage of the fact that Native Americans did not understand land sales since in their own society there was no custom of selling land. Hence, there were incidents, such as in 1755 in South Carolina, when more than 500 Cherokees met with a similar number of settlers. Gifts were exchanged and meals were served in silver bowls and cups. The Cherokees were very happy and declared that the tribe wished to give 'all their Lands to the King of Great Britain' and make him 'the owner of all their Lands and Waters'. This was a metaphorical use of language, a way to be nice to outsiders. This was especially clear when the Cherokees refused to take any payment for their offer. But the offer was too good for the settlers to allow qualms about metaphorical speech to get in the way. To make this into a contract, the settlers persuaded the Cherokees to take a small payment, which they accepted out of politeness. Little did they realize that they were about to lose all their land.[1]

I mentioned at the start how altruism is important for economic prosperity but, in our literal interpretation of the invisible hand

---

[1] The larger implications of this kind of 'contract' for mainstream economics is discussed in my book, *Beyond the Invisible Hand: Groundwork for a New Economics* (Princeton University Press 2010; Penguin India 2011).

proposition, this has been overlooked. There is now a lot of research highlighting the importance of 'pro-social' behaviour. Let me close by presenting the reader a game that I published in 1994, called the Traveller's Dilemma. The game has come to acquire a bit of a life of its own, with laboratory experiments run on it in several American universities. What has, however, not been talked about enough is the role of altruism it highlights.

In the Traveller's Dilemma, two travellers (who do not know each other) happened to have gone to a remote island and bought an identical antique each. When they arrive at their home airport, they discover that the airline has mishandled the baggage and that their antiques are broken. So they ask for compensation. The airline manager, not knowing the value of these 'strange objects', offers them the following payment scheme. Each passenger, without consulting with the other, has to write down a number (an integer) between 2 and 100. If they both write the same number, the manager will pay them both that number in rupees. If the two write different numbers, he will give both travellers the lower number, but with a correction. He will give the 'good' person, who wrote the lower number, an extra Rs 2, and the 'bad' person who wrote the higher number, Rs 2 less. So, if person A writes 47 and B writes 60, A gets Rs 49 and B Rs 45.

If both players want to make the most money for themselves, what should they write?

Note that if they both write 100, each gets Rs 100. But, in that case, if one player deviates to 99, he will get Rs 101. By this reasoning, both will change to 99. But, now, if one player changes to 98, he can do better. By this logic, both will switch to 98. This logic turns out to be relentless. If each traveller single-mindedly tries to make as much money as possible for himself, they will both end up writing 2 and earning only Rs 2. If each showed some respect for and altruism towards the other and not 'ditch' the other passenger for a single dollar, they could both have earned Rs 100. The invisible hand of self-interest drives them not to prosperity but indigence.

Trust and Development

WHEN SHE WAS IN HER SIXTIES, my father's youngest sister once shared with me a puzzle about her health that had clearly been troubling her. 'I don't know why I keep such poor health, I eat nothing but sweets.' To me, the diagnosis was contained right in that sentence.

I remembered her remark recently, reading about the endless debates on economic growth. From the Washington Consensus to the more recent Growth Commission of the World Bank, experts have debated the determinants of growth and tried a slew of policies. But large tracts of sub-Saharan Africa, much of South Asia, and big chunks of Latin America have proved stubborn beyond expectation. It is noteworthy that all these prescriptions have had to do with economic variables—monetary policy, fiscal rules, and trade regimes. Is it possible that therein lies the flaw?

I believe the answer is yes. What the conventional wisdom has overlooked is that the absence of economic growth is often because of our preoccupation with economic variables. In reality, economic growth owes much to non-economic variables—to culture and social norms, to our habits and collective beliefs; in brief, to variables that traditional economic theory sweeps under the carpet as unimportant. There is fortunately some new research trying to uncover the links between social norms and economic growth. I shall here dwell on one such theme—trust.

There can be no denying that industrialized societies have a higher level of trust and trustworthy behaviour among their citizens than poor nations. What I am suggesting is that this is not mere coincidence. It could not have been otherwise. Unless these societies had inculcated minimal standards of personal integrity and trustworthiness, they would not have succeeded in achieving high economic growth. The phenomenal success of the East Asian economies through the 1960s and 1970s owes credit to good economic policy, but it also owes a lot to the norms of honesty and trustworthiness that had come to be a part of East Asian life. If we want India to have sustained development, we must try to instil norms of personal integrity in the citizenry. Clearly, the country has some distance to go on this score.

The crux of a prosperous economy is efficient contract enforcement. In industrialized societies, people often get into agreements and plan on exchange, some of which play out over long stretches of time. In the mortgage market, for instance, we take a loan in an instant and promise to pay it back over decades. In societies in which contracts are poorly enforced, people quickly learn not to get into contracts. Since modern, industrial societies depend on contracts and agreements, societies that fail to enforce them will fail to become modern and industrialized. It is not surprising that India's mortgage market developed only after we had in place a system for enforcing long-term mortgage contracts. And without such enforcement, many people who now own homes would never have been able to do so.

There are, however, limits to how much government can do. There are hundreds of situations in life where minor contracts and expectations need to be fulfilled, where it is impossible to have a third party, like government, check them all out. When we eat in a restaurant, we need to be able to trust that the kitchen is clean. When we fly an aeroplane, we need assurance that the engines are in order. Hence, a nation in which people are innately honest and trustworthy has a great advantage and, conversely, a nation without these traits is handicapped.

These valuable traits cannot, however, be developed by repeating simple mantras, like 'Honesty is the best policy.' For one, that is a lie. Teaching people to be honest by propagating a lie is unlikely to be successful. For each person, individually, honesty is not always the best policy. If it were, we would not have to work so hard to persuade people about it.

The problem arises from the fact that traits like trustworthiness, honesty, and industry are treated by most human beings as group characteristics. Hence, we talk of 'Protestant ethics' and 'Confucian values', we think of some groups as being more industrious than others and some nations being more trustworthy than others. And when this happens, it is not in your interest to develop these traits because you will anyway be judged, at least in part, by your group identity.

Hence, we cannot develop these desirable characteristics by appealing to self-interest. They have to be nurtured as ends in themselves, as innate moral qualities. A huge responsibility for this lies with our leaders in government, industry, and other walks of life. A vast majority of our politicians and industry leaders make for poor role models. Fortunately, there is a minority that is different. Let us hope that the size of this minority grows. Ordinary people could learn from them. Once good norms are in place, the rewards for the economy as a whole can be enormous.

Where India Is Ahead of China

IT MUST BE BECAUSE OF THE 19TH NATIONAL CONGRESS of China's Communist Party last month that there has been a flurry of conferences, meetings and discussions in recent weeks on the growth prospects of emerging economies, particularly China.

Both as a consequence of Donald Trump's dismal performance and Xi Jinping's remarkable leadership, China is beginning to rival US's global political influence. But, in terms of the economy measured by GNP or per capita income, China still has a long way to go.

One particularly interesting meeting I participated in was on the relative growth prospects of China and India. China's economic performance has been so good since 1978 to now, that the tendency for most analysts is to extrapolate that and put China ahead of India in terms of prospects. Yet, I have come to believe that, in terms of long-run economic prospects, there is reason to place India ahead of China. Since this is a contrarian view, it needs explanation.

China's economic performance in 1969, a year in which its growth rate was an unbelievable 16.9 per cent, and more relentlessly after 1978, has been outstanding. One reason for the success is the coercive power of its leaders. This enabled China to push through tough reforms. India's cacophonous democracy placed many more restraints on the leaders and often made it impossible for them to make essential reforms.

But I believe that these same traits that helped China grow risk becoming its Achilles' heel. Conversely, India's early investment in secularism, cultural openness, freedom of speech, which did make the early years difficult for economic growth, is now in a position to pay off.

According to the tenets of neoliberal economics, China's economy should not be growing. But since we have hard evidence of its growth, that debate should be treated as settled: neoliberal economics is wrong. However, there are puzzling questions about China's phenomenal performance. A disproportionate amount of its GDP is produced by the state-owned sector, and the Communist Party has representatives on the boards of private companies. It is a top-down system that failed in most countries but seems to have succeeded in China.

What China's experience shows is that a coercive system, run by intelligent leaders, can yield dividends. Mao Zedong made big mistakes but it was under his leadership that the country invested in health and education, which has given China a remarkably talented workforce. Under Deng Xiaoping's leadership, critical space was created for market forces and, at the same time, a clever interventionist policy was devised for exchange rates, which promoted exports. And in Xi Jinping we see an extraordinary capacity for management and control as well as for global engagement.

Why, then, do I have concerns about China? Because a coercive, top-down system, after a while, acquires its own raison d'être and, when that happens, the interests of those at the top run contrary to the interests of the nation. The coercive structure is then used to preserve political power rather than to promote development.

The key lesson is: a top-down coercive system may work for a while, but tends to backfire in the long-run. In a fascinating TedTalk, the celebrated British music conductor, Charles Hazlewood, pointed out how coercion and the dictatorship of the conductor can produce good music; but truly great music requires personal freedom for individual players and trust between the conductor and the orchestra. This is true not just for orchestras but for corporations and governments.

In societies like China and India, a special problem pertains to the control of corruption. Because corruption is so pervasive, leaders, even if they are genuinely keen on controlling it, face a choice of who they will go after, friends or the opposition. There is a natural tendency, stemming from the instinct of self-preservation, to go after the latter. Soon, the anti-corruption drive becomes an instrument of silencing dissent. Both India and China face this risk but it is bigger for China because of the absence of free media.

The Chinese top-down system is so all-embracing that it may be impossible to dismantle. Like in so many countries through history, when there is some malfunctioning of such a system, the economy gets short shrift over political power preservation. And therein lies India's strength. Thanks to the nation's early commitment to democracy, openness and free media, it is now in a position to reap the benefits. India's high growth from 2005 has many drivers but those early (and undoubtedly costly) social and political investments are prominently among them. For this reason, I believe India is likely to outstrip China not in the next few years, but in the long run. Its system, with vents open for continuous dissent, may make growth a little slower but, for that very reason, surer.

Democratic nations can, of course, take wrong turns. We have seen this happen in the US in the early 1950s during the McCarthy years, in India in 1975–7 when Indira Gandhi imposed Emergency. But the traditions of freedom, and in particular the anonymous ballot, play an important role in bringing these to an end, as happened in the US and in India. That is the reason for my optimism for India's economy.

All forecasts, however, come with caveats; things can go wrong. I am not talking about a wrong policy intervention, such as the ill-conceived demonetization of last November or the poor design of the otherwise desirable GST. India's big risk is the rise of right-wing religious vigilantism in recent years. These acts are led by people with a deep sense of inferiority about their own nation and so they like to shout from roof tops about their greatness five millennia ago and imitate fundamentalist and supremacist groups of other societies. The silencing of dissent and the free media, and the use of threats and even actual violence that has emerged from this group is a genuine risk for India. There is a small probability that this group, by its own insecurity and viral hatred of the other, will cause India to stall and stagnate. But I remain optimistic, and believe that this is just a phase.

seven

Conundrums of Finance and Economics*

Burning Cash: A Finance Conundrum

HERE IS A QUESTION FOR MONETARY-POLICY wonks and for the laity interested in logic puzzles. Earlier this week, when the Reserve Bank of India (RBI) announced tough policy measures for controlling inflation, the Sensex took a tumble of over 500 points. There were complaints that this meant a loss of wealth for individuals, corporations, and, hence, the nation. The question I want to ask is: Is this necessarily so? After all, Sensex points are not apples and oranges. Its decline does not connote a direct loss of goods and services as happens when a building burns down or crops are damaged by floods.

---

* 'Burning Cash: A Finance Conundrum' was first published in *Hindustan Times*, 2 August 2008. 'Why Some Financial Products Should Be in Prescription' was first published as 'Prescription Financial Products', in the Project Syndicate website on 21 September 2009. 'Financial Scams and Ponzis' was first published as 'India's Lessons from Satyam', in *BBC News Online*, 26 January 2009. 'Acquiring Land for Industry' was first published as 'Not Losing the Plot', in *Hindustan Times*, 14 August 2009. 'Bureaucratic Reform in India' was first published as 'Who Keeps Us behind China? Babus

To put this in sharper relief, consider a related problem. A rich man, travelling by ship, loses Rs 1 crore when his trunk-load of cash is washed away in a typhoon. Clearly, he is worse off; and since no one else was involved in this, we would be tempted to conclude that society as a whole loses wealth equal to Rs 1 crore. But, on further thought, that is not obvious. Since the total amount of apples, oranges, homes, etc., is unchanged, it is arguable that there is no loss of real wealth in society. This man's loss must be balanced by small, indirect gains of other individuals. But on even further thought, this also may not be right. Most economists (I have tried this on many) would tell you that, since this person now has less cash, he will spend less on apples, oranges, homes, etc., which will cause the manufacturers of these goods to produce less and so there will indeed be a net shrinkage in total output.

Let us suppose this is correct. Then if, instead of a storm causing him to lose money, a fairy goddess (or the RBI, if you so prefer) gave him notes worth Rs 1 crore, freshly minted for him, then the entire society would be better off. After all, getting Rs 1 crore is no different from not losing Rs 1 crore.

If the creation of Rs 1 crore notes creates more real wealth, another Rs 1 crore printed and gifted to another person must do the same, and so must another crore and another.... But this, we know, is not the case. This will cause ruinous inflation and impoverish society, as happened in Germany in 1923, Hungary in 1946, and during Mohammad bin Tughlak's reign in fourteenth-century India. It follows that there are situations where the loss of a trunk-load of cash increases total output (since there are situations where the injection of a trunk-load of cash causes total output to fall). The link between monetary assets and real wealth is evidently not a

and Judges', in *Financial Express*, 20 October 2008. 'Labour Market Reform in India' was first published as 'Why India's Labour Laws are a Problem', in *BBC News Online*, 18 May 2006. 'Whither Social Progress?' was first published in *BBC News Online*, 31 August 2009. 'Same-Sex Preference and Rights' was first published in *Hindustan Times*, 14 October 2007. 'Evidence-Based Policy Mistakes' was first published in the Project Syndicate website on 30 November 2017. 'The ABC of Doing Business' was first published in the Project Syndicate website on 28 February 2018.

unidirectional one. The tracking of this link remains one of the big open problems of economic theory.

Some of these complexities carry over to the connection between the value of shares and real wealth in a nation. The deflation of the value of stocks can, in some situations, be concomitant with an increase in aggregate prosperity.

Take the downturn of the Indian stock market following the announcement of RBI's anti-inflationary package—the raising of the repo rate and the cash reserve ratio. First of all, it is not at all certain that the two are causally connected; some would argue that the Indian stock market was reacting to the Dow Jones. But let me leave this aside for now. The RBI intervention has been described in the press as a policy meant to curb inflation at the cost of growth. The response of the Sensex is treated as evidence that growth is being compromised. In reality, it is not at all clear that this is the right way to analyse this. It is arguable that the opposite is the case. If this inflation were left unchecked, growth in the long run would decline. In 1972, India had an inflation of 10 per cent; in 1973, 20 per cent; and in 1974, 25 per cent—the highest ever in independent India. By letting inflation rise to such a height, did we get good growth? No, 1974 was one of India's worst years. The gross domestic product (GDP) grew by only 1.2 per cent, which means per capita income declined. Hence, checks on inflation can push up aggregate growth in the future to levels that are higher than what they would be if inflation were allowed to rise unabated.

I do not say this as the final word on the subject. Monetary policy requires a strange combination of engineering skills and artistry and intuition. The only rule that we can be sure of is to be wary of those who claim to know exactly what the right policy is.

Why Some Financial Products Should Be on Prescription

ONE POSITIVE FALLOUT OF THE FINANCIAL crisis that began in 2007–8 is our realization that financial products can be as complex and dangerous as drugs. This realization has, in turn, led to innovative ideas and experimentation with new laws, regulations, and institutions around the world. In India, the government has announced the establishment of the Financial Stability and Development Council (FSDC) to address inter-regulatory co-ordination issues and provide macro-prudential supervision. In the US, the Dodd-Frank Wall Street Reform and Consumer Protection Act and new initiatives to monitor the safety of financial products could alter the architecture of finance.

Several proponents of these new ideas have openly used the analogy with drugs. It has been argued that if, in 2007, there had been a *Financial* Products Safety Commission, the way the US has the Food and Drugs Administration, we would not have had the flooding of the market with teaser mortgages that got millions of households tangled in predatory credit.

What is especially sophisticated about these new ideas cropping up in the US, Europe, India, China, and all over the world is the recognition that, in financial products, like in drugs and toys, it is impossible to say in advance what products we should allow and what we should not, because we cannot even conceive of all the products that can and will eventually come on the market. Hence, the need for a judgemental body that can look at a new product and form an opinion about its desirability.

While these are innovative ideas, there is one worrying aspect to them. They have to tread a narrow path between reckless freedom for financial institutions, which contributed to the recent global financial crisis, and over-caution that can suffocate innovation and create inefficiencies. Consider a teaser loan, which initially charges a low or even zero interest rate, and then has a ballooning of interest burden at a later date. This is a dangerous product, true, and it did cause many families to fall into an unsustainable debt trap. Yet, it can be of great value to sophisticated firms and households that may have good reason to believe that their future earnings profile will be higher than the current one. Such entities would be able to make investments with teaser loans, which would not be possible otherwise.

This is just one example. It is impossible to anticipate the numerous financial products that human ingenuity can create and which can be, at the same time, dangerous to use but of great value to some. The risk with many of the regulatory measures under consideration in today's crisis-scarred world is that they may end up over-regulating our markets to the point of blocking the emergence of valuable new products.

Is there a way out of this conundrum? The answer is yes. In creating new financial regulation we need to take the medical analogy one step further. The secret is to create the equivalent of the prescription. Instead of banning all dangerous products or freely allowing all, we need to identify products that are valuable to some customers but not all—call them 'prescription financial products'—and create a body of registered finance professionals (RFPs) who are empowered to certify the purchase of these products by individuals.

You are planning to buy a house. Your local bank offers you what is certified to be a teaser loan, that is, it is a prescription product. You can take such a loan, provided that an RFP signs off on such a contract. In brief, what I am saying is that, just as we do not ban steroids because they are dangerous, but put them on the list of prescription drugs, we should have room for the same when it comes to financial products. Having this option can vastly shorten the list of products that will need to be banned.

There is, however, one aspect in which I would recommend staying away from the medical convention—at least, as prevails in industrialized nations, where each medicine is either over-the-counter or prescription, irrespective of who is buying the product. In order to keep the system lean, I would recommend that there should be a provision for declaring some individuals and firms as being exempt from having to get an approval before buying a prescription financial product. In other words, all financial products will be classified as either over-the-counter or prescription. But, in addition, we may want to designate some individuals and firms as sophisticated enough to be able to handle their own affairs or well off enough to be able to deal with financial failure. They should be allowed to buy prescription financial products without an RFP's approval.

The reason I argue for this exemption provision is my experience in India, having recently moved here from the US. This is one aspect of life in which India has less bureaucracy and is, I believe, in the lead. A few months ago I went and met our new local drugstore owner. Without encumbering him with any prescription, I told him somewhat sheepishly that I was going on an extended foreign travel and wanted to keep a precautionary strip of antibiotic tablets with me. He looked me up and down, sized me up, and then said, 'Since you are going for so long, I would suggest you keep two strips.'

Financial Scams and Ponzis

WHAT A TRAGIC FALL. B. RAMALINGA RAJU, founder of Satyam Computer Services and an icon of India's software success, is now a prisoner in Hyderabad's Chanchalguda jail for what can only be described as daylight robbery.

It appeared initially that he had done what he confessed to, namely, fudged the balance sheets of his company to show higher profits and greater reserves in order to bolster shareholder confidence and rake in more investor money. It turned out, however, that he had not committed that crime. His company did have the large profits and reserves that he had shown on the books. The real crime was that he pilfered that money—an astonishing $1 billion. The shareholders had, in that sense, not been deceived with wrong information but simply had their money stolen.

In some ways this more blatant crime may be the saving grace for India. By turning out to be not one of those pure budget-fudging crimes that leave investors and customers wondering if the entire industry is tainted, this may do less damage to the larger reputation of India's software industry. Nevertheless, now that India, with all its recent economic reforms, is breaking away from the shackles of the

Licence Raj, it has to be prepared to grapple with the more novel crimes associated with market capitalism—the crimes that come from giving more licence to the Rajus.

The fundamental crime that appears in a variety of forms in modern market economies and is often difficult to detect because it can appear in so many guises is the Ponzi scheme. It is possible to argue that what Ramalinga Raju initially claimed was that he was guilty of a Ponzi fraud.

The classic Ponzi is what was recently done by America's Bernard Madoff. His investment company collapsed with an outstanding liability of $50 billion, leaving hundreds of thousands of investors stranded with all their money gone. He promised investors high returns. Then, instead of using the money received from investors to create wealth, he kept a large part for himself, got more money from new investors, and used this to pay the promised high returns to the early investors. As his reputation spread, more and more people gave their money to him and he continued with the same strategy. With each wave of fresh money received, he kept a large share for himself and used the rest to pay off old investors.

The trouble with this scheme is that it can survive only by continuously expanding the number of investors. Since the human population is finite, it is a matter of arithmetic that a Ponzi scheme has to eventually collapse. That happened in the case of Bernie Madoff; it happened to Charles Ponzi (1882–1949), who has the honour of having this particular fraud named after him, though schemes of this kind go back to antiquity; it happened to the scamsters who ran Kolkata's infamous Sanchaita Finance Company in the 1970s.

What makes Ponzis difficult to detect is that they often come intertwined with serious investment. Take a company like Satyam. To start with, this is a productive company that actually converts investor money into valuable goods and services. Suppose in a year of faltering profit, this company nevertheless gives out good returns to its shareholders by utilizing the money received from new investors. It is now beginning to mix productive activity with Ponzi. In fact, since the new investment is not used productively, but to payoff early shareholders, it is possible that, by this very act, the next year's profits will be low and the company will be under pressure to expand its Ponzi activity.

Such hybrid-Ponzis are difficult to identify. After all, companies occasionally do some returns-smoothing to stabilize some of the year-to-year profit fluctuations. In small measure this does no harm, and can in fact be a desirable form of insurance against market vagaries. It is when this practice becomes addictive that one is in trouble. Just as there is no easily detectable time when a heavy drinker becomes an alcoholic, the start of corporate budgetary crimes is difficult to pin down.

These are some of the hazards that India has to be prepared to deal with. One hopes that a part of the safeguard against this will be the individual integrity of business leaders. But, as we know from history and experience from around the world, there will always be the black sheep in a group, whether it be the software sector, pharmaceuticals, or banks; and for this, a newly industrializing nation needs carefully crafted laws and continuous vigilance.

Acquiring Land for Industry

THE LAND ACQUISITION BILL, CURRENTLY ON hold with the Lok Sabha, has given rise to deep political fissures. At the heart of this is the following question: In harnessing land for large-scale industrialization, should we leave it all to the free market, whereby industrialists and farmers are left to discuss land price and voluntarily come to an agreement, or should we have provision for government to utilize state power, fix a reasonable price, and acquire land?

Modern economic theory sheds light on this; and, somewhat unexpectedly, comes out on the side of government intervention. As a consequence, even some of the most aggressively market-oriented nations in the world, such as the US, have provisions that allow the state to intervene and acquire land for large-scale industrial or commercial use.

The economic argument shows that, left entirely to voluntary transactions, many socially desirable industrialization projects would never get implemented. This so-called 'hold-up problem' was briefly touched upon by Amartya Sen in his Penguin Lecture on 'Justice and India' in Kolkata on 5 August 2009, though he did not elaborate on it.

The essential idea is simple, though it has an impressive intellectual heritage in game theory and, in particular, the work of John Nash.

We know that for big industrial projects, such as a new automobile factory, a large amount of contiguous land is needed. Getting some parts of this land and not others would make the project unviable. Suppose a large project is being considered by an industrialist called T for which he needs to buy two plots of neighbouring land, currently owned by farmers M and B (I am trying to use letters which are meaningful). Assume the industrial project can generate gross profit of Rs 10 and the farms are fallow and yield no benefit to the farmers. Hence, this is clearly a viable project. If, for instance, T gives Rs 3 to each of the farmers, they gain (Rs 3 each) and T gains (Rs 4).

Since, in reality, hundreds of farmers are likely to be involved, it is reasonable to assume that all the bargaining cannot be done simultaneously. I shall mimic this here by assuming that T has to strike a deal first with M and then with B.

Assume that each farmer demands the maximum she can get within the limits of what the industrialist will be willing to pay. It can be proved that the project will not be undertaken. For ease of exposition, I shall assume that all payments are made in integers; in other words, there is never any payment in paisas.

In the first stage, the bargain is between T and M. The argument will go through no matter what M asks for. Note that if M asks for more than 9, T will reject it, and if she asks for less than 1, it is not in her own interest. So let me simply assume that M asks for some amount between 1 and 9.

Next—in stage 2—he talks to B, who knows that if she says no, the project will not occur. Recall that T needs both plots for the project to be viable. So, if B agrees to a deal, the profit generated is 10, and if B does not, then the profit is 0. In brief, B has the power to hold up the entire project. So as long as B charges any amount less than Rs 10, it is in T's interest to accept the offer. Recall that whatever T spent in stage one is now sunk cost and cannot be recovered. Therefore, B will charge 9, and T will accept the deal.

However, this means that over the two stages, T would have spent 10 or more acquiring the land and so his net profit will be zero or negative. Interestingly, we know this even without knowing the exact deal struck in stage one. Since a loss or, at best, zero profit is foretold for the industrialist, he will not start the process of negotiation with the first farmer. Hence, no industrialization occurs even though all of them could have gained from it.

Some may counter that large-scale land acquisitions have taken place, prominently in Gujarat, with no state interventions. I have two words of caution on this. First, many seemingly voluntary land acquisitions are actually based on subtle intimidations and threats to poor farmers. Second, for every such deal that goes through, there are many that never get initiated for the aforementioned reasons.

My argument must not be construed as giving government licence to acquire land at will. China's policy of using the strong arm of the state to confiscate large amounts of agricultural land that the farmers cannot question is not worth emulating. We must have a law that specifies the limits of state engagement. The industrial project has to be of demonstrable social worth. And it should be mandatory that the landowners are compensated handsomely, well above the market price.

India's labour-intensive industrial sector is poised for development. Once a proper legal and institutional backdrop is provided, we should see enormous growth in this sector, which can have a larger impact on poverty alleviation and the mitigation of unemployment than many a piecemeal intervention.

Bureaucratic Reform in India

THANKS TO THE GLOBAL FINANCIAL CRISIS and slowdown of the American economy, India's growth forecast for this year has been lowered to 7 per cent—my own expectation is that it will go even lower. But there is reason to expect that, within two years, India will be back on the 9 per cent per annum growth path that it has been on during the last four years.

This is good performance but still well below China's annual growth of 11 per cent. However, now that India is saving and investing 35 per cent of its national income—a statistic that even 10 years ago, when our savings rate held steady around 23 per cent, would have been unthinkable—it is possible to think of strategies for catching up with China's growth performance. Just as the human body has several organs, all important but one or two that are vital, a nation's economy also has, among its myriad components, one or two vital ones, which, managed properly, can help a nation to course ahead. A country's bureaucracy and judicial system are examples of such critical components. Many other parts of the economy can be left on auto-pilot, if these are run effectively.

Take, for instance, loans for buying cars or fertilizer or tractors or, for that matter, any transaction that engages two or more agents over a certain period of time. There would not be need for government to set up separate organizations and have teams of bureaucrats to provide these if the government had an efficient legal system, whereby individuals could sign contracts and rely on the judiciary to enforce these contracts quickly and fairly. Individuals would lend to each other much more freely and they would perform trade and exchange without the need for government to directly provide these services. In other words, if the government provides the institutional foundations for the market to function, it does not have to be engaged in doing all the work that the market can do.

An efficient judiciary and bureaucracy cannot, however, be wished into existence. They need careful design, determination, and some initial expense of reorganization, but once done, they can

TABLE 7.1   DOING BUSINESS IN DIFFERENT NATIONS

Country	No. of Days to Start Business	No. of Days to Enforce Contract	No. of Months to Close Business
India	33	1,420	120
China	35	406	20
Singapore	5	120	10
South Korea	17	230	18
Pakistan	24	880	34
Thailand	33	479	33
Malaysia	24	600	28

Source: *Doing Business* (2008), The World Bank.

help government cut back on so many other separate expenses and initiatives. How has India been doing in terms of its bureaucracy? Over the last few years there has been a useful data set put out by the World Bank that allows us to answer this question without having to resort to impressionistic tales and hand-waving. Some of the most recent data on this is reproduced in Table 7.1.[1]

The first step in running a business is of course to get the basic paperwork done and to acquire the necessary permissions from the government. As Table 7.1 shows, this takes 5 days in Singapore, 17 days in South Korea, and 33 days in India. As already discussed, a vital function of government in an economy is the enforcement of contract. If we cannot rely on contracts, there are a thousand activities that we are unable to undertake. In the event of a contract lapse, how long does it take to enforce it? The answer is 120 days in Singapore, 230 days in South Korea, and a whopping 1,420 days in India. For this and for the time that it takes to close a business, Table 7.1 shows that India is at the bottom of the list—the worst performer. There is little surprise that there is not a greater rush of new firms entering India's labour-intensive manufacturing sector.

Singapore and South Korea, which are among the world's best-performing economies, hold the top two ranks for all the three

---

[1] Statistics for some of the same items, four years earlier, appear in Chapter 3, in the section 'India Globalizing'.

indicators in Table 7.1. This is not a coincidence. These economies do well because they have such efficient bureaucracies. Further, having a cumbersome bureaucracy may not be too big a hurdle for large corporations that have their legal departments and enough in-house personnel to handle this. But this handicaps greatly small businesses and self-employed individuals, thwarting enterprise and, ultimately, hurting the whole economy.

The story of India's judiciary is not very different. In response to a query lodged under India's Right to Information Act, 2005, the Home Ministry's Department of Justice revealed that, in 2007, there were 26.3 million cases pending in the nation's lower courts and 3 million were pending in India's 21 high courts. (The only good news for the rest of the nation was that a quarter of all pending cases were in Allahabad High Court.) In the same year, a quarter million under-trials were languishing in jails, of whom 2,069 had been in jail for over five years. Apart from the gross injustice of this system, such inefficiencies work as a huge deterrent for the economy. This is what makes me believe that, if the bureaucracy and the judiciary can be made more efficient, India can close the gap with China.

There is evidence from some sub-sectors that we can reform these sectors and the effect of this on the economy will be salutary. Following the financial sector reforms of the early 1990s, India introduced the Debt Recovery Tribunal (DRT) to enable banks and other financial institutions to quickly recover loans that they had given out to individuals and firms. Only large loans—those exceeding Rs 10 lakh—came under the purview of the DRTs.

There were hurdles in setting up the DRT. In July 1994, the Delhi Bar Association challenged the validity of DRTs and the Delhi High Court issued a stay on their operations. They could resume function only after the Supreme Court gave orders for them to do so in 1996. How successful have the DRTs been and have they had an effect on general economic functioning? These questions are asked and answered very persuasively in a recent paper, 'Legal Reform and Loan Repayment: The Microeconomic Impact of Debt Recovery Tribunals in India' by Sujata Visaria, economist at Boston University.

By 31 January 2002, 57,000 cases had been filed with the DRTs. By 31 March 2003, loans worth Rs 79 billion had been recovered as a consequence. Visaria's study shows that while the verdicts reached by the DRTs and high courts are very similar, the DRTs have been vastly more efficient than the regular courts. In the case of high courts, summonses went out on average 449 days after the filing of a case. DRTs took 56 days to do the same. For hearing and presentation of evidence and first arguments, the high courts took a little over thrice as much time as a DRT.

The most interesting finding is that this greater judicial efficiency has an impact on economic variables. The mere presence of a DRT improves the timely repayment of loans and lowers the interest rate that banks charge. The lower interest rate is a direct response of the market to the lower transactions cost that arises from the more effective judicial system.

This small experiment illustrates both that it is within our powers to make the judicial process more efficient, and that this can be expected to have a positive impact on the economy as a whole. The time is ripe for India to overhaul its management of the courts and bureaucracy, so that the nation does not rank so poorly on indicators like those illustrated in Table 7.1. And that, in turn, will automatically ensure that the nation moves up also on the ranking tables of economic performance.

Labour Market Reform in India

WHILE THE INDIAN ECONOMY IS BOOMING, there is evidence that workers are not partaking in the boom adequately. Employment is not growing as fast as working age population, nor are wages rising as rapidly as per capita income.

There are many reasons for this—some to do with forces of globalization that are beyond the Indian government's policy reach. But much of it has to do with the 'culture' that pervades our labour markets, which in turn is a consequence of the complicated and ill-conceived laws that govern the labour market.

The travails of Kolkata's famous Great Eastern Hotel illustrate nicely much of what is wrong. The hotel, founded in 1840 by a British confectioner, David Wilson (and originally named Auckland Hotel), prospered for a long time; but began to flounder in the early 1970s. Worried about the many workers of the hotel, the Congress government took over its management in 1975; and, driven by similar concerns, the Left Front government nationalized it in 1980.

Protected from the vicissitudes of the market, the hotel's quality continued to decline and staff size grew. According to some back-of-the-envelope calculations I did some time ago, it came to have such a high staff-to-rooms ratio that it was not clear why the hotel needed customers. If it moved its staff members into the hotel, it would be a self-sufficient housing complex, if slightly over-crowded. Fortunately, the government has since taken restructuring measures and there are hopes of the hotel's revival. But what happened for over 30 years is a mirror to much that ails Indian labour.

I have written on this subject before, but given its importance, it merits a revisit. In India there are 45 laws at the national level and close to four times that at the level of state governments that monitor the functioning of labour markets. Some of these date almost as far back as the founding of the Great Eastern Hotel. They were meant to control conflict and keep the labour market efficient.

Unfortunately, the experience has been to the contrary. According to recent World Bank estimates, in 2004, there were 482 cases of major work stoppages, resulting in 15 million human days of work loss. Between 1995 and 2001, around 9 per cent of factory workers were involved in these stoppages. The figure for China is close to zero. On the other hand, the wages of Chinese workers are rising much faster than that of India's. These facts are not unrelated.

Most of India's labour laws were crafted with scant respect for 'market response'. If X seemed bad, the presumption was that you had to simply enact a law banning X. But the fact that each law leads entrepreneurs and labourers to respond strategically, often in complicated ways, was paid no heed.

In a poor country, no one with any sensitivity wants workers to lose their jobs. So what does one do? The instinct is to make it difficult for firms to lay off workers. That is exactly what India's Industrial Disputes Act, 1947, did, especially through some later amendments, for firms in the formal sector and employing more than 100 workers.

But in today's globalized world, with volatile and shifting demand, firms have responded to this by keeping their labour force as small as possible. It is little wonder that in a country as large as India, less than 10 million workers are employed in the formal private sector.

Some commentators have argued that India's labour laws could not have had much of a consequence since most of them apply to only the formal sector. What they fail to realize is that one reason the formal sector has remained miniscule is because of these laws (and also the culture that the laws have spawned).

What is needed now is not a law that allows employers to fire workers at will but one that allows for different kinds of contracts. Some workers may sign a contract for a high wage but one that requires them to quit at short notice; others may seek the opposite. This would allow firms to employ different kinds of labour depending on the volatility of the market they operate in.

Flexibility in hiring and firing is not the only problem. India's complex web of legislation leads to a system of dispute resolution that is incredibly slow. Data from the Ministry of Labour reveal that in 2000, there were 533,038 disputes pending in India's labour courts; and, of these, 28,864 had been pending for over 10 years.

If India is to be a vibrant global economy, this has to change. Much of the debate on labour laws has been misconstrued. We do not need changes in labour laws and policy to elicit sacrifice from organized labour, as some economists have suggested. Indian workers, whether they be in the organized sector or the unorganized sector, are too poor for that. We need changes in order to create greater private-sector demand for labour, which will boost wages and employment.

In brief, we need to move to a system that (i) makes room for more flexible contracts in the labour market, (ii) has a minimal welfare net for workers who are out of work, and (iii) resolves labour market disputes more quickly.

Whither Social Progress?

IN THE HEADY TIMES THAT FOLLOWED India's independence, India may not have done well economically, but in social and political matters—ranging from untouchability to divorce—India implemented a number of progressive policies and laws. In some of these matters, India was actually ahead of many industrialized nations.

Our current situation is quite the opposite. The economy is surging with infusions of foreign capital and rises in productivity, but on the social and political front there is little to report. (I am not counting the spread of jeans and hamburgers, and the peppering of speech with 'like' as social advance.) Our attire may be modern and cars placed on better shock absorbers, but in some fundamental ways the contemporary Indian is more communal and blinkered and more intolerant than our forefathers.

Nehru used to talk and write openly about his atheism. In a letter to Gandhi he wrote, 'It is all very well for the likes of Sapru and me (a curious combination!) to…bless the movement for temple entry when neither has the remotest desire to go within a hundred miles of a temple, except, so far as I am concerned, to see the architecture and the statuary!' It is a tribute to the tolerance of the times and, even more, to Gandhi—as devout a believer as there ever was—that this did not get in the way of Nehru's political life or closeness to Gandhi. It is difficult to think of a person with such views, so openly aired, winning an election today in India.

August being the month of India's birth is a good time to take stock of these larger questions. Even as we pursue modernity in economics, it would be good to see some initiative and activism on the part of government in social and institutional matters. And issues there are by the dozen—child labour, gay rights, stem cell research, caste discrimination, gender discrimination. There is scope for policy initiative on each of these matters and, since money is not a major factor for some of these, there is no reason why India cannot actually be ahead of richer nations. With Bush at the helm of the US, the bar has anyway been lowered considerably.

Well over 10 per cent of all Indian children between the ages of 9 and 15 years are labourers. Surely this is unacceptable in a nation that prides itself on its economic progress. I have been doing research on this and hope to write about it in future. Let me here consider another subject on which policy changes are long overdue. This concerns IPC 377—that is, Section 377 of the Indian Penal Code. This decrees homosexual love as not just illegal but criminal.

There has been effort to amend this law so that homosexual love, *when it is between consenting adults and conducted in private*, is not treated as criminal. To me such an amendment would be a sign of civilization. Tolerating behaviour that does not have a negative externality—that is, does not adversely affect a third party—is a key ingredient of a civilized society and such tolerance has a long tradition in India from Buddha to Ramakrishna. But previous Indian governments have staunchly resisted amending this law, taking the line that homosexuality is perverse and an import into India from the West.

The truth is different. There is evidence from ancient Indian writings and carvings on temple walls that same-sex love is not alien to India. It is true that this law is seldom used to actually prosecute, but it is used to harass same-sex partners and to inflict on them a sense of unnaturalness and deviation. Moreover, it is a hindrance in the control of AIDS and the spread of HIV, since people are often forced to keep their sexual histories hidden even from doctors for no other reason but the fear of IPC 377.

The urge not to feel unnatural is natural enough. I realized this at a gay wedding in New York. It was between an Indian and an American woman. They could not, of course, formally get married because New York law does not recognize such marriages but it was a ceremonial occasion. A young rabbi, with a palpable spiritual presence, presided over the wedding. At the end of the ceremony, with readings from religious texts from around the world and the poetry of Tagore, he declared the couple 'married in the eyes of all', he paused deliberately and added with emphasis, *'enlightened* human beings'.

That evening there was a party where most couples were of the same sex. A charming young woman asked me what my 'partner' did. I replied, 'My partner is a demographer,' taking care to omit all pronouns—such is the human urge to be accepted. We continued to chat for a while about our 'partners', with me feeling increasingly hypocritical, till my wife came and joined us and I had to come out.

Same-Sex Preference and Rights

IN THESE EXHILARATING DAYS OF ECONOMIC growth and Sensex surges, it is easy to forget that India still has a great distance to go on social and political matters—dismantling caste discrimination, ensuring women's rights, and mitigating poverty. Interestingly, the situation now is the reverse of the decade after independence. Economic growth was negligible then, but it was a time of great social activism. Nowadays, India is growing at a rapid clip, but one cannot help feeling that we are becoming less tolerant and abandoning the virtue of inclusion.

Let me draw your attention to the shameful piece of legislation discussed in the last section—Section 377 of the Indian Penal Code (IPC), which makes homosexuality not just illegal but a criminal offence. I find it morally repugnant to have a law that passes judgement on another human being's personal preference when that preference has no negative consequences for others.

Sticklers for precision will point out that what IPC 377 declares criminal is the act of sodomy. While that is indeed what the fine print says, there is no getting away from the fact that in terms of both its original intent and current usage it is nothing but an instrument for punishing gays. Other defenders of this legislation will tell you that to legalize same-sex love is to give in to Western ways, that India is an inherently tolerant society and so there is no need to worry about bigotry, and that there are more urgent problems that we should attend to instead.

The first of these claims is patently wrong. What is alien to India is the legislation. It was drafted by Macaulay in the 1860s to inculcate Victorian values in Britain's prize colony. Moreover, whether or not a law like this has religious roots is unimportant. As for the second assertion, it is true that, in many ways, we are a tolerant society. For instance, the personal lives and proclivities of our politicians do not impinge on their electoral prospects, as happens in many Western nations. On the other hand, there is plenty of evidence of harassment of gays, especially among the poor and in prisons. Apart from anything else, this law has handicapped the fight against AIDS.

Finally, while it is true that India has more pressing problems, the decriminalization of same-sex love has significance that goes beyond repealing an archaic law. It is a statement of moral integrity, a declaration that heterosexuality has no claims to moral superiority. To repeal this law is a signal against bigotry of all kinds and a message of inclusion to all minorities—of religion, caste, and sexual orientation.

Immediately after independence, when Nehru fought to introduce the Hindu Code Bill, which would put women and men on an equal footing in matters of inheritance and abolish the rules of caste in sanctifying marriage, there were religious fundamentalists who argued that these changes went against Hinduism and some even objected that the bill was being piloted by Ambedkar, an untouchable.

My own view is that when reason and our innate sense of justice go against religious doctrine, we must accept the former. My sympathies are with the person who wrote that India's rule-chanting priests deserved to be banished 'because they would never mend, their hearts would never become big. They are the off-springs of centuries of superstition and tyranny.' The writer in question was Vivekananda and he wrote this in a letter to Alasingha, dated 10 July 1893.

Coincidentally, today, after I began writing this, I heard the Dalai Lama in a jam-packed indoor sports stadium at Cornell. The atmosphere was electric. One questioner asked, 'If a scientific finding went against a religious doctrine, which one should be rejected?' His response came effortlessly. If, on verification, the scientific finding was confirmed, it was the religious doctrine that would have to go.

Evidence-Based Policy Mistakes

AFTER YEARS OF STRESSING THE IMPORTANCE of evidence-based policymaking, economists have clearly had some influence on politicians. What economists now need to do is to impress upon those same politicians that citing any evidence before adopting any policy is not evidence-based policymaking.

Turkish President Recep Tayyip Erdoğan has thrown around numbers to defend his decision to flood the Turkish economy with state-guaranteed credit. But the truth is that the policy was a politically motivated effort to win public support by engineering short-term growth (at the cost of driving inflation to a nine-year high of 12 per cent).

Likewise, US President Donald Trump cites simplistic trade-deficit figures to justify *protectionist policies* that win him support among a certain segment of the US population. In reality, the evidence suggests that such policies will hurt the very people Trump claims to be protecting.

Now, the chair of Trump's Council of Economic Advisers, Kevin Hassett, is attempting to defend congressional Republicans' effort to slash corporate taxes by claiming that, when developed countries have done so in the past, workers gained 'well north of' $4,000 per year. Yet there is ample evidence that the benefits of such tax cuts accrue disproportionately to the rich, largely via companies buying back stock and shareholders earning higher dividends.

It is not clear whence Hassett is getting his data. But chances are that, at the very least, he is misinterpreting it. And he is far from alone in failing to reach accurate conclusions when assessing a given set of data.

Consider the oft-repeated refrain that, because there is evidence that virtually all jobs over the last decade were created by the private sector, the private sector must be the most effective job creator. At first glance, the logic might seem sound. But, on closer examination, the statement begs the question. Imagine a Soviet economist claiming that, because the government created virtually all jobs in the Soviet Union, the government must be the most effective job creator. To find the truth, one would need, at a minimum, data on who else tried to create jobs and how.

Moreover, it is important to recognize that data alone are not enough to determine future expectations or policies. While there is certainly value in collecting data (via, for example, randomized control trials), there is also a need for deductive and inductive reasoning, guided by common sense—and not just on the part of experts. By dismissing the views and opinions of ordinary people, economists may miss out on crucial insights.

People's everyday experiences provide huge amounts of potentially useful information. While a common-sense approach based on individual experience is not the most 'scientific', it should not be dismissed out of hand. A meteorologist might detect a coming storm by plugging data from myriad sources—atmospheric sensors, weather balloons, radar, and satellites—into complex computer models. But that does not mean that the sight of gathering clouds in the sky is not also a legitimate sign that one might need an umbrella—even if the weather forecast promises sunshine.

Intuition and common sense have been critical to our evolution. After all, had humans not been able to draw reasonably accurate conclusions about the world through experience or observation, we would not have survived as a species.

The development of more systematic approaches to scientific inquiry has not diminished the need for such intuitive reasoning. In fact, there are important and not obvious truths that are best deduced using pure reason.

Consider the Pythagorean Theorem, which establishes the relation among the three sides of a right-angled triangle. If all conclusions had to be reached by combing through large data sets, Pythagoras, who is believed to have devised the theorem's first proof, would have had to measure a huge number of right triangles. In any case, critics would likely argue that he had looked at a biased sample, because all of the triangles examined were collected from the Mediterranean region.

Inductive reasoning, too, is vital to reach certain kinds of knowledge. We 'know' that an apple will not remain suspended in mid-air, because we have seen so many objects fall. But such reasoning is not foolproof. As Bertrand Russell pointed out, 'The man who has fed the chicken every day throughout its life at last wrings its neck instead, showing that more refined views as to the uniformity of nature would have been useful to the chicken.'

Of course, many policymakers—not just the likes of Erdoğan and Trump—make bad decisions not because of a misunderstanding of the evidence, but because they prefer to pursue politically expedient measures that benefit their benefactors or themselves. In such cases, exposing the inappropriateness of their supposed evidence may be the only option.

But, for the rest, the imperative must be to advocate for a more comprehensive approach, in which leaders use 'reasoned intuition' to draw effective conclusions based on hard data. Only then will the age of effective evidence-based policymaking really begin.

The ABC of Doing Business

THE WORLD BANK'S ANNUAL *Doing Business* (DB) report is probably its most-cited publication. It is also the Bank's most contentious, and with the release of 'Doing Business 2018' last October, the controversy surrounding the report has reached new heights, with some critics accusing it of obfuscation, data rigging, and political manipulation.

I was closely involved with the DB report from 2012 to 2016, so I had to restrain myself from jumping into the debate on the topic. But now, a review of the DB index and annual report seems worthwhile.

I first became familiar with the DB report when I was an adviser to the Indian government and would look to it for ideas about how to cut India's notoriously cumbersome bureaucratic red tape. So, when I moved to the World Bank and learned that I would be overseeing the DB team, it was like a regular restaurant patron suddenly being asked to supervise the kitchen.

The upshot was that I learned all that went on behind the scenes. And although I had some conceptual disagreements, I was impressed by the integrity of the process.

The DB index aims to measure, across countries, the ease of starting a business, obtaining the relevant permits, accessing essential infrastructure, and so forth. It comprises 10 indicators, each of which is based on various sub-indicators, and all of which are aggregated, according to a fixed rule, into a final score that determines a country's ranking among 190 economies. According to the 2018 report, New Zealand and Singapore are the world's best and second-best places to do business, and Eritrea and Somalia are the worst, at 189 and 190, respectively.

Although there were aspects of the DB rankings that I did not like, I do not find the recent charges of data rigging to be credible. Having personally supervised much of the process, which involves a very large team compiling economic data from around the world, I can vouch for the multiple layers of checks and balances that are in place.

Nevertheless, there certainly are ways to influence the rankings without cooking up data. With any big operation—whether it is the DB or an effort to measure GDP (gross domestic product)—one occasionally discovers conceptual flaws. For example, when I first took over the process, I disagreed with the prevailing assumption that a higher tax rate is necessarily worse for an economy.

After all, the same logic dictates that the lower the tax rate, the better, which implies that a tax rate of zero is optimal. But that is obviously absurd. Even if one ignores the moral dimensions, a very low tax rate leaves a country more exposed to the threat of severe fiscal crises, which are a nightmare for business. Steps were taken to make some minimal corrections that would not be too disruptive.

Still, recognizing such problems poses a dilemma. It is never ideal to have to change a yardstick that has been used to track changes over time; but nor is it right to rely on an assumption that one knows to be flawed. At the end of the day, it is a judgement call.

For my part, I mitigated against possible biases by not even looking at the final result until I had first decided, using abstract reasoning, which changes were essential.

In this year's DB, the two big controversies concern India's rise and Chile's fall. Between 2016 and 2017, India moved from 130th to 100th place. I no longer have inside information on the data, but I can see two reasons why this could occur.

First, if a country is determined to move up the ranking, it can do so by focusing on the 10 indicators that determine the final score, though this is not a national economic strategy that I would recommend.

Second, any change in ranking can be driven either by what a country does relative to other countries, or by measurement changes that the DB may have instituted in a given year—changes like those mentioned above. For example, when India moved from 142nd to 130th place between 2014 and 2015, the DB team and I computed that only four of the 12 positions that India had climbed reflected changes India had made, with the remainder attributable to changes in the DB methodology.

As for Chile, which slipped from 48th to 57th place between 2015 and 2016, and is now ranked 55th, it is worth noting that there is a lot of cheek-by-jowl competition at the higher end of the ranking. Small changes by countries that neighbour one another in the index can result in a sharp reordering.

But it is also true that Chilean President Michelle Bachelet's government has placed greater emphasis on social indicators than on economic indicators. To my mind, that is a cause for praise, not criticism.

Having worked with Bachelet on the World Bank's 2018 *World Development Report* on education, I know that she is that rare politician who is genuinely committed to improving social welfare.

Many countries and political leaders make the mistake of equating the DB ranking with overall welfare. But the DB merely measures what it says it measures: the ease of doing business. That is certainly important for an economy, but it is not everything. In fact, one of the first lessons of economics is that all good things in life involve trade-offs. It would be a pity to see more countries focusing only on 'doing business' to the exclusion of other indicators of well-being.

eight

Medley*

Are We Becoming Over-Cautious?

EARLIER THIS SUMMER—BEFORE THE MUMBAI train blasts and before the heightened tension in Heathrow—I was taking a flight within India. Security was lax; a genial security officer did a cursory pat down and waved me on. I asked him if he did not need to do a more thorough check. His response: 'Aajkal to kuch nahi hota' (Nowadays nothing untoward happens).

This is no doubt a case of the oriental fatalism act overdone. But, at times, I wonder if the world is not going too far in the other direction. Given the rise of terrorism the world over, of course, airport frisking will be extra-diligent, and parking a car to drop off passengers at airports will cause security personnel to go edgy. These are quite understandable.

* The first section, 'Are We Becoming Over-Cautious?', was first published as 'Are There Too Many Warnings in Life', in *BBC News Online*, 27 September 2006. The second section, 'My Worst Lectures', was first published as 'Economist? Whatever...', in *Hindustan Times*, 26 April 2008. The third section, 'India at 60', was first published in *India Today*, 2 July 2007.

But there is an aspect of caution in life that deserves scrutiny. What concerns me is that, through a combination of forces, ranging from the fear of litigation to the rise of genuine risks in everyday life, we are erring on the side of caution. If you read the warning labels on products, you will know what I mean. My printer ink cartridge, for instance, has a warning that I should not drink it. I do not know whether I should thank the company that produced it for its touching concern for my health or send a letter to the product manager asking him what he thinks my IQ is.

The husk of psyllium, popularly known in India as isabgol, that grows in abundance in the Kutch region of Gujarat, has been known from ancient times for its medicinal value. Two spoonfuls stirred with water and taken at night act as a mild (and soothing, some diehards would insist) laxative. Recent research has also suggested that isabgol may lower cholesterol. In India, isabgol is widely used, adults and children gulping it down with water and without a thought. In the US, it can be bought over the counter under various brand names, such as Metamucil. But alas, when you are about to down one of these, your mind, far from being put to rest, has every reason to be on alert, for you are told: 'Taking this product without adequate fluid may cause it to swell and block your throat or esophagus and may cause choking.'

Travelling by British Airways from Kolkata, via London, to New York last month, I could understand the severe limits placed on what we could carry, and the meticulous checks that our baggage was subjected to at each airport. In fact, it was comforting to have that drill. But what about the routine, chilling instruction (crafted by the International Air Transport Authority and so covers all airlines) we get at the start of each airplane flight, such as how to get into the 'brace position' in the event of an emergency? I wonder if this is not overdone and also poor economics.

On the cost side is the fact that it ruins the journey for thousands of air-travellers who are already uncomfortable about flying, by reminding and in effect exaggerating to them the risks involved. If, every time you got into a car, you had to hear a recitation of the risks of driving and of how, in an accident, the airbags will open up and how you should respond to such an eventuality (for instance, not have your knitting needle pointing towards the airbags), we would have much less traffic and many more hypertension patients.

What about the benefits? It is true that in some events this instruction can save one. But to see how miniscule that probability is, note first that the chance of an emergency, where the need arises to get into the brace position, is tiny; and, second, if the need does arise, the most likely outcome is that one will meet one's end in a brace position, and there is nothing to commend that.

The probability that the brace position is needed and will save you is therefore microscopically small. So, if we do a serious cost-benefit analysis of these alarming announcements, my guess is that we will cease to bother passengers with them. And the hazard warning does not end there. If, after settling into your seat, you reach into your pocket for one of those refreshment strips, 'Cool Mint Listerine Pocket Paks', for instance, you will notice a word of caution in bold. WARNING: THE CARRYING CASE MAY CAUSE A CHOKING HAZARD. In case you were tempted to eat not just the candies but the carrying case, I suppose that is a useful warning.

Weighed down by these thoughts, last evening I tried to put all the dangers surrounding me out of my mind, and relax with a book and a glass of soda. And what better than ginger ale, caffeine-free, Canada Dry, to soothe the nerves? But no sooner had I sunk into the sofa and picked up the bottle, my eyes fell on a warning on the side of it: 'Contents under pressure. Cap may blow off causing eye or other serious injury. Point away from face or people.'

My Worst Lectures

THE WORST LECTURE I EVER GAVE was to a kindergarten class in Princeton. I had just arrived from India as a visiting scholar at the Institute for Advanced Study and the principal of my son's elementary school invited me to speak on India—its culture, its geography, and 'of course some economics', he added politely. Aware that kindergarteners suffer from acute attention deficit disorder, I decided to capture their interest at the start with an arresting account of how to save oneself in the event of a bear attack in an Indian forest. My teacher had told me when I myself was in KG that the trick was to lie on the ground motionless, holding one's breath, and pretending to be dead. Bears have little interest in corpses; so it would sniff and then walk away. The children listened riveted.

Seizing the opportunity, I moved to more serious topics, beginning with India's large population. But before I could say 'million', a little hand went up. Could I please tell him how he should save himself in an Indian forest if he were attacked by a tiger? Not wanting to scare a little mind with the truth—'there is no chance in hell'—I said that he should aim for the animal's eyes. Once he had gouged them out (the presumption being the tiger will sit quietly like a customer on a barber's stool), the tiger would not know where to bite and the boy could simply walk away. They all laughed at how easy it was.

I realized I was making it a bit too interesting because no sooner had I finished on the topic of the tiger than I was asked about the art of escaping from a snake attack. And then we were on to the rhino, the elephant, the lion, an elephant and a snake together, and other imaginative coalitions. The teachers and the principal watched me, in bewilderment, devoting a full 45 minutes to the art of fending off attacks in the Indian wild, no doubt wondering what kind of economics research I did and also why anyone ever died in an Indian forest.

My second-worst lecture was at a school for the poor, a few miles outside Kolkata. I had just finished my PhD from London and returned to India. My mother, with her unwavering urge to help less-fortunate children and equally absolute belief in my ability to deliver on that, persuaded the school's principal, whom she had met somewhere once, that he should invite me to speak so that I could inspire the children to go on to higher education and to contribute to the world. The principal was reluctant, but my mother was strong willed.

My mother came on that occasion and over tea in the principal's office, told him how brilliant and famous I was; he nodded in courteous agreement. We then went to the classroom, a cavernous hall with some 50, rowdy children in their early teens. The atmosphere was that of a correctional facility. The principal began by saying how they were lucky to have me speak to them, that I was dedicated to spreading education in India, that I was an economist committed to change. He went on and on, describing me more than once as 'this famous economist'. I did puzzle about the length and content of the introduction but did not realize that the poor man was prevaricating while waiting for that light-bulb moment. It never came. He eventually had no choice; he turned to me and asked, 'Excuse me, what is your name?'

The children were poor but not unintelligent. The class broke out in a roar; I was destroyed and gave an incoherent lecture.

My mother is now about to turn 90. So many years on, she continues to be an optimist—for India, for the world. She also remains steadfast in her belief that I am doing good work. Her only sign of age is the occasional tripping up on words, such as confusing between 'economist' and 'Communist'. On a recent visit to Kolkata, I told her that I would soon be on my way to Delhi for an international conference of economists, exaggerating its importance a little to make her feel happy. She listened with great interest and, as soon as I stepped out of the room, I heard her phone a favourite cousin of hers and tell her that I was headed to Delhi to participate in a conference, where 'leading communists from all over the world were gathering to discuss how to make the world a better place'.

India at 60

IT IS A REASONABLE FORECAST THAT 30 to 40 years from now, India will be a developed country. And when that happens, I believe it is the 1990s that will be viewed as the decade when the nation broke from its past.

The decade had not started out well. The shock waves of the first Gulf War caused remittances into and exports out of India to take a nosedive, and this triggered a spiralling economic crisis during 1991–2. That year the nation's per capita income recorded a negative growth rate.

The crisis turned out to be a blessing in not too much of a disguise. As a nation we had fallen into a groove—nurturing a mindless bureaucracy in the name of socialism, repeating the same tired policies, and refusing to admit the need for change. It was like Mr Needleman, who, in a Woody Allen short story, leaned out from his balcony seat during an opera and fell into the orchestra pit. And then, as Mr Allen puts it, 'Too proud to admit that it was a mistake, he attended the opera every night for a month and repeated it each time.'

It needed courage to break the logjam. Tribute has to go to the then finance minister, Manmohan Singh, for ushering in what was arguably the most dramatic policy shift in independent India's history. India's notorious licensing system was dismantled, the mindlessly high import tariffs lowered, and exchange controls eased. The gamble paid off. The economy turned round from the brink of major chaos and international debt default. And by 1994, the economy was booming. The next three years would be the best that independent India had seen till then, with gross domestic product (GDP) growing at above 7 per cent per annum. There was a small dip after that as the whole of East Asia plunged into a major economic depression. But the growth rate picked up again after two years, and currently the economy seems to be cruising at a remarkable 8 per cent per annum average rate.

India's balance of payments used to be forever crisis-ridden. From the late 1970s to the early 1990s, the nation's foreign exchange reserves were stuck at what, to use a tired expression, could be described as the 'Hindu foreign exchange balance'—around $5 billion. The reforms did the impossible. By 1994, the balance rose to $25 billion, by 2002 to $75 billion, and now it is close to $200 billion.

While the reforms were critical for the turnaround of the economy, we would be remiss not to recognize that there were

Kaushik Basu

other factors of importance. India's savings rate had risen sharply in the 1970s, following the bank nationalization of 1969, and this was critical for the success of the economy. As a nation we had for a long time over-invested in higher education, producing more engineers than the economy could absorb, more English-language skills than would be recommended on narrow utilitarian grounds. But once the technology revolution in America's Silicon Valley occurred, there was a surge in global demand for these resources and the over-investments paid off unexpectedly and handsomely.

This shows that the argument that the success of the reforms proves the Nehruvian policy to be wrong and India should have adopted the 1990s' reforms 40 years ago, need not be valid. While it is true that India had been excessively stubborn about policy and experimented too little, the success of the particular policy package adopted in the early 1990s depended on several complementary pre-conditions. There are many Latin American nations that had undertaken similar reforms in the 1960s and 1970s and plunged into crisis and political instability. For one, cutting deals with multinationals is a challenging task. The contracts can run into hundreds of pages and a nation that ventures to this before acquiring the necessary expertise can end up unwittingly losing more than it gains. History is replete with instances of such 'voluntary' impoverishment.

Finally, I consider the 1990s to be a decade of critical political and social change. In global politics, India has come to occupy a strategic space that it never had before. With the rise of China and the decline of Russia, it is now evident that the US and China confront a future where they will either have to live with a bilateral face off or have the comforting presence of a third pole, which India can provide. This is in the interest of both China and the US and an advantage handed to India on a platter. India has also come to occupy a critical space, beyond its own making, in America's anti-terrorism strategy.

Even more importantly, this was a decade of critical social change. It saw the rise of a new class of honourable people (albeit still very few) in business and politics. In the psyche of middle-class India, 'business' has long been a dirty word. The arrival of people like

Mr Narayana Murthy of Infosys sent a message to a whole generation of youngsters that to be an entrepreneur you do not have to be corrupt and a money-hawk. In politics, Manmohan Singh represented a rare combination of intelligence and personal integrity.

New research in economics shows that one important trait that helps a nation or a community prosper economically is trust. Cross-country studies suggest that nations where the citizens are known to be trustworthy tend to do better. The reason is not difficult to see. Not every deal and contract in life can be enforced by the courts and the police (certainly not our police). Hence, when we cut deals relating to trade or any transaction with people, we often have to rely on the expected innate integrity and trustworthiness of the people.

On the flip side, being trustworthy means having to give up some quick short-term gains, but one can expect to do better in the long run. Hence, trustworthiness and integrity are forms of 'social' investment. One foregoes immediate gains but benefits in the long run. With the rise in this kind of investment, one can not only hope for more economic development but also a decline in corruption.

India's financial investment is on the rise—we have data on that. My belief is that even our social investment (in being more dependable and trustworthy) is on the rise, though, admittedly, it is difficult to produce hard data on this. The trend was started in the 1990s. And if my conjecture is right, the benefits of this will accrue for many decades to come.

Mother at 90[1]

M Y MOTHER TURNED 90 ON 28 February 2009. I am now convinced that it is a myth that people lose their hair,

---

[1] This piece has not been published before. I rarely wrote a diary before December 2009, and cannot quite recall what made me write this one diary entry in early March 2009. My mother died on 7 October 2010.

sight, and digestive ability with age. My mother's head seems to have sprouted more hair than in her youth, she reads the morning newspaper without glasses, and eats more than any of us siblings can muster up digestive juices to handle.

It is true that she cannot come to America any more; the long flight, which till even five or six years ago she undertook gleefully, she can no longer handle. Ever the environmentalist, she would collect all the disposable cups and plates and spoons that came her way, occasionally even reaching out to wasteful but good-natured co-passengers in her quest, during the long journey and bring the booty cheerfully along to our home in upstate New York.

My mother now lives alone in Kolkata. She has good household help and a day-nurse to assist her with some of the chores that she finds difficult. My three sisters who live in Kolkata take turns to make sure one of them drops in each day. As for me, whenever I go to anywhere in Asia, I try to make a diversion to stop by and spend a few days with her in Kolkata, which elates her spirits more than anything else. Old age is not easy, especially when none of the children live under the same roof. To keep boredom at bay, we got her to play a couple of rounds of Chinese Checkers each day with her nurse. When I asked her how that was going, she said, 'Very well. The nurse is improving and even defeats me occasionally.'

My mother was always the epitome of unaffected self-confidence. I recall, several years ago, my wife, sisters, and I discussing guilt feelings with my mother. I told them how guilt feeing was an emotion I did not know, my sisters said they rarely had guilt feeling, and my wife said how she, on the contrary, was well acquainted with this emotion. My mother then caught us all by surprise, telling us how she was extremely prone to guilt feeling. She then added that she had however never felt guilty, because she had 'never done anything wrong'. That is my mother for you.

While the health and the mind are fine, what goes with age, I am now convinced, is political correctness. During this last year, some of my mother's utterances on age, sex, and religion would make Larry Summers appear a font of moderation and correctness. Details on this will, however, have to go unreported.

The other thing that goes is short-term memory. She now routinely confuses the word 'economist' with 'Communist', boosting my reputation among Bengal's left intelligentsia. She, like so many women of her age, is totally apolitical.

Some time ago, when I phoned my mother, she lamented that she was no longer what she used to be and did not enjoy going out anymore. But that week she felt she would go to see an uncle of mine, who was one of her favourite cousins. These were times of such uncertainty, she added to justify the excursion, that she worried she would not get to see her favourite people anymore. Since this cousin of hers had just turned 75, she said she could not help feeling apprehensive that she would suddenly one day hear that he was no more. My mother was about to turn 90.

part three

Contemporary Policy Excursions

nine

India and the World*

In India, Black Money Makes for Bad Policy

O N 8 NOVEMBER, THE INDIAN GOVERNMENT announced an immediate ban on two major bills that account for the vast majority of all currency in circulation. Indians would have until

---

* 'In India, Black Money Makes for Bad Policy' was first published in *New York Times*, 27 November 2016. 'India and the Visible Hand of the Market' was first published in *New York Times*, 29 June 2017. 'Resisting the Moral Retreat' was first published in *Indian Express*, 22 June 2017. 'Anger Is Not Enough' was first published as 'Economic Graffiti: Anger Isn't Enough' in *Indian Express*, 14 July 2017. 'Trump's Gift to China' was originally published in the Project Syndicate website on 9 March 2017. 'Facing the Slowdown' was first published in *Indian Express*, 25 January 2018. 'In the Name of Education' was first published as 'Economic Graffiti: In the Name of Education' in *Indian Express*, 23 February 2018. 'Reviving India's Economy' was originally published in the Project Syndicate website on 19 September 2017.

the end of the year to change those notes for other bills, including newly minted ones.

On Wednesday, the government released via a smartphone app called 'Narendra Modi', named after the prime minister, the results of a survey purporting to show 90 per cent support for its so-called demonetization policy.

The poll was rightly criticized. In the two weeks after the measure was announced, millions of Indians stricken with small panic rushed out to banks; ATMs and tellers soon ran dry. Some 98 per cent of all transactions in India, measured by volume, are conducted in cash.

Demonetization was ostensibly implemented to combat corruption, terrorism financing, and inflation. But it was poorly designed, with scant attention paid to the laws of the market, and it is likely to fail. So far its effects have been disastrous for the middle- and lower-middle classes, as well as the poor. And the worst may be yet to come.

India has a large amount of what is known as 'black money', meaning cash or any other form of wealth that has evaded taxation. According to a 2010 World Bank estimate, the most reliable available, the shadow economy in India makes up one-fifth of the country's GDP. (A 2013 study by McKinsey, the consulting firm, puts the figure at more than one-quarter.)

Black money tends to exacerbate inequality because the biggest evasions occur at the top of the income spectrum. It also deprives the government of money to spend on infrastructure and public services like health care and education. According to the World Bank's most recent estimate, from 2012, India's tax-to-GDP ratio is about 11 per cent, compared with about 14 per cent for Brazil, about 26 per cent for South Africa and about 35 per cent for Denmark.

The government's wish to tackle these problems is laudable, but demonetization is a ham-fisted move that will put only a temporary dent in corruption, if even that, and is likely to rock the entire economy.

Many Indians have been scrambling to change their old notes, causing snaking queues in front of banks and desperation among the poor, many of whom have no bank account and live from cash earnings.

Anyone seeking to convert more than 250,000 rupees (about $3,650) must explain why they hold so much cash, or, failing that, must pay a penalty. The requirement has already spawned a new black market to service people wishing to offload: large amounts of illicit cash is broken into smaller blocks and deposited by teams of illegal couriers.

Demonetization is mostly hurting people who are not its intended targets. Because sellers of certain durables, such as jewellery and property, often insist on cash payments, many individuals who have no illegal money build up cash reserves over time. Relatively poor women stash away cash beyond their husbands' reach, as savings for the children or the household.

Small hoarders often fear being questioned about the source of their money—they are accustomed to being harassed by tax collectors, among others—and may choose instead to forgo some of their savings.

People have also been skimping in response to the new policy, causing demand for certain basic goods to fall, which has hurt farmers and small producers and could eventually lead them to scale back on their activities.

And even more pain is around the corner. With so much money in circulation suddenly ceasing to be legal tender, India's economic growth is bound to nose-dive. Another risk is that the Indian rupee could depreciate as a result of people and investors moving to more robust currencies.

The government's demonetization dragnet will no doubt catch some illicit cash. Some people will turn in their black money and pay a penalty; others will destroy part of their illegal stashes in order not to draw attention to their businesses. But the overall benefits will be small and fleeting.

One reason is that the bulk of black money in India is not money at all: it is held in gold and silver, real estate, and overseas bank accounts. Another is that even if demonetization can flush out the black money that is held in cash, with no improvement in catching and punishing tax evaders, people with ill-gotten gains will simply start saving in the new bills currently being issued.

When the government announced demonetization, it also justified the measure as a way to curb terrorism financing that relies on counterfeit rupee notes, as well as to dampen inflation.

Both these justifications are flawed. Catching fake notes already in circulation neither helps trap the terrorists who minted them nor prevents more such money from being injected into the economy. It simply inconveniences the people who use it as legal tender, the vast majority of whom had no hand in its creation.

There also is no evidence that black money actually is more inflationary than white money; nor in theory should it be. Black money is just money held by people instead of the government. It is an excessive money supply that tends to create inflation; whether that money is white or black makes little difference.

Demonetization may have been well-intentioned, but it was a major mistake. The government should reverse it. It could at least declare that 500 rupee notes, which many poorer people frequently use, are legal again.

And if the government really does want to limit the amount of black money in circulation, it would do better to move India towards becoming a more cashless society. About 53 per cent of adult Indians have a bank account, but many signed up at the government's initiative and so quite a few of the accounts are dormant. On the other hand, more than one billion people in India have a cell phone, and this could be tapped to encourage more active banking, in the form of mobile banking.

India's push to issue a unique ID number to all Indians based on their biometric information is a major step in the right direction. More than one billion people have already been registered, according to the government, potentially enabling them to use an app to collect pensions, for example.

Tackling corruption also goes beyond currency, cash, or even banking. It requires changing institutions and mindsets, and carefully crafting policies that acknowledge the complexity of economic and social life. The government could start by increasing penalties for tax evasion and amending India's outdated anti-graft laws.

In a country like India, where the illegal economy is so intimately intertwined with the mainstream economy, one inept government intervention against shadow activities can do a lot of harm to the vast majority, who are just trying to make a legitimate living.

India and the Visible Hand of the Market

IN 1776, ADAM SMITH DESCRIBED THE POWER of the market's 'invisible hand'. Although some economists have since overstated this power, dismissing the role of government regulation, it is true that the market, when left to itself, often manages to meet a society's economic needs in ways that no one fully understands. It is a mistake for the state to disrupt it wantonly and for bureaucrats to try to do its job.

And that is just the mistake India made last fall.

On 8 November 2016, the Indian government suddenly declared that as of midnight that night all bills in denominations of 500 and 1,000 rupees would cease to be legal tender. 'Demonetization', as the policy is called, applied to 86 per cent of the value of all currency in circulation. It was a state intervention of historic proportion.

The goal, the government said, was to eliminate fake Indian currency notes, force people to bring out wealth they had hidden to avoid paying taxes on it—so-called black money—and help India switch from cash to digital money. To counter the criticism that erupted, the government later pointed to eight other countries that had adopted similar measures in recent times. Unfortunately, the list includes Iraq, North Korea, and Venezuela.

Nearly eight months later, a lot of data is now available to help us assess what demonetization has actually wrought. Here it is, in a word: demonetization failed to do what it was supposed to do, and although the immediate disruption it caused was less severe than feared at first, the policy's impact is turning out to be more protracted than initially expected.

Very little black money has been caught. The truly corrupt hold their black money not as money at all, but as real estate and bank balances abroad. The government had authorized people to trade in up to 4,000 rupees in the cancelled notes, so some parcelled their 500- and 1,000-rupee bills into small bundles and got multiple agents ('money mules') to change them, no questions asked. The government's freshly minted 2,000-rupee notes promptly became the new stash currency of choice.

In the first weeks, even months, following demonetization, there was visible chaos. Soviet-era-style queues snaked in front of banks and ATMs. The informal sector—mostly small traders, farmers, and small unregistered businesses, which often do not have bank accounts—reeled from cash shortages. But the immediate damage caused, though large, was not as large as some of us had feared. GDP growth in the last quarter of 2016 was 7 per cent and manufacturing activity continued to grow.

On the other hand, there may be greater long-term side effects than expected.

The problems appeared unexpectedly when agricultural products arrived on the market. In January, with cash shortages in full swing, demand plunged and food prices collapsed. By February, potato prices in Uttar Pradesh were just over half of what they had been during most of 2016 (at around 350 rupees per quintal, instead of over 600 rupees per quintal). Tomato prices were less than one-third. Onion prices in May were half of what they had been a year before. The cost of onions in India is notoriously volatile—and often influenced by politics and elections—but the likeliest culprit for this year's drop was demonetization.

The outcome was curious: widespread suffering in the midst of plenty. Incomes crashed and distress mounted among farmers, a group in India already affected by high suicide rates because of mass indebtedness.

And the downturn has hit more than the farming sector.

The Indian economy was on a good trajectory until last year, and the government deserves credit for that. It had taken major steps to cut the costs of doing business and unify taxes on goods and services. With, in addition, the drop in world oil prices (which meant huge savings for India, an oil importer) and the rise of labour costs in China (which made Indian manufacturing and exports more competitive), there was every reason to believe that the Indian economy would soon get back to where it was before the 2008 world financial crisis: growing at over 9 per cent per year.

Instead, India's growth in the first quarter of 2017 was 6.1 per cent, down from 7.9 per cent in the fiscal year 2015–16.

An economy is a complex machine, and there is no way to be absolutely certain that the cause of all this is demonetization. But there is a tell-tale sign: much of the slowdown originated in the financial sector. Rural loans increased by only 2.5 per cent between October 2016 and April 2017, compared with 12.9 per cent a year before. The rate of growth in overall bank credit declined.

The growth in industrial output in April was a paltry 3.1 per cent, down from 6.5 per cent the previous April. In the first quarter of 2017, the construction sector actually shrank, by 3.7 per cent, over the previous quarter.

All this augurs poorly for the months to come: as the agriculture sector slows down in response to low crop prices and the credit shortage begins to bite, overall growth will likely fall further. The state-engineered shock of demonetization will continue to course through the economy.

Demonetization did boost the use of digital money, which is more efficient than paper money. But the government did not need to put 86 per cent of the currency out of circulation to achieve that. Demonetization was too coarse an approach, and it accomplished too little while causing too much collateral damage.

India's economy has enormous strengths—such as high rates of savings and investment—and this crisis will pass. But just as sailors heading to sea disregard the winds and waves at their peril, economic policymakers cannot ignore the laws of economics, and intervene in the market with a blunt and heavy hand, without risking shipwreck.

Resisting the Moral Retreat

A SPECTRE IS HAUNTING INDIA—OF HEIGHTENED HATRED, communalism, and a retreat from knowledge, science, and creativity. Left unchecked, these forces can engulf our better sense and harm India, not just in terms of society and culture, but even economic development and growth.

India has long been a poor country, inching up from what the World Bank officially labelled as 'low-income' to the 'lower-middle income' category in 2007. Yet we had a disproportionate presence in the world's intellectual space, in the domain of culture, cinema, science, and religion.

As a researcher working in Delhi in the 1980s, I remember going to international conferences and being surprised by the large presence of Indians. For a low-income country, this was indeed most remarkable. It was a tribute to India's intellectual achievement and open-society character. As if this early intellectual investment was ultimately paying off, the Indian economy began to grow well from the mid-1990s, picking up steam in 2003 and again in 2005, after which it remained for several years on a high growth path, well over 9 per cent per annum, which took the country to the middle-income cluster.

Unfortunately, in recent times, its global stature in the world of knowledge, science, and culture seems to be eroding. A disproportionate amount of global news and writings on India is now related to cow slaughter, *gau rakshaks*, anti-Romeo squads, banning momos, and religious intolerance. There is a noticeable drop in India's visibility in important global debates, from diplomacy and international economic and monetary policy to other urgent concerns of our time.

After Independence, India veered an unusual course. Whereas other poor countries were often dictatorial, trying to whip their nation into rapid growth, with some succeeding but most crashing into ignominy, India made some unexpected choices. India had little success in terms of the economy, at least till the 1990s, but it stood out as a poor country which was, nevertheless, a vibrant democracy. Visitors would get taken aback by the culture of free speech and the impressive and argumentative media. Indian university campuses were like American ones, and maybe more, where people freely debated controversial issues, criticized government, questioned religion. With the exception of 1975–7, Indira Gandhi's Emergency years, India never deviated from this path.

Whether this was the right sequence of choices for a newly independent nation may be debated. But what is certain is that India made the harder investments—free speech, openness to cultures from around the world, democracy—early. Now that India is growing well, these are great assets that can make it a vibrant society and also help make the economic growth sustainable. To destroy this capital will be folly.

This is why people, and most importantly political leaders, who want India to do well and flourish ought to sit up and try to change course before the damage becomes endemic. This new communalism and xenophobic aggression stems, paradoxically, from a sense of inferiority about one's own community and nation. People suffering from this, sadly, begin to imitate the very nations and groups they castigate and criticise.

I remember years ago listening to a politician visiting my father ranting that too many Indian women wore western clothes, adding: 'Why should we imitate westerners? They do not imitate us.' I recall even as a child being embarrassed by how blatantly he was imitating the West.

The tragedy is that what the Hindu fundamentalists and bhakts are pushing India towards is a travesty of the original bhakti movement which began in Tamil Nadu in the sixth century, and stressed the personal nature of religion and emphasized the philosophy and syncretism of Hinduism.

In the mid-nineteenth century, Karl Marx marvelled at the remarkable resilience of Hinduism. Whereas in many developing countries, as colonialism spread, the early religions vanished, in India, Hinduism withstood repeated attacks and domination. It was non-aggressive but strong. Every time the foreign powers left, there was Hinduism, sometimes a little wilted but ready to sprout again.

Growing up in a traditional Hindu household, I learnt to appreciate this. I was taught by my parents that the caste system, whether or not it is part of Hinduism, is detestable and ought to be rejected. But beyond this, Hinduism appealed because, like the ideas that emerged from classical Greece, the Vedas were imbued with a sense of philosophical wonder and mysticism, treating nothing as too sacred to question. With no central authority, Hinduism is meant to be an open religion, tolerant of diversity. The fact that in my early teens I concluded that the world as we see around us is logically inconsistent with the existence of the kind of God that most religions teach us did not bother my older relatives, who were devout Hindus.

What we are doing now is attacking the religion from within. Marx may have been right about Hinduism's resilience to outside attacks but what we risk now is irreparable damage by the very people who claim to be its champions. Hyper-nationalism is a manifestation of an insecurity about one's place in the world, whereby you want to shape your country and religion in the image of the very countries and religions you claim to detest.

India deserves to flourish as an open multi-cultural society, in which people feel included, irrespective of their race, religion, and sexual orientation. If we want to take on important moral causes, we should strive to end caste discrimination, repeal Section 377 of the Indian Penal Code, which discriminates against gays and, for that reason is immoral, and continue to work to raise the status of women.

Among the newly independent nations of the last century, India stood out as a moral leader in terms of openness to race and religion, and Nehru carried this to the global stage. This was the vision that

Rabindranath Tagore wove into his writings. It will be sad to see India retreat from this into narrow backwaters.

If this does not persuade the trolls, there is one more reason. The standard response of the trolls on social media to anybody who questions their ideology is to tell them to go away to Pakistan. Looking at the list of Indian intellectuals, scientists, and thinkers who have come under this kind of attack, one thing is clear. If this advice is taken seriously, Pakistan will become the world's highest IQ nation.

Anger Is Not Enough

CORRUPTION IS AMONG THE MOST DEBILITATING economic illnesses that afflicts large parts of the world. It damages the quality of life for ordinary people, destroys the moral fabric of society, and slows growth. The reason we see less corruption in high-income countries than in low- and middle-income ones is not that those countries are innately more moral, but countries that manage to combat corruption are the ones more likely to progress.

Transparency International provides us with data on corruption across nations and over time. Of the 142 countries it ranks in terms of the perceived levels of corruption, Denmark and New Zealand tie for the first position, and Mauritania is at the other end, with the highest corruption. The two big emerging economies, China and India, had the same score in the most recent table and are ranked 79th. In both China and India, data shows that corruption has not only been high since 2000, but it has been increasing fairly steadily. This raises the question: why is corruption so persistent?

To control corruption, we need determination and passion, but we also need analysis and a modicum of understanding of economics, law, and psychology. My belief is that it is the deficiency of the latter that allows corruption to flourish and persist. The anger and agitation against corruption that we often see in the streets are genuine. But the reason this does not translate into less corruption is because anger is not enough.

Let me give two examples of insights that can come from analysis.

There are many examples from around the world of strong leaders, like Xi Jinping of China, who genuinely wanted to banish corruption when they first came to power, but did not do so. From the logic of political economy, it is not hard to see why this happens.

All political leaders rely on overt loyalty. Further, the so-called strong leaders tend to have an aversion to public criticism. It is not hard to see that, for such leaders, nothing is as advantageous as pervasive corruption. When that happens, it becomes easy for the leader to silence dissent and encourage public display of loyalty. This is because when there is pervasive corruption, the leader has the option of arresting almost anyone on corruption charges. This gives the leader the capacity to arrest those who publicly oppose him, not for the criticism, or at least not openly so, but on the grounds of corruption. If this is done systematically, then criticism can be stopped and public display of loyalty can be engineered, since people know that if they oppose the leader they will be arrested for corruption.

The ubiquity of corruption gives a political leader a leash to curb dissent without having to openly say he or she is curbing dissent.

For the second example on the power of analysis, I want to return to a suggestion I had made in 2011 and unwittingly stirred up controversy. Nothing came of my proposal but I do think it ought to be considered by any government serious about controlling corruption, especially bribery.

The idea in a nutshell is the following. Let us call a bribe a 'harassment bribe', when a person has to give it to a bureaucrat or police in order to get something that she has the right to receive. If after you pass the driving test, the official who takes your test asks for a bribe, then that is a harassment bribe.

To curb bribery, India's Prevention of Corruption Act, 1988, asks for severe punishment for anybody caught in a bribe exchange with the punishment for the bribe giver and the taker being the same. This well-meaning law is, however, founded on weak logic. What the law does is to unify the interest of the bribe giver and the taker, once the bribe has been paid. Both the giver and the taker have an interest in colluding to hide the fact of bribery.

My proposal to break this collusion, at least in the case of harassment bribery, was to amend the 1988 law and declare the act of giving such a bribe legal but the act of taking the bribe illegal and maybe to increase the punishment for the government servant who takes the bribe. With such an amendment, the bureaucrat trying to take a bribe will know that, after the bribery, the bribe giver will have much less hesitation is admitting to having given a bribe, and this fear will make it less likely that the bureaucrat would ask for the bribe in the first place. This is called backward induction in game theory.

I had proposed this based on pure reason and had little evidence to offer, one way or the other then. But evidence has come in in many forms since. First, laboratory experiments done by Klaus Abbink, Utteeyo Dasgupta, Lata Gangadharan, and Tarun Jain, published in the *Journal of Public Economics*, show that while my argument is not without caveats, asymmetric punishment does tend to curb bribery.

More recently, there are some fascinating findings from China. Three researchers, Maria Berlin, Bei Qin, and Gianca Spagnolo, discovered that in 1997, the Criminal Law of the People's Republic of China was changed in ways that altered the criminal responsibility for bribery between the bribe taker and the bribe giver. Interestingly, they also find that there is sharp decline in bribery after 1997 in China. The results are not without ambiguity but this break in the law creates the possibility of empirical work that we did not have earlier.

My aim here is not to make a case for a particular reform but to stress, first, that the main culpability for corruption lies with not ordinary citizens but government officials who are supposed to enforce the law; and, second, the importance of data and analysis in designing corruption control. If the anger citizens feel against corruption can be matched with expertise and design, we may be able to make a dent in the incidence of corruption, the major economic malaise of our times.

Trump's Gift to China

US PRESIDENT DONALD TRUMP'S PROTECTIONIST threats against China have spurred much concern. If he follows through on his promises and, say, officially labels China a currency manipulator or imposes higher import tariffs, the short-run consequences—including a trade war—could be serious. But, in the longer term, a turn towards protectionism by the US could well be a blessing in disguise for China.

There is no doubt that China is going through a difficult phase in its development. After three decades of double-digit GDP growth—an achievement with few historical parallels—the pace of China's economic expansion has slowed markedly. The combination of rising labour costs and weaker demand for Chinese exports has reduced China's annual GDP growth to 6.9 per cent in 2015 and 6.7 per cent last year. The Chinese government has now lowered its growth target for 2016–2020 to 6.5–7 per cent.

This is still a respectable pace, but it is not the best China could do. As Justin Yifu Lin and Wing Thye Woo have noted, in 1951, when Japan's per capita income relative to that of the US was the same as China's is today, Japan was experiencing sustained growth of 9.2 per cent.

One impediment to such growth for China is a heavy debt burden. A stress-test analysis by the McKinsey Global Institute found that if China continued to pursue its debt- and investment-led growth model, the ratio of nonperforming loans could rise from 1.7 per cent today (according to official figures) to 15 per cent in just two years. That said, the risk of non-performing loans is not news to the People's Bank of China, which will, the evidence suggests, take steps to mitigate it.

Unfortunately, debt is not China's only problem. Its dominance in global exports—the main engine of its growth in recent decades—has eroded. India's trade-to-GDP ratio overtook China's last year. And, while labour productivity is rising steadily in China, it remains less than 30 per cent of advanced-country levels.

Given these challenges, it may seem strange to assert that China may now be on the verge of ascending to a new level of global influence. But, because of Trump's policy approach, China has a new and important opportunity to do just that. While trade and capital flows require regulation, openness, on balance, does vastly more good than harm. Trump's 'neo-protectionist' policies—which aim to limit the flow of goods, services, and people to the US—are rooted in nothing other than myopic xenophobia. In the end, this will isolate the US far more than China or Mexico.

History bears this out. On the eve of World War I, Argentina was among the world's wealthiest countries, behind the US, but ahead of Germany. Since then, Argentina's economy has deteriorated substantially for two reasons: inadequate investment in education (a mistake that Trump may also make) and heightened protectionism.

The rise of nationalism in the 1920s culminated in 1930, when far-right nationalist forces overthrew Argentina's government. The new government—which was bitterly opposed to liberalism, not to mention foreigners—raised tariffs sharply in several sectors. On average, import tariffs rose from 16.7 per cent in 1930 to 28.7 per cent in 1933. Jobs in traditional sectors were saved, but productivity declined. Today, Argentina is not even among the top 50 economies worldwide.

So Trump's policy approach can be expected to do great damage to the US economy and have far-reaching implications, given America's prominent global role. But self-imposed economic isolation, combined with an inward-looking 'America first' foreign-policy approach, will also create space for other countries—including China, India, and Mexico—to increase their own international clout.

Consider Trump's withdrawal from the Trans-Pacific Partnership (TPP), the mega-regional trade deal involving 12 countries in the Asia-Pacific region, but not China. The TPP certainly had its flaws—not least that it would have conferred disproportionate and unfair benefits on large corporations. But it had plenty of redeeming qualities, and was being celebrated in countries like Malaysia and Vietnam for the access it would give to the US market.

Now that the rug beneath these countries' feet has been pulled out, China can lend a helping hand. Already, China has boosted its regional investments considerably, including through its 'One Belt, One Road' initiative. Without the TPP facilitating capital flows among its member countries, China is likely to overtake the US as the largest source of foreign direct investment for the ASEAN countries. China is also seeking to deepen its economic ties with TPP signatories Australia and New Zealand.

Likewise, China has seized the opportunity afforded by Trump's ill-conceived plan to build a wall on the US border with Mexico to reach out to America's southern neighbour. Just over a month after Trump's election, Chinese State Councillor Yang Jiechi met with Mexican Foreign Minister Claudia Ruiz Massieu, pledging to deepen diplomatic ties and increase flight connections and trade. China is already Brazil's top trading partner. It can now aim for the same position in Mexico, and perhaps all of Latin America.

As Trump adopts increasingly closed-minded and xenophobic rhetoric, Chinese President Xi Jinping is toning down his nationalist language and sounding increasingly like a global statesman. China, he seems to recognize, now faces the chance not just to achieve another round of economic expansion, but also to secure a far more prominent role in global decision-making and policy.

Facing the Slowdown

The Indian government recently lowered its economic growth forecast for 2017–18 to 6.5 per cent, and there is reason to be concerned. That the economy would suffer a slowdown after demonetization was inevitable, as all professional economists could see. But growth dropping to 5.7 per cent and 6.3 per cent in, respectively, the first two quarters of this financial year, when oil prices were roughly half of what they were in 2014, is a sharper decline than expected.

I believe that the long-run prospect for India is excellent and may be better than that of any other emerging economy. It is, therefore, incumbent upon us to try to dissect why the economy is doing poorly now, and to make policy corrections.

To begin with some history, India had many achievements to be proud of during the first four decades after its independence—a vibrant democracy, secularism and freedom of speech, comparable to many advanced economies—but economic growth was not one of them. India's growth picked up only after 1990 and in three broad steps. It began with the reforms initiated by Manmohan Singh, with Narasimha Rao as prime minister, in the early 1990s, which got India growing annually at nearly 7 per cent, which, at that time, was quite an achievement. The second uptick happened around 2003, and a part of the credit for this goes to Atal Bihari Vajpayee as PM. India's savings and investment rates picked up and the annual growth rate moved to the 8 per cent range. The final step was in 2005 when India began growing at an unbelievable rate of 9.5 per cent per annum, and kept this up for three consecutive years, all the way till the global financial crisis of 2008.

Some may be tempted to dismiss these as episodes. But if we compute the average growth of the last 30 years, it turns out to be 6.6 per cent. It follows that India is now performing below the average of not just the last five or 10 years, but the last 30 years. Given that during these three decades the trend of the growth rate has been steadily positive, this is indeed reason for concern.

One can see this slowdown in various dimensions, such as the international sector, where India is performing below capacity. With China ceding space because of rising labour costs and the abandonment of its low-exchange rate policy, India should have done much better in terms of exports.

An additional concern on the international front stems from the expected liquidity tightening by the US Fed. IMF research shows that this will cause a drop of $70 billion of portfolio capital flows to emerging economies over the next two years.

This will be a result of the Fed's balance sheet reduction and likely interest rate hike. Even if interest rates are not raised significantly by the Fed, which is a possibility given the low interest rate policy followed by Japan, the Eurozone, and other regions, there will be an expected decline in capital flows of $55 billion, as a consequence of purely the balance sheet action. This can cause turbulence in emerging economies, and India has to use professionally (not politically) drafted policies to minimize the negative shock.

However, the big worry for India lies elsewhere—it has to do with jobs and inequality. Because these numbers, unlike those pertaining to foreign exchange flows and stock market indices, do not fluctuate from day to day, they do not attract enough attention. But India's inequality—and especially wealth inequality—is rising, with the rich getting steadily richer and, at the other end, the slowdown in job creation is hurting not just the destitute but even the middle classes.

In fairness, job creation has been weak for a while, including during India's high-growth years, 2005–8. But this is beginning to hurt now. In 2004, agriculture and related activities provided jobs for 56.7 per cent of the working population. Ten years later, this number had dropped to 43.7 per cent. The shrinking of the agricultural sector as a provider of jobs is not unnatural. What hurts are lopsided controls imposed on this sector in the name of protecting consumers and aiding the suppliers of fertilizer and other agricultural inputs. Farmers are getting squeezed between these two interventions. And further, even though global prices are high, Indian farmers are not allowed to access this route.

Workers leaving agriculture normally get picked up by other sectors, and often the export industry. But that does not seem to be happening. India's exports grew by 12.3 per cent during April to November 2017. However, a dissection of this number helps us understand what is happening. If we break up the exports into the labour-intensive segment and the rest, we find that the bulk of export growth occurred in the latter. The growth in exports of labour-intensive goods, such as electronic products, textiles and agricultural items, was a paltry 4.4 per cent. It is this failure in job creation which is India's big policy challenge.

What should be done? There are some green shoots. Recent data on the Purchasing Managers' Index and industrial production show some improvement. The challenge is to capitalize on these. Among other things, we need to step up savings and investment. By 2008 and 2009, India's investment rates were hovering close to 40 per cent and India was beginning to look like a fast-growing East Asian economy. This indicator has now slid sharply. It is the responsibility of the government to rectify this, in the absence of which there will be no sustained success in job-creation. My belief is if our monetary and fiscal policies are too tight-fisted on liquidity, it will hurt growth. We can and must spend to invest and create jobs.

India's economy is not doing well. Carefully crafted policy reforms can turn it around. But for that we need to see the slowdown in the eye, and not get into a denial mode, which will be the surest way to turn the green shoots brown.

In the Name of Education

E conomists have written a lot about the importance of investment and capital for economic growth, and we have measures to track how many different kinds of capital are growing. We know, for instance, that the investment-to-GDP ratio in India has been falling over the last three or four years (which can cause a serious growth slowdown). However, the most important form of capital, namely, human—the education, vocational skills, and creativity a population possesses—is one of the hardest to measure.

For that reason, the Annual Status of Education Report (ASER), which began in 2005, has established itself as one of the most vital documents for analysing the long-run prospects of India's economy. As a data source on the state of children's education across the nation, it has no peers. It gives us a broad sense of what is happening to human capital in India. ASER 2017, which was released last month, is focused on the age group 14 to 18 years. This constitutes roughly

10 per cent of India's population. This is a group that will be in the driver's seat over the coming decades.

Reading ASER 2017 is a depressing experience. Of the 14- to 18-year-olds, 86 per cent are enrolled in a school or a college. However, 25 per cent of them cannot read a basic text meant for children, five to seven years old, in their mother tongue; 57 per cent of them are unable to do basic division—a three-digit number to be divided by a single digit number, such as 999 divided by 3. Of the 18-year-olds enrolled in colleges and schools, 60 per cent can read English, though one-fifth of those cannot tell you what they read. And 36 per cent of rural adolescents could not correctly name India's capital, with some of them thinking it is 'Pakistan'. Bhakts clearly have some work to do here.

These disturbing numbers hide large inter-state differences, which is both good news and bad. Consider the percentage of youth with the ability to read basic English. At the top end we have states like Kerala with an impressive 94.9 per cent and Himachal Pradesh with 82.4 per cent. But at the other end we have Uttar Pradesh, with less than 50 per cent, and Rajasthan, with less than 40 per cent. If someone dismisses this on the ground that English is an alien language, we can look at the ability to solve simple division problems (I hope no one will dismiss division as a foreign imposition). We see similar gaps. In Kerala and Himachal, 67.1 per cent and 58.4 per cent, respectively, can do division whereas the figures for Uttar Pradesh and Rajasthan are approximately 35 per cent. (I should clarify that these data are not based on full random sampling of the states and so should be interpreted with some caution.)

Turning to the causes behind these dismal numbers, the first thing we must try to avoid is to put it all at the doorstep of one party or one political leader. The numbers suggest a collective failure and an accumulation of faulty policies over a long time. However, matters are being made worse now. There is a surge of hyper-nationalism in India in recent years that, in the name of respecting our ancient wisdom, is making the mistake of putting it on a sacred pedestal. This can do great harm to modern education and scientific learning. There are groups perpetuating superstition and decrying modern knowledge, not recognizing that we must embrace the best ideas no matter when or where they originated.

What this is doing is enhancing the importance of form over content in our educational system. The gross enrollment ratio for those in the age group 18 to 24 (that is, the per cent of population of that age that is enrolled in educational institutes) has gone up from 11.6 per cent in 2005 to 24.5 per cent in 2015. Likewise, the number of students enrolled in standard eight has gone up from 11 million a decade ago to 22 million now. These are impressive increases but where they are not being matched by improvements is in the main purpose of going to school, which is to learn.

The rising enrolment shows that the desire to get a certificate or a degree is high in India. What is falling by the wayside is the content behind the degree. For long-run development what matters is what we actually learn and whether we have the scientific temper, the courage and intellect to challenge old ideas and texts. The importance of the ASER report lies in the fact that it draws attention to precisely these fundamentals.

POSTSCRIPT   Luckily, the worship of the degree has its comical side. While mulling over the above depressing numbers, my mind drifted back to my PhD days at the London School of Economics. I had become friendly with a new student (who will have to remain unnamed) who came for the one-year MSc degree from another country (that will also remain unnamed). A warm and friendly person, with poor educational background, he used to come to me for help with economics and calculus. But to no avail. At year's end he failed the exam. Determined and always full of good cheer, he decided to stay on another year, telling me: 'All I need are three letters—M, S, and C. That is enough to fool the masses.'

And he struggled on; another year passed. Then the day the MSc results came out, walking past his apartment in the evening, I saw a party in full flow, with champagne popping. My friend was in the centre, with the room full of his country folks. I decided to walk in and congratulated him. He thanked me and introduced me to the others as his 'teacher'. He said he was happy he could now go back home. Then putting his arm around me, he walked me out to the balcony and said, 'You have been so kind to me, spending so many hours teaching me, I must tell you what no one in that room knows. I have failed again.'

Reviving India's Economy

NOT LONG AGO, INDIA WAS A POSTER CHILD for political stability and economic growth among emerging economies. Though the country had a long way to go to eradicate poverty and extreme inequality, when it came to steady GDP growth, it was among the world's strongest and most consistent performers. Not anymore.

In the second quarter of 2017, India's growth rate fell to 5.7 per cent. It is now tied with Pakistan—behind China, Malaysia, and the Philippines—on the list of major economies for which *The Economist* provides basic economic data. Neighbouring Bangladesh, which is not on that list, is now growing at over 7 per cent per annum (and Bangladesh's per capita income now exceeds Pakistan's).

Given the Indian economy's massive size and extensive global linkages, its growth slowdown is a source of serious concern not just domestically, but around the world. But it is not too late for India to reverse the trend. The key will be carefully crafted policies that address both short- and long-term challenges.

In the short term, policymakers must address declining demand for Indian products, both among domestic consumers and in export markets. All signs point to falling consumer and business spending in India. In fact, India's index of industrial production grew by a meagre 1.2 per cent in July, compared to 4.5 per cent a year earlier. Output of consumer durables fell by 1.3 per cent; a year earlier, it grew by 0.2 per cent.

Meanwhile, annual export growth has fallen in recent years to just 3 per cent, compared to 17.8 per cent in 2003–8, India's rapid-growth phase. This is partly a result of a stronger rupee, which has raised the price of Indian goods in foreign markets. And, indeed, imports have risen sharply as well, as the rupee's appreciation lowers the relative price of foreign goods: in the first half of this year, nominal merchandise imports grew by 28 per cent.

But there is another potential driver of the sharp rise in imports: people may be over-invoicing, in order to shift money abroad. This could indicate that big traders expect a correction in the rupee's exchange rate, at which point they plan to sell the dollars that they are now accumulating for a larger sum of rupees.

This possibility should worry the Indian authorities—and spur them into action. To boost domestic demand in the short term, India needs Keynesian interventionist policies. To mitigate the rupee's appreciation, thereby boosting external demand, the Reserve Bank of India (RBI)—one of India's most respected institutions, populated by qualified professionals—must be given greater policy space and autonomy.

My advice would be for the RBI to lower interest rates further, thereby aligning India's monetary policy more closely with that of the world's other major economies. While the current tendency towards very low interest rates is not ideal from a global perspective, the fact is that as long as India remains an outlier, it will encourage the so-called carry trade, which artificially drives up the rupee's value.

The bigger challenge facing India will be to nurture and sustain rapid growth in the long run. To figure out how to achieve that, it is worth considering the efforts of another major emerging economy: China.

As part of its industrial policy, China's government has identified specific economic sectors to boost. India can adopt a similar approach, with health and education being two particularly promising sectors.

Despite its success, India's medical tourism industry still has plenty of untapped potential—not least because health-care costs are rising around the world. The income earned from such tourism could help the country to shore up its own health system, ensuring that all Indians—including the poor and especially children, among whom malnourishment remains rampant—have access to quality health care.

Likewise, India can become a hub for higher education. For the government, the imperative is to create more regulatory space and provide a facilitating ethos for the private sector. An education boom would bring huge returns for the entire Indian economy.

The final piece of India's long-term growth puzzle is investment more broadly. The experience of East Asian countries, not to mention economic theory, shows that capital investment is among the most effective drivers of sustained economic growth. Even in India, the sharp uptick in growth from 2003 occurred alongside a surge in overall investment.

Yet India's investment-to-GDP ratio is now slipping, from over 35 per cent in the last eight years to around 30 per cent today. This can be explained partly by an increase in risk aversion among banks, which are concerned about non-performing assets. Falling business confidence may also be a factor.

If India implements policies that boost short-term growth, while laying the groundwork for long-term performance, confidence should rise naturally. Once investment picks up, India will be able to recapture its past rapid growth—and sustain it in the coming years. That outcome would benefit not just India, but the entire global economy.

ten

Inequality and Labour Pains*

The Insecurity of Inequality

GLOBAL INEQUALITY TODAY IS AT A LEVEL last seen in the late nineteenth century—and it is continuing to rise. With it has come a surging sense of disenfranchisement that has fuelled alienation and anger, and even bred nationalism and xenophobia. As people struggle to hold on to their shrinking share of the pie, their anxiety has created a political opening for opportunistic populists, shaking the world order in the process.

* 'The Insecurity of Inequality' was originally published in the Project Syndicate website on 11 April 2017. 'Experts and Inequality' was originally published in the Project Syndicate website on 23 August 2017. 'Inequality in the Twenty-First Century' was originally published in the Project Syndicate website on 15 December 2017. 'The World Economy's Labour Pains' was originally published in the Project Syndicate website on 4 January 2016. 'Profit Sharing Now' was originally published in the Project Syndicate website on 28 September 2018. 'Can You Be Rich and Left-Wing?' was originally published as 'The Rich Can Fight Inequality, Too' in the Project Syndicate website on 22 March 2019.

The gap between rich and poor nowadays is mind-boggling. Oxfam has observed that the world's eight richest people now own as much wealth as the poorest 3.6 billion. As US Senator Bernie Sanders recently pointed out, the Walton family, which owns Walmart, now owns more wealth than the bottom 42 per cent of the US population.

I can offer my own jarring comparison. Using Credit Suisse's wealth database, I found that the total wealth of the world's three richest people exceeds that of all the people in three countries— Angola, Burkina Faso, and the Democratic Republic of Congo— which together have a population of 122 million.

To be sure, great progress on reducing extreme poverty—defined as consumption of less than $1.90 per day—has been achieved in recent decades. In 1981, 42 per cent of the world's population lived in extreme poverty. By 2013—the last year for which we have comprehensive data—that share had dropped to below 11 per cent. Piecemeal evidence suggests that extreme poverty now stands just above 9 per cent.

That is certainly something to celebrate. But our work is far from finished. And, contrary to popular belief, that work must not be confined to the developing world.

As Angus Deaton recently pointed out, extreme poverty remains a serious problem in rich countries, too. 'Several million Americans— black, white, and Hispanic—now live in households with *per capita* income of less than $2 per day', he points out. Given the much higher cost of living (including shelter), he notes, such an income can pose an even greater challenge in a country like the US than it does in, say, India.

This constraint is apparent in New York City, where the number of known homeless people has risen from 31,000 in 2002 to 63,000 today. (The true figure, including those who have never used shelters, is about 5 per cent higher.) This trend has coincided with a steep rise in the price of housing: over the last decade, rents have been rising more than three times as fast as wages.

Ironically, the wealthy pay less, per unit, for many goods and services. A stark example is flying. Thanks to frequent flier programs, wealthy travellers pay less for each mile they fly. While this makes sense for airlines, which want to foster loyalty among frequent fliers, it represents yet another way in which wealth is rewarded in the marketplace.

This phenomenon is also apparent in poor economies. A study of Indian villages showed that the poor face systematic price discrimination, exacerbating inequality. In fact, correcting for differences in prices paid by the rich and the poor improves the Gini coefficient (a common measure of inequality) by 12–23 per cent.

The better off also get a whole host of goods for free. To name one seemingly trivial example, I cannot remember when I last bought a pen. They often simply appear on my desk, unintentionally left behind by people who stopped by my office. They vanish just as often, as people inadvertently pick them up. The late Khushwant Singh, a renowned Indian journalist, once said that he attended conferences only to stock up on pens and paper.

A non-trivial example is taxation. Rather than paying the most in taxes, the wealthiest people are often able to take advantage of loopholes and deductions that are not available to those earning less. Without having to break any rules, the wealthy receive what amount to subsidies, which would have a far larger positive impact if they were allocated to the poorest people.

Beyond these concrete inequities, there are less obvious—but equally damaging—imbalances. In any situation where, legally, one's rights are not enforced or even specified, the outcome will probably depend on custom, which is heavily skewed in favour of the rich. Wealthy citizens can not only vote; they can influence elections through donations and other means. In this sense, excessive wealth inequality can undermine democracy.

Of course, in any well-run economy, a certain amount of inequality is inevitable and even needed, to create incentives and power the economy. But, nowadays, disparities of income and wealth have become so extreme and entrenched that they cross generations, with family wealth and inheritance having a far greater impact on one's economic prospects than talent and hard work.

And it works both ways: just as children from wealthy families are significantly more likely to be wealthy in adulthood, children of, say, former child labourers are more likely to work during their childhood.

None of this is any individual's fault. Many wealthy citizens have contributed to society and played by the rules. The problem is that the rules are often skewed in their favour. In other words, income inequality stems from systemic flaws.

In our globalized world, inequality cannot be left to markets and local communities to solve any more than climate change can. As the consequences of rising domestic inequality feed through to geopolitics, eroding stability, the need to devise new rules, re-distribution systems, and even global agreements is no longer a matter of morals; increasingly, it is a matter of survival.

Experts and Inequality

TOWARDS THE END OF 2008, THE WORLD glimpsed the first clear signals of an economic crisis that, a year later, would be in full swing, creating economic hardship of a kind not seen since the Great Depression of the 1930s. The deep recession that followed the nearcollapse of the global financial system in 2008 caught nearly everyone by surprise—including the experts who were presumably the best equipped to see it coming.

In November 2008, less than two months after the failure of the US investment bank Lehman Brothers, a visibly irate Queen Elizabeth II, visiting the London School of Economics, famously asked, 'Why did nobody notice it?'

Over the last decade, a range of answers has been offered, with experts being blamed for arrogance, complicity, or being just plain overrated. And the context was dire, with jobs lost and balance sheets shrinking. The queen's own personal wealth had fallen by £25 million ($32.1 million) since the start of the crisis (though the decline was from a very high base.)

Now, with the perspective offered by the post-crisis decade, we may be in a better position to answer Queen Elizabeth's question. But we must first consider more broadly the challenges confronting economists and financial experts in today's world—challenges that remain poorly understood, by contemporary economics' critics and defenders alike.

The first problem is that for certain types of economic phenomena—such as financial recessions, stock-market crashes, or exchange-rate fluctuations—it is logically impossible for anyone to be known to be forecasting accurately far in advance. This does not mean that no one has the ability to foresee a crash, but rather that no one can be known for having that ability. If someone does have such a reputation, their predictions can become self-fulfilling prophecies: if they predict, say, a stock-market crash, everybody will begin to sell their shares, bringing about the predicted outcome.

A second problem of expertise arises from the fact that it is not always in the interest of experts to reveal what they do and do not know. Most people would prefer to show off their expertise, perhaps exaggerating how wide a field it covers.

Of course, this does not negate the value of experts. For example, when I was an adviser to the Indian government, a decision was taken to sell some 3G spectrum. Some of us argued that the government should use professionally designed auctions—an area where economists have expertise akin to engineers—instead of selling the asset for a pre-determined price. India's political leaders listened, and the spectrum, which had been valued by bureaucrats at $7 billion, sold for an astonishing $15 billion.

But there are many fields where economists' knowledge is highly imprecise and comes with significant provisos, which may not be fully understood. This may be because decision-makers choose not to pay attention; but it may also be because economists themselves do not spell out the risks.

This risk is all the more acute in a world where scientific and technological progress is taking us into uncharted territory. The decisions that must be taken in response to these developments—

those related to the nature of the world or those we have created ourselves—require as much accurate information as possible.

Increasing complexity is reflected in contemporary law and policy. It is common nowadays for people to conclude contracts that are so long and convoluted that signatories do not know what they entail (this was a major factor contributing to the subprime mortgage crisis in the US, which fuelled the global economic crisis and subsequent Great Recession). Likewise, central banks nowadays intervene in ways that often are poorly understood by those most affected.

The upshot is that we are increasingly reliant on experts. And experts may decide to use their know-how not just to address the challenges ahead, but also to serve their own interests.

This is an age-old problem. In the seventeenth century, the economist and investor Sir William Petty was tasked with surveying large swaths of army land, much of which lay fallow, in Ireland. He did a good job, using some truly innovative methods. But he also ended up personally owning much of the land he had surveyed.

This 'Petty problem' is likely to become worse, as the world's complexity—and, thus, its reliance on expertise—increases. This will do nothing to endear experts to ordinary people. Already, many parts of the world, from the US to India, are experiencing a surge in right-wing populist sentiment that is rooted at least partly in mistrust of experts, who are perceived as selfserving.

It is not immediately clear how the Petty problem can be solved. But we must acknowledge its existence—and recognize that it is intimately connected to high and rising inequality in much of the world. Moreover, we must address inequality head on, by limiting the gap between the richest and poorest. If, for example, it becomes impossible for a CEO to earn more than a certain multiple of what the average worker in his or her firm is paid, there will be a limit to how much ingenuity the CEO directs towards pure self-enrichment.

Of course, imposing caps on executive compensation is a blunt instrument for fighting inequality. But more nuanced policymaking—often based on the misguided assumption that companies can be trusted, or induced, to self-regulate—has failed. The time has come for measures that everyone can understand.

Kaushik Basu

Inequality in the Twenty-First Century

A T THE END OF A LOW AND DISHONEST YEAR, reminiscent of the 'low, dishonest decade' about which W.H. Auden wrote in his poem 'September 1, 1939', the world's 'clever hopes' are giving way to recognition that many severe problems must be tackled. And, among the severest, with the gravest long-term and even existential implications, is economic inequality.

The alarming level of economic inequality globally has been well documented by prominent economists, including Thomas Piketty, François Bourguignon, Branko Milanović, Tony Atkinson, and Joseph E. Stiglitz, and well-known institutions, including OXFAM and the World Bank. And it is obvious even from a casual stroll through the streets of New York, New Delhi, Beijing, or Berlin.

Voices on the right often claim that this inequality is not only justifiable, but also appropriate: wealth is a just reward for hard work, while poverty is an earned punishment for laziness. This is a myth. The reality is that the poor, more often than not, must work extremely hard, often in difficult conditions, just to survive.

Moreover, if a wealthy person does have a particularly strong work ethic, it is likely attributable not just to their genetic predisposition, but also to their upbringing, including whatever privileges, values, and opportunities their background may have afforded them. So there is no real *moral* argument for outsize wealth amid widespread poverty.

This is not to say that there is no justification for any amount of inequality. After all, inequality can reflect differences in preferences: some people might consider the pursuit of material wealth more worthwhile than others. Moreover, differential rewards do indeed create incentives for people to learn, work, and innovate, activities that promote overall growth and advance poverty reduction.

But, at a certain point, inequality becomes so severe that it has the opposite effect. And we are far beyond that point.

Plenty of people—including many of the world's wealthy—recognize how unacceptable severe inequality is, both morally and economically. But if the rich speak out against it, they are often shut down and labelled hypocrites. Apparently, the desire to lessen inequality can be considered credible or genuine only by first sacrificing one's own wealth.

The truth, of course, is that the decision not to renounce, unilaterally, one's wealth does not discredit a preference for a more equitable society. To label a wealthy critic of extreme inequality as a hypocrite amounts to an *ad hominem* attack and a logical fallacy, intended to silence those whose voices could make a difference.

Fortunately, this tactic seems to be losing some of its potency. It is heartening to see wealthy individuals defying these attacks, not only by openly acknowledging the economic and social damage caused by extreme inequality, but also by criticizing a system that, despite enabling them to prosper, has left too many without opportunities.

In particular, some wealthy Americans are condemning the current tax legislation being pushed by Congressional Republicans and President Donald Trump's administration, which offers outsize cuts to the highest earners—people like them. As Jack Bogle, the founder of Vanguard Group and a certain beneficiary of the proposed cuts, put it, the plan—which is all but guaranteed to exacerbate inequality—is a 'moral abomination'.

Yet, recognizing the flaws in current structures is just the beginning. The greater challenge is to create a viable blueprint for an equitable society. (It is the absence of such a blueprint that has led so many well-meaning movements in history to end in failure.) In this case, the focus must be on expanding profit-sharing arrangements, without stifling or centralizing market incentives that are crucial to drive growth.

A first step would be to give all of a country's residents the right to a certain share of the economy's profits. This idea has been advanced in various forms by Marty Weitzman, Hillel Steiner, Richard Freeman, and, just last month, Matt Bruenig. But it is particularly vital today, as the share of wages in national income declines, and the share of profits and rents rises—a trend that technological progress is accelerating.

Kaushik Basu

There is another dimension to profit-sharing that has received little attention, related to monopolies and competition. With modern digital technology, the returns to scale are so large that it no longer makes sense to demand that, say, 1,000 firms produce versions of the same good, each meeting one-thousandth of total demand.

A more efficient approach would have 1,000 firms each creating one part of that good. So, when it comes to automobiles, for example, one firm would produce all of the gears, another producing all of the brake pads, and so on.

Traditional antitrust and pro-competition legislation—which began in 1890 with the Sherman Act in the US—prevents such an efficient system from taking hold. But a monopoly of production need not mean a monopoly of income, as long as the shares in each company are widely held. It is thus time for a radical change, one that replaces traditional anti-monopoly laws with legislation mandating a wider dispersal of shareholding within each company.

These ideas are largely untested, so, much work would need to be done before they could be made operational. But as the world lurches from one crisis to another, and inequality continues to deepen, we do not have the luxury of sticking to the status quo. Unless we confront the inequality challenge head on, social cohesion and democracy itself will come under growing threat.

The World Economy's Labour Pains

THE ONGOING GLOBAL ECONOMIC SLOWDOWN, which began in 2008 with the financial crisis in the US, could set a new endurance record. What is certain is that with growth stalling in Japan and slowing in China, and with Russia in deep crisis and the Eurozone still barely recovering, the world economy is not yet out of the woods.

This 'persistent recession', as well as some of the world's political conflicts, are manifestations of a deeper shift in the global economy—a shift driven by two kinds of innovations: labour-saving and labour-linking.

Although labour-saving innovation has been with us for a long time, the pace has picked up. Global sales of industrial robots, for example, reached 225,000 in 2014, up 27 per cent year on year. More transformative, however, is the rise of 'labour-linking' technology: digital innovations over the last three decades now enable people to work for employers and firms in different countries, without having to migrate.

These changes are captured by a remarkable statistical trend in high- and middle-income countries. Total labour income as a percentage of GDP is declining across the board and at rates rarely witnessed. From 1975 to 2015, labour income dropped from 61 per cent to 57 per cent of GDP in the US; from 66 per cent to 54 per cent in Australia; from 61 per cent to 55 per cent in Canada; from 77 per cent to 60 per cent in Japan; and from 43 per cent to 34 per cent in Turkey.

For emerging economies, the challenge of labour-saving innovation is mitigated in the medium term by labour-linking technologies. Emerging economies with cheap labour that can organize themselves well enough to provide basic infrastructure and security can benefit greatly from this global structural change.

We see this in the numbers. In 1990, just 5 per cent of the Fortune 500 corporations were from emerging economies; now 26 per cent are.

Chinese corporations feature prominently on the list. India's information technology sector has taken off since the 1990s, lifting the entire economy's growth rate. With business in 35 countries, Malaysia's Petronas, founded in 1974, is now described as one of the new 'seven sisters'—energy companies that dominate the global market.

To be sure, several emerging economies are beset by corruption and falling commodity prices; Brazil, where GDP is expected to contract by around 3 per cent in 2015, is a prime example. Nonetheless, the only countries' recording high rates of annual GDP growth are emerging economies, including Vietnam (6.5 per cent), India, China, Bangladesh, and Rwanda (around 7 per cent), and Ethiopia (over 9 per cent).

What we are likely to see in 2016 and beyond is disparate performance, with emerging economies that are able to adapt to the new world forging ahead. Even while this happens, high- and middle-income countries will come under strain, as their workers compete for jobs in the globalized labour market. Their income disparities will tend to rise, as will the frequency and intensity of political conflict. To respond to this by blocking outsourcing, as some politicians propose, would be a mistake, for such countries' higher production costs would cause them to be out-competed in global markets.

As the march of technology continues, these strains will eventually spread to the entire world, exacerbating global inequality—already intolerably high—as workers' earnings diminish. As this happens, the challenge will be to ensure that all income growth does not end up with those who own the machines and the shares.

It is a challenge comparable to what the UK faced during the Industrial Revolution in the early nineteenth century. Until then, child labour was rampant and viewed as normal; workers routinely laboured for 14 hours or more per day, with conservatives arguing that continuous toil helped build character (other people's, needless to say). The activism of progressive groups, the writings of intellectuals, and the enormous effort that went into crafting the Factory Acts curtailed these abhorrent practices, enabling the UK to avert disaster and become a powerhouse of growth and development.

How dramatically our thinking has changed can be seen from archival records. In 1741, promoting his new roller spinning machine, John Wyatt pointed out how his innovation would enable factory owners to replace 30 adults with 'ten infirm people or children'. The attorney general who granted the patent went further, noting that 'even Children of five or six Years of age' could operate this machine.

The time has come for another round of intellectual and policy reform. One great injustice of our world is that the bulk of human inequality occurs at birth, with children born into destitute households facing malnutrition and stunting from the start, while a small number come into the world as heirs to large stores of accumulated wealth and income. As labour income is squeezed, this disparity will widen, causing a variety of economic and political crises.

Heading them off will require, above all, greater effort to spread education, build skills, and provide universal health care. Innovative thinking will be needed to achieve these goals. But we also need to think of new ways to bolster labour income.

One example is certain forms of profit sharing. If workers have a stake in their companies, technological innovations will not be a source of anxiety, because wage losses will be compensated by the rise in equity income.

Several economists and legal scholars have written on this subject. But, as with all innovations, a lot of research is needed to get it right. What we learned in 2015 is that we do not have the luxury of doing nothing.

Profit Sharing Now

AT THE BRITISH LABOUR PARTY'S ANNUAL CONFERENCE in Liverpool this month, the shadow chancellor of the exchequer, John McDonnell, proposed a profit-sharing scheme that would grant workers equity in the firms where they are employed.

McDonnell raised this idea in what was decidedly a political speech, and policy experts and economists have reacted sceptically. While a poorly executed profit-sharing programme could do serious damage, that is no reason to reject the idea altogether. It is in fact a good sign that the idea is being publicly defended by a political leader.

Many mainstream economists, from Martin Weitzman and Richard B. Freeman to Joseph E. Stiglitz, Debraj Ray, Robert Hockett, and Kalle Moene, have proposed variants of the concept. And with many advanced economies at a critical juncture, with unconscionable levels of inequality threatening to shred the very fabric of democratic politics, 'equity for the poor' is an economic principle whose time has come.

As this month marks the tenth anniversary of the collapse of Lehman Brothers, it may help to go back a decade and pick up the story from there. The post-2008 Great Recession affected all sections of society, including the rich. In fact, it was a rare period when the number of millionaires in the world actually declined. But fret not for the wealthy. They have recovered well: whereas the world's richest 1 per cent of households owned 42.5 per cent of all wealth in 2008, they own 50.1 per cent today.

No matter how you slice the data on wealth and income, the super-rich are doing very well, and the gap between them and median-income earners—not to mention the poor—continues to widen. The near-unprecedented levels of inequality within countries today helps to explain the past decade of political upheaval and social strife, from the open-ended conflicts in the Middle East to the rise of populism and xenophobia in the West.

The rise in inequality today is largely due to technological change, such as rapid advances in robotics and digital technology, and it has been aggravated by heightened awareness on the part of the poor. For much of history, the powerful managed to persuade the slaves, outcasts, and downtrodden that their poverty was a 'natural' result of their own inferiority, laziness, and—testing the limits of human gullibility—sins committed in past lives. But with the diffusion of information technology, the poor no longer have the wool pulled over their eyes.

Economic change is thus necessitating new ideas—and not for the first time. The Industrial Revolution is often remembered for its 'Satanic mills', but it was also a time of radical new thinking in economics, spearheaded by Adam Smith, John Stuart Mill, David Ricardo, Antoine Cournot, and many others. Governments eventually pursued revolutionary reforms of labour laws and other social-welfare measures. Moreover, it was during this earlier period of change that the income tax was introduced. Until then, income taxes had been used only sporadically to raise funds for wars. But in Britain in 1842, the income tax became a systemic, permanent feature of the economy. Many at the time rejected the policy altogether, warning that it would destroy incentives and bring the economy to a halt. Fortunately, their hue and cry went unheeded.

Owing to today's technological advances, the share of total income accruing to labour (as opposed to capital) is declining worldwide. It is only reasonable, then, that workers should be granted the right to some share of the economy's profits. That is why McDonnell's proposal deserves consideration, provided that we remain alert to incentives and the laws of the market.

To that end, it would be better to pursue a fractional form of profit sharing, rather than large-scale nationalization. If all of a country's wealth were to be aggregated into one pot, the temptation for looting would be too great. In the case of the Soviet Union, a small group quickly captured the pot. The history of the Soviet Union has alerted us that the last stage of communism may well be crony capitalism.

A better alternative is to address the problem with a scalpel, rather than an axe, by having the state grant workers equity, from which they can earn a supplementary income. The standard objection—that people are robbed of their dignity when they are given money without having to work—is ahistorical. Under feudalism and slavery, suzerains and plantation owners grew enormously wealthy from the unremunerated work of serfs and slaves. No one ever pitied them for missing out on the 'dignity of labour'.

For whatever reason, it does however make a difference psychologically whether one earns by dole or ownership. That is why I personally have reservations about a universal basic income. Equity and a claim on some share of profits, however, would bypass the problem completely. Workers would have a genuine sense of ownership, which will become increasingly important in a world of diminishing work.

Much will depend on how such profit-sharing schemes are designed and implemented. But, whatever we think of proposals like McDonnell's, we no longer have the luxury of dismissing the idea as a non-starter.

Can You Be Rich and Left-Wing?

WHEN WEALTHY PEOPLE ESPOUSE LEFT-WING CAUSES, such as redistribution of wealth, those on the right often label them hypocrites. 'If you are so concerned about equality, why do you not give up some of your own income first?' is the usual retort.

This response can have a powerful dampening effect. Most people do not like to think of themselves as hypocrites. So the wealthy are faced with a choice: either give away some of their assets and then campaign against inequality or just keep quiet. Most prefer the second option.

This is unfortunate, because global inequality is reaching intolerable levels. What is more, wealth tends to remain in families over time. Inequality is becoming dynastic, with some people born rich and vast numbers who are poor from the moment they appear on Earth.

The injustice of this is so grotesque that just thinking and talking about it should prompt us to demand corrective action. But by stopping the most influential segment of society from expressing dissent, the right has stymied the first step in this process.

We now have plenty of statistical evidence of inequality. For example, Oxfam's latest annual report estimates that the 26 richest people on earth own the same wealth, or have the same net worth, as the 3.8 billion people who comprise the bottom half of the world's wealth distribution. Moreover, according to Oxfam, the combined wealth of the world's billionaires grew by $900 billion last year, or nearly $2.5 billion per day.

Inequality within countries is also spiking. The *World Inequality Report 2018* estimates that the sharpest increases in wealth concentration at the top are occurring in the US, China, Russia, and India.

True, a certain amount of inequality is both inevitable and essential to drive the economy. But inequality today far exceeds this 'Goldilocks' level. Regardless of the continuing debate about how exactly to measure wealth and income inequality, there can be little doubt that both are unconscionably high. Walking through big-city slums in developing countries, witnessing the squalor and misery of the poor and homeless in rich countries, and looking at the homes and lifestyles of the rich anywhere, the need to address the current situation becomes clear.

Moreover, the right to call attention to that need must not be restricted to the poor. The right-wing response that silences rich people with left-leaning views may look reasonable at first, but it is a non-sequitur. You can be well-off, rich, or super-rich, and unwilling to give up your wealth unilaterally, yet still think the system that has allowed you to earn and accumulate so much is unfair. There is no contradiction or hypocrisy in such a stance.

Some of the world's finest thinkers concur. The British philosopher Bertrand Russell famously argued (clearly with himself in mind) that smoking good cigars should not debar one from being a socialist. And American economist Paul Samuelson made a similar point in 'My Life Philosophy', an essay he published in 1983. Samuelson became quite wealthy thanks to the phenomenal success of his textbook *Economics*, which was required reading for undergraduate students all over the world for decades. But he was clear about where he stood politically. 'Mine is a simple ideology that favors the underdog and (other things equal) abhors inequality', he wrote.

At the same time, Samuelson admitted that when his 'income came to rise above the median, no guilt attached to that'. And he wrote with striking frankness that, although he rejected giving up his wealth unilaterally, 'I have generally voted against my own economic interests when questions of redistributive taxation have come up.'

Arguably the most famous historical example of a rich person striving for greater equality was Friedrich Engels, whose father owned large textile factories in the greater Manchester area of England and elsewhere. Young Friedrich became radicalized seeing child labour and the suffering of the working classes.

Later in life, Engels returned to work for his inherited business so that he could support the efforts of his friend, Karl Marx, to put an end to that kind of profit. No matter what one thinks of the desirability or viability of Marx's precise proposal, the yearning to rectify gross social inequalities is surely admirable.

There is hope today, too. Several of the super-rich, in the US and elsewhere, openly support the broad left and its objective of curbing extreme inequalities. They are willing to endure allegations of hypocrisy for this larger goal, which makes their cause morally powerful.

Progressive individuals who willingly give up their own income advantage are admirable. But, whether or not they take that step, they need not be silent on the need for collective action to tackle extreme inequality, one of the most pressing global issues of our time.

eleven

The Global Challenge*

America's Dangerous Neo-Protectionism

U S PRESIDENT DONALD TRUMP IS ABOUT TO MAKE a policy mistake. It will hurt—particularly in the short run—countries across sub-Saharan Africa, Latin America, and Asia, especially emerging economies like China and Sri Lanka (which run large trade surpluses vis-à-vis the US) and India and the Philippines (major outsourcing destinations). But none will suffer more than the US itself.

* 'America's Dangerous Neo-Protectionism' was originally published in the Project Syndicate website on 13 February 2017. 'A Currency Crash Course for Politicians' was originally published in the Project Syndicate website on 24 July 2018. 'Why Is Democracy Faltering?' was originally published in the Project Syndicate website on 25 October 2018. 'The Case for a Global Constitution' was originally published in the Project Syndicate website on 18 April 2019. 'The Language of Conflict' was originally published in the Project Syndicate website on 24 July 2019. 'A Thimbleful of Optimism' was originally published as 'A Thimbleful of Optimism—at the End of 2018' in the Project Syndicate website on 31 December 2018.

The policy in question is a strange neoliberal protectionism—call it 'neo-protectionism'. It is, on the one hand, an attempt to 'save' domestic jobs by slapping tariffs on foreign goods, influencing exchange rates, restricting inflows of foreign workers, and creating disincentives for outsourcing. On the other hand, it involves neoliberal financial deregulation. This is not the way to help the US working class today.

American workers are facing major challenges. Though the US currently boasts a low unemployment rate of 4.8 per cent, many people are working only part-time, and the labour-force participation rate (the share of the working-age population that is working or seeking work) has fallen from 67.3 per cent in 2000 to 62.7 per cent in January. Moreover, real wages have been largely stagnant for decades; the real median household income is the same today as it was in 1998. From 1973 to 2014, the income of the poorest 20 per cent of households actually decreased slightly, even as the income of the richest 5 per cent of households doubled.

One factor driving these trends has been the decline in manufacturing jobs. Greenville, South Carolina, is a case in point. Once known as the Textile Capital of the World, with 48,000 people employed in the industry in 1990, the city today has just 6,000 textile workers left.

But the economics driving these trends is far more complex than popular rhetoric suggests. The major challenge facing labour today lies only partly in open trade or immigration; the much bigger culprit is technological innovation and, in particular, robotics and artificial intelligence, which have boosted productivity substantially.

From 1948 to 1994, employment in the manufacturing sector fell by 50 per cent, but production rose by 190 per cent.

According to a study conducted at Ball State University, if productivity had remained constant from 2000 to 2010, the US would have needed 20.9 million manufacturing workers to produce what it was producing at the end of that decade. But technology-enabled productivity growth meant that the US actually needed just 12.1 million workers. In other words, 42 per cent of manufacturing jobs were lost during that period. While some forms of targeted protection may be able to play a role in supporting US workers, neo-protectionism is not the answer. And it would not just be ineffective; it would actually do substantial harm.

The simple fact is that, thanks to everything from efficient and safe shipping lanes to digital technology and the Internet, a large pool of cheap labour is available to global producers. American attempts to stop domestic firms from tapping that resource would not change that reality, or stop companies elsewhere from doing so. As a result, US producers would become less competitive vis-à-vis those from, say, Germany, France, Japan, and South Korea. Meanwhile, financial-sector deregulation would exacerbate economic inequality within the US.

An effective solution to the problems facing American workers must recognize where those problems' roots lie. Every time a new technology enables a company to use less labour, there is a shift from the total wage bill to profits. What workers need, however, is more wages. If they are not coming from employers, they should come from elsewhere.

Indeed, the time has come to consider some form of basic income and profit-sharing. Finland has experimented with this. In the emerging world, India, in its most recent economic survey, has outlined a full scheme.

In the same vein, the tax system should be made much more progressive; as it stands, there are far too many loopholes for the ultra-wealthy in the US. Investment in new forms of education that enable workers to take on more creative tasks, which cannot be completed by robots, will also be vital.

Some on the American left—for example, Senator Bernie Sanders—have called for such policies. They understand that the conflict is one of labour versus capital, whereas the neo-protectionists harp on competition between US and foreign labour. But it is the neo-protectionists who have gained the most power, and they are now threatening to pursue an agenda that will clip the wings of US producers, ultimately undermining America's position in the global economy.

When Greenville saw its manufacturing sector's competitive advantage begin to wane, it could have tried creating artificial incentives to protect companies. But, instead, it created incentives for other kinds of businesses to move in. This diversification bolstered the city's economy, even as it lost the majority of its textile-manufacturing jobs.

That is how the US should be thinking today. Had US presidents in the past used the neo-protectionist policies now being proposed to hold onto low-skill jobs when those jobs first began to move to developing countries, the US economy today might well have a larger, labour-intensive manufacturing sector. But it would also look a lot more like a developing economy.

A Currency Crash Course for Politicians

ONE MAJOR IMPETUS BEHIND US PRESIDENT Donald Trump's protectionist policies is his belief that China has artificially weakened its currency in order to dump goods in the US. Trump harped on this issue often during his presidential campaign. But now that he is taking action to reduce America's bilateral trade deficit with China, there could be grave consequences for the world economy. Trump is making a mistake. And yet his views about China's currency should not come as a surprise, given that exchange-rate management is one of the most complex areas of economic policymaking.

I learned this the hard way while serving as an adviser to the Indian government from 2009 to 2012. After Standard & Poor's downgraded the US's long-term sovereign credit from AAA to AA+ on 5 August 2011, I was surprised to see the dollar begin to strengthen. It took me a while to understand what was happening.

Investors were worried that the downgrade could cause global turbulence and began to pull their money out of emerging markets. In earlier times, investors would then have parked some of their money in strong European economies. But, because most of those countries had handed over monetary policy to the European Central Bank and could no longer print their own money, there was a heightened risk of default.

By contrast, the US had its own currency and central bank, allowing it to make good on its debt under almost any circumstances. And investors were also reassured by the fact that the world's second most powerful economy, China, had a vested interest in a relatively strong, stable dollar, owing to the fact that a large portion of its massive stock of foreign-exchange reserves was held in dollars. Hence, the paradox: though the source of the problem was the US, money went rushing to the US, strengthening the dollar.

I have had a keen interest in exchange-rate management ever since that episode. In May 2013, when I was chief economist at the World Bank, my colleague Aristomene Varoudakis and I published a study examining different exchange-rate policies across a wide range of countries. We found that almost all countries occasionally buy and sell on foreign-exchange markets in order to increase or lower the value of their own currency. In most cases, this is not done directly, but rather by commercial banks acting at central banks' behest.

China, for its part, has pursued an interesting exchange-rate policy over the decades. Through the 1980s and 1990s, there is no doubt that China kept its currency artificially undervalued so that it could sell more goods internationally. From the mid-1990s to 2005, the renminbi was virtually pegged to the US dollar in nominal terms, and the dollar did experience real appreciation. The logic was simple: by buying dollars, China could cause the relative value of the dollar to rise, which meant that the value of the renminbi would fall. Accordingly, the People's Bank of China accumulated enormous dollar reserves during this time.

As it happens, Switzerland pursued a similar—albeit shorter-lived—strategy after the 2008 global financial crisis, and particularly after September 2011. During that time, the Swiss National Bank managed to hold down the Swiss franc's value while accumulating a huge volume of foreign-exchange reserves.

Is this a good strategy? In China's case, it certainly allowed domestically based firms to export more, but only because they were selling at below-cost prices, thus incurring losses. This approach makes sense if one is selling habit-forming goods, because you can raise prices and make up for earlier losses once the customer has become dependent on the product. Hence, if you were starting a newspaper in the print era, it was generally wise to underprice it until you had built up a large base of loyal readers.

Like certain products, buying from a country can also be habit-forming. Once you have mastered all of the rules and regulations, as well as the culture and politics, of a trading partner, you have an interest in continuing to do business with that country.

With the US and many other nations now hooked on buying from China, Chinese policymakers no longer need to maintain an undervalued currency. And, indeed, China has been spending down its foreign-exchange reserves since mid-2014. Though the renminbi was once kept artificially weak, there are now many economists who believe that it is actually overvalued. That, after all, is what one would expect for the seller of an addictive good.

In this context, Trump's tariff war comes far too late, and will prove utterly self-defeating. But let us assume that Trump is right— that China is still selling its products to US consumers at a loss. In that case, my advice to him is simple. He should send a thank-you note to Chinese President Xi Jinping.

Why Is Democracy Faltering?

JAIR BOLSONARO, THE FRONTRUNNER FOR THE Brazilian presidency, is a far-right, gun-loving, media-baiting hyper-nationalist. The fact that he would be right at home among many of today's global leaders—including the leaders of some of the world's major democracies—should worry us all. This compels us to address the question: why is democracy faltering?

We are at a historical turning point. Rapid technological progress, particularly the rise of digital technology and artificial intelligence, is transforming how our economies and societies function. While such technologies have brought important gains, they have also raised serious challenges—and left many segments of the population feeling vulnerable, anxious, and angry.

One consequence of recent technological progress has been a decline in the relative share of wages in GDP. As a relatively small number of people have claimed a growing piece of the pie, in the form of rents and profits, surging inequality of wealth and income has fuelled widespread frustration with existing economic and political arrangements.

Gone are the days when one could count on a steady factory job to pay the bills indefinitely. With machines taking over high-wage manufacturing jobs, companies are increasingly seeking higher-skill workers in areas ranging from science to the arts. This shift in skill demand is fuelling frustration. Imagine being told, after a lifetime of body-building, that the rules have been changed and the gold medal will be awarded not for wrestling, but for chess. This will be infuriating and unfair. The trouble is that no one does this deliberately; such changes are the outcome of natural drift in technology. Nature is often unfair. The onus for correcting the unfairness lies on us.

These developments have contributed to growing disparities in education and opportunity. A wealthier background has long improved one's chances of receiving a superior education and, thus, higher-paying jobs. As the value of mechanical skills in the labour market declines and income inequality rises, this difference is likely to become increasingly pronounced. Unless we transform education systems to ensure more equitable access to quality schooling, inequality will become ever-more entrenched.

The growing sense of unfairness accompanying these developments has undermined 'democratic legitimacy', as Paul Tucker discusses in his book *Unelected Power*. In our deeply interconnected globalized economy, one country's policies—such as trade barriers, interest rates, or monetary expansion—can have far-reaching spill-over effects. Mexicans, for example, do not just have to worry about whom they elect president; they also need to concern themselves with who wins power in the US—an outcome over which they have no say. In this sense, globalization naturally leads to the erosion of democracy.

Kaushik Basu

Against this background, the ongoing transformation of politics should not be surprising. The frustration of large segments of the population has created fertile ground for tribalism, which politicians like Trump and Bolsonaro have eagerly exploited.

Mainstream economics is founded on the assumption that human beings are motivated by exogenously given preferences—what economists call 'utility functions'. Though the relative weights may differ, all individuals want more and better food, clothes, shelter, vacations, and other experiences.

What this interpretation fails to account for are 'created targets' that arise as we move through life. You are not born with an essential drive to kick the ball through a goal post. But once you take to soccer, you become obsessed with it. You do not do it to get more food or clothes or houses. It becomes a source of joy in itself. It is a created target.

Even becoming a sports fan is similar. Nobody is *essentially* a devotee of Real Madrid or the New England Patriots. But, through family, geography, or experience, one might become deeply connected to a particular sports team, to the point that it becomes a kind of tribal identity. A fan would support players not because of how they play, but because of the team they represent.

It is this dynamic that is fuelling tribalism in politics today. Many who support Trump or Bolsonaro do so not because of what Trump or Bolsonaro will deliver, but rather because of their tribal identity. They have created targets related to being part of 'Team Trump' or 'Team Bolsonaro'. This damages democracy by giving political leaders a license they did not have earlier. They can do what they want without being constrained by the will of the people.

It is not immediately clear how we can rectify these problems, protect the vulnerable, and restore democratic legitimacy. What is clear is that business as usual will not cut it.

The Industrial Revolution—another major turning point for humankind—brought massive changes in regulations and laws, from the various Factories Acts in the UK to the implementation of income tax in 1842. It also brought the birth of modern economics, with major breakthroughs by the likes of Adam Smith, Augustin Cournot, and John Stuart Mill.

But we are at a historical juncture where the subject of political economy deserves a rethink. The dinosaur did not have the capacity for self-analysis and headed towards extinction 65 million years ago. We, too, run the risk of civilizational collapse. But, luckily we are the first species with the capacity for self-analysis. Therein lies the hope that, despite all the turmoil and conflict we see around us, we will ultimately avert the 'dinosaur risk' and pull ourselves back from the brink.

The Case for a Global Constitution

IN MY BOOK *The Republic of Beliefs: A New Approach to Law and Economics*, I was eager to demonstrate how the methods that have emerged from the long and fruitful dialogue between these fields could, with a little help from game theory, be applied to multilateral disputes and multi-jurisdictional conflicts. So, I included a section on the challenge of creating a global constitution. This is an idea with quite a long history.

In the fourteenth century, for example, Italy's semi-autonomous city-states developed the 'statutist doctrine' for resolving the problems that arose with trade and commerce across multiple legal jurisdictions. As Stephen Breyer, an associate justice of the US Supreme Court, suggests, in the absence of institutional dispute-resolution mechanisms, a case brought against a Florentine native by a native of Rome could have pulled both states into war.

Or, consider the Dutch East India Company's seizure of a Portuguese merchant vessel, the *Santa Catarina*, in the Strait of Singapore in 1603. That episode gave rise to such fraught multi-jurisdictional questions that the Dutch jurist Huig de Groot (Grotius) had to be brought in to mediate, leading to one of the earliest attempts to codify international law.

Despite this long history, attempts at establishing international law have met with only limited success. Creating a system that is sensitive to the well-being of all individuals—what the University of Chicago's Eric Posner calls the 'welfarist approach'—quickly runs into the problem of nation-state sovereignty. As the sole enforcer of the law and guarantor of citizens' rights within its jurisdiction, the nation-state has the prerogative to ignore or overrule laws or rights recognized by third parties.

Still, we cannot simply wait around for academic debates on such matters to reach a conclusion. The world is mired in disputes that cut across jurisdictions, not least the UK's Brexit debacle. How will the flow of goods and people between the European Union and Britain, and between Northern Ireland and the Republic of Ireland, be managed? Neither British Prime Minister Theresa May nor anyone else has a decisive answer. The outcome of Brexit remains uncertain, even as the likelihood of May's own exit becomes a foregone conclusion.

Meanwhile, in another domain, there is a growing realization that current antitrust laws may be insufficient for managing the issues raised by the digital economy. Though the US is home to 12 of the world's 20 largest tech companies, it has failed to curb their worst practices. In the absence of an international framework, national and regional governments such as the EU have begun to pursue unilateral regulatory action, at the risk of stoking tensions with US President Donald Trump's dithering administration.

Likewise, from the Mediterranean Sea to the US–Mexico border, the flow of people with different customs and beliefs, from countries with different legal frameworks, is stretching existing immigration systems to the limit. Some of these differences can be comical. A pest-control technician treating my house in Delhi, India, once assured me that my home would be termite-free because he was using strong chemicals, and added, for further reassurance, 'ones that are totally banned in the US'. But there are also more serious conflicts of beliefs and customs, not least those involving clashes of religions. Unabated sectarian conflict in an age of sophisticated weapons and cyber warfare could be catastrophic.

While the details of international law will continue to be debated indefinitely, we can—and urgently must—adopt a global constitution in the here and now. At a minimum, such a compact would outline basic rules of behaviour that all can agree to follow, and authorize enforcement by a third party that is actually empowered to carry this out.

We often appeal to individual morality and basic human decency when trying to resolve political and cultural conflicts. The assumption is that if everyone would just respect everyone else's right to practice their own religion, many of our problems would disappear. In fact, such conflicts are often intractable, for there are some customs and practices that are fundamentally incompatible with one another.

Imagine two societies. In one, the dominant religion requires everyone to drive on the left; in the other, everyone must drive on the right. Were they forever to exist on separate islands, there would be peace. But with globalization and the movement of people between the two islands, the seeds of conflict will have been sown.

Societies can either perpetuate such conflict through war and domination, or they can agree to a common code. Some parties may need to be compensated for their sacrifices, or each party may need to offer concessions on some issues in exchange for favourable terms on others. That is the point of negotiation and compromise, for which there is no alternative other than enduring conflict.

Compromise is rarely easy, especially where interest and identity overlap. But given the extent to which globalization has already progressed, we cannot simply stay in our lane and hope for the best. The US, long a leader in establishing global norms, is retreating behind a psychological wall. We will need ordinary citizens, members of civil society, and, indeed, religious leaders to recognize the need for global collaboration and demand that policymakers take the initiative.

The Language of Conflict

I WAS HAVING LUNCH IN AN ITHACA RESTAURANT with my mother-in-law, who was visiting from India, when the Chinese waitress serving us asked her where she came from. 'Kolhapur,' my mother-in-law replied, referring to the small town in Maharashtra where she was born. Much to my surprise, the waitress looked overjoyed. 'I lived there for several years,' she said.

They hit it off. My mother-in-law said that the world's best ice cream comes from there, and the waitress agreed that she had never had better ice cream since she left. After a while, I realized what was happening: my mother-in-law was talking about Kolhapur, and the waitress about Kuala Lumpur. But all their facts matched perfectly, so I decided not to spoil their joy.

Language is a strange thing. It is an enabler of human progress and happiness (including through amusing misunderstandings like the one in Ithaca), but it can also be a source of conflict and an instrument of oppression.

The connection between language and conflict is not as far removed from the social sciences, including game theory, as many think. By exploring this important link more closely, economists and other researchers could perform a great service towards understanding the contemporary world.

We live in the best of times. We live in the worst of times. The world has never been as rich as it is today. Yet it is coming apart at the seams, amid increasing political polarization, great-power rivalry, and xenophobia.

Today's mix of rising prosperity and deepening divisions is reminiscent of the Industrial Revolution that began in the mid-eighteenth century and lasted nearly a hundred years. Unsurprisingly, that era coincided with major theoretical breakthroughs in political economy, from Adam Smith's *The Wealth of Nations* in 1776, to the contributions of Antoine Augustin Cournot and Léon Walras. Theirs were not everyday research findings. Like the later seminal work of John Hicks, Paul Samuelson, and Kenneth Arrow in the twentieth century, they produced deep insights that provided sudden, blinding clarity about how the economy works, and how politics interacts with markets and economic well-being.

Although we cannot predict the path of future political-economy research, past experience suggests it will be in multiple directions. Language is likely to be one of them. Some scholars have already provided critical insights into the political economy of language, such as Princeton University's Stephen Morris on political correctness. But there is much more to be done, particularly on the connection between language and conflict.

Signs of this link are evident in the US, where, earlier this month, President Donald Trump made statements which seem patently racist. He said that four Democratic non-white congresswomen should 'go back' to the countries they came from—even though three were born in the US and the fourth is a naturalized citizen who arrived as a child refugee. And yet Trump's appeals to white identity appear to have cost him few supporters. I do not believe all his supporters are racists. The generous interpretation is that they use language differently from Trump's critics.

Because what a speaker means and what a listener hears can be very different, language can be an instrument to foment trouble. Much of the problem stems from the fact that the real world is extremely varied and granular, whereas language is coarse by comparison. Some political leaders seek to exploit this to control and subjugate the population.

George Orwell's *1984* describes a team of bureaucrats working on the eleventh edition of the Newspeak Dictionary to 'cut language down to the bone'. As Orwell puts it, one of them 'bit hungrily into his bread,' and said, 'It's a beautiful thing, the destruction of words.'

If, for example, people regard the words 'socialism' and 'communism' as synonymous, rather than describing different systems of political economy, then it can become impossible to talk about the former without stoking fears of the latter. Similarly, a right-wing group in Israel can silence dissent by promoting the view that criticism of the group is equivalent to anti-Semitism (or self-hatred, in the case of Jewish critics). This would prompt many people who would hate to be anti-Semitic to desist from criticizing the group.

In India, some groups label anyone espousing ideas to the left of the extreme right as an 'urban Naxal', referring to a violent revolutionary group with which few want to be associated. In a similar vein, the Indian columnist Mrinal Pande has highlighted how the use of modern Hindi to promote a chauvinist culture and totalitarian ideas creates division and also damages the reputation of the language itself.

Digital technology and the continued growth of social media are increasing the scope for conflict and political mischief by bringing together large numbers of people from different cultural and political backgrounds. For many of them, the same word may have a different emotional or political valence, and the same sequence of words may be interpreted in different—even contradictory—ways.

As words acquire new meanings, many people stop using certain words in order not to be seen as sitting on the fence. As the fence shifts, this becomes a dynamic process producing increasingly polarized societies. Understanding these dynamics will require a combination of logic, equilibrium analysis, philosophy, and creativity.

The world is changing as rapidly as it did during the late-eighteenth and early-nineteenth centuries, if not more so. It is time for economists to venture out in novel directions as their illustrious predecessors did.

A Thimbleful of Optimism

At the end of this year of political trauma and conflict, I found myself feeling an unexpected sense of hope, sitting in Mumbai, where I could see the Arabian Sea stretching westward towards the Gulf of Aden and Africa, as well as the vast Indian subcontinent extending eastward to the Bay of Bengal and the lands beyond.

To be sure, one must not gloss over the ongoing catastrophes of 2018. In Yemen, millions of civilians, including children, are suffering starvation and indiscriminate violence. On the southern border of the US, refugees fleeing misery and conflict do not know if they will be met with sanctuary or bolted gates and tear gas.

Around the world, hyper-nationalist politicians and egomaniacs are launching trade wars, stoking hatred, and veering towards fascism.

If I feel optimistic, it must be because, over the last month, I have been on the road, and somewhat sheltered from the news, from the US to Mexico, China, and, now, India. Through it all, I have chatted with roadside vendors, students, and strangers in cafes, and when one does this it is impossible not to be struck by how similar people are across the planet. We may not look, dress, or speak the same, but our shared humanity becomes evident through conversation and interaction. At a time when hatred of the 'other' is on the rise, this is comforting.

Travel also reminds us of our shared history. Walking in Mexico City's Roma Norte area, amid the old colonial homes with wrought-iron balconies and murals of Alfred Hitchcock, Sigmund Freud, and others, I came across a sign reading 'M.N. Roy'. It was a nightclub named after the Indian revolutionary M.N. Roy, who lived in Mexico with his American wife, the social activist and Stanford University student Evelyn Trent, in the early twentieth century.

Mexico was then a hub of intellectuals, artists, and radicals with bohemian visions of a new world. Though Roy was born in Arbelia, a tiny hamlet outside of Kolkata, he was a restless soul with phenomenal intellectual powers, who lived all over the world, writing, and speaking. He was one of the founders of the Communist Party of Mexico. Later in life he changed his mind, becoming a radical humanist. I was keen to find out more about the nightclub, but it keeps rather revolutionary hours, opening at 23:15 and closing at four in the morning.

From Mexico, I travelled to the other side of the world, where I addressed a congress in Xiamen, in China's Fujian Province. I was anxious, having recently heard the story about an American economist in China who doubted that a joke he was about to relate in a public lecture would survive translation. He was delighted when the audience roared with laughter. At dinner he learned that the joke had been translated as: 'The American economist is telling a joke. Please laugh.'

Fortunately for me, no translation was needed, because all lectures at Xiamen University are now delivered in English. I was being hosted by the new, pragmatic China, where English is adopted not for its own sake, but to position China as a global power. While the US under President Donald Trump retreats behind an unbuilt wall, China's pragmatism is propelling it forward.

From my hotel window in Xiamen, I could see the 'piano island', Gulangyu, a beautiful, pedestrian-only space that serves as a cultural melting pot. The name comes from the fact that many Europeans once settled there in large homes with pianos. And, interestingly, law and order was maintained by Sikh policemen from British India.

After Xiamen, I travelled to neighbouring Quanzhou, an even older melting pot. It was not only, for a while, the home of Lao Tzu, the founder of Taoism, but also the landing port for Marco Polo.

While on the road, I did encounter some news, and not all of it was bad. In Mexico, I liked the new president, Andrés Manuel López Obrador, and his vision of a more equitable society. There are risks that he will make policy mistakes. But in a world increasingly ruled by mendacity, a leader with good intentions is a welcome addition.

I also found some hope in the growing likelihood that Trump will be ousted from power, and in recent victories over the nationalism and populism of recent years. In India's regional elections in November and December, ordinary people—including Hindus— soundly rejected the chauvinist Hindutva ideology peddled by nationalist politicians such as Yogi Adityanath. Even one of the most prominent Hindu monastic orders rejected fundamentalism. On Christmas Eve, Swami Suparnananda, a leading figure in the Ramakrishna Mission, stood together with the Catholic Archbishop of Calcutta and reminded people the 'great message of Swami Vivekananda that a good Hindu is a good Christian, a good Christian is a good Hindu, a good Musalman is a good Christian'.

Finally, I found hope in reading *Sapiens: A Brief History of Humankind*, the historian Yuval Noah Harari's 443-page pass at the last 2.5 million years on Earth. I began reading it with scepticism, but soon was hooked. Written with a philosopher's flair and interspersed with humour, it brought to mind my teenage encounter with Bertrand Russell's sweeping *A History of Western Philosophy*. By reminding us that humans occupy a vanishingly small niche in the universe, it achieves what few books do: it puts us in our place.

part four

Literary Translations

t w e l v e

By Debt if Need Be⋆

THIS IS A MASTERPIECE FROM THE OEUVRE OF humorous short stories by Shibram Chakraborty (1903–80). Written in the middle of the twentieth century, it captures, as always with his stories, some essential features of Bengali *bhadralok* society. But in this case, it also has a bit of non-dismal economics. I have often used summary versions of this tale in development economics and game-theory classes at the Delhi School of Economics and at Cornell University to illustrate some intricacies of moneylending and the debt trap. I looked around for long for an English translation and, not finding one, decided that interested readers will have to make do with mine till someone more skilled in literature comes along.

I am not indebted to anybody. Whoever else may say so, I would not. In fact, I believe no one, apart from a *kabuliwallah*, can make

⋆ This is the author's translation of the original short story 'Rnam Krttva' by Shibram Chakraborty in Bengali. The translation was first published in *The Little Magazine*, vol. 6, 2008.

such an assertion.[1] The path to heaven is punctuated by strife. And unless one dies prematurely young, one has to take a loan some day or the other.

In my case it was in fact more than a loan that was weighing on my mind. I had not paid my house rent. It was not too much, just Rs 500, but, nevertheless, my shark-like landlord showed up at my doorstep: 'I have given you a lot of time and am not willing to entertain any more excuses...'

'Just think for yourself,' I pleaded. 'For a mere Rs 500 you are making such a fuss. But years later, when I am no more, people will point to your house and say, "such and such famous author used to live here". Won't that be gratifying?'

'Used to live here?' He cut me off abruptly. 'Look, I have no interest in such imagined glory. Let me say this clearly. If by midnight today I don't have the money, then it won't be many years later. From tomorrow itself people will say that.'

With those words, the landlord left. But where would I find this much money at such short notice? Most people stay away from writers precisely because of the risk that they will sooner or later be touched for a loan. And among writers, I was known to be a particularly acute case.

Should I go to Harshavardhan? I pondered. To him and his ilk, Rs 500 is trivial.

When I finally mustered up courage and raised the matter with him, he said, 'Certainly. If I don't give to you, to whom should I give?'

I have to say I got a start; I could not quite fathom his tone.

'You are not too close a friend of ours, right?' he half questioned, half asserted.

'If we are to talk of friendship....,' I tried to butt in somewhat meaninglessly.

[1] A *kabuliwallah* is, literally, a person from Kabul. During the late British period in India, kabuliwallahs, in their long robes and characteristic turbans, were a regular presence in Indian cities, especially Calcutta (now Kolkata). They were essentially moneylenders and, in those days of limited formal banking, were very much part of the Calcutta economy.

'Yes, I am talking of friendship. You are not our friend. And the popular saying is: one must not lend to a friend. That way you risk losing the friend and the money.' He paused, 'But, yes, if it is a friend you want to get rid of, then in fact it is a good idea to give him a small loan. You can be sure you will never see him again.'

If only I was this latter kind of a friend to him, I mused with a sigh.

'But you are not a friend; you are a writer. No one wants a writer for a friend.'

'And a writer, in turn, has no friend,' I added pointlessly.

'Anyway, since you are not a relative and not a friend, there is no problem; I am happy to give you money. How much do you want?'

'Not much, only 500 rupees. And I am not asking for charity. Today is Wednesday; I'll return you the money on Saturday morning.'

I made the promise. And what option did I have? With the imminent threat of homelessness, I had to make it. But by Saturday morning, I was, of course, in trouble again.

Burdened by debt, engrossed in thought, I was walking down the main street when I unexpectedly bumped into Gobardhan.

'Brother Gobardhan, will you do me a favour? If you agree, I'll tell you what.'

'What favour?'

'If you promise me you will not tell your brother, I will tell you.'

'Why on earth should I tell my brother? What makes you think I tell him everything?'

'Well in that case...the favour is...Can you loan me 500 rupees... Just for a few days. Today is Saturday, right? By Wednesday evening I will return it to you.'

'Just this?' With that brief remark, Gobar reached into his pocket and handed me five crisp 100-rupee notes.

Money in hand, I headed straight to Harshavardhan.

'See I kept my word. I may be a poor writer who plays around with words, but when it comes to keeping my word, there can be no failing.'

Harshavardhan quietly put away the money.

'I am sure you thought you had lost your money, that you would not see me again in this life,' I said.

'No, no, not at all. I didn't think so. In fact I had forgotten about the money. Believe me, I didn't think twice after I gave you the money. But now that you have returned the money, I am thinking.'

'You are thinking that, by having returned these 500 rupees I have established my respectability and will soon come back for a thousand. Isn't that so? And then, returning that thousand, I'll be back for two thousand. And in this manner I will raise my debt to ten thousand rupees; and then I will do the vanishing trick. Right? It is this thought that is weighing on your mind?'

I planted this thought in his head; and realized I also planted it in mine.

'No, no,' he insisted, 'I have no such thoughts. I am thinking, you returned my money so promptly, how did you manage to solve your financial problem so easily. ... Anyway if you have any need in the future, please don't hesitate to ask me.'

'You don't have to worry about any hesitation on that score.' Needless to say, those were words uttered in my head. Writers are not known for their hesitation.

On Wednesday, the need arose again. I had to, of course, take the money from Harshavardhan, and I paid back Gobardhan.

'How are you brother, Gobar?' I said gleefully. 'See how well I keep my word. Here, take the money. Thank you very much.'

Saturday, I had to go back to Gobar.

'Brother Gobar, I told you last week I would return your money on Wednesday. I did return it, didn't I? Was there even a day's delay?'

'Why are you saying this?' Gobardhan asked, bewildered.

'Well, I need the money once more. Five hundred rupees once again. I'll return it to you on Wednesday...without fail.'

In this manner my life trundled on. Harshavardhan to Gobardhan, Gobardhan to Harshavardhan—Saturday and Wednesday...from one to the other, ceaselessly, I continued weaving an elaborate dhariwal blanket, when one day, in the middle of the high street, crisis occurred. I bumped into both of them at once.

The two brothers were coming down that road. They stopped on seeing me. There was a questioning look in their eyes.

Maybe they were simply curious about where I was off to, how I was doing—some such mundane matter. But I had a sinner's mind, so all I could see in their eyes was an urgency to clear up all pending matters.

'Harshavardhan sir, brother Gobardhan,' I swallowed. 'I have been meaning to…to say something to the two of you. Brother Gobardhan, you…every Saturday will give Harshavardhan sir 500 rupees. And Harshavardhan sir every Wednesday you will give brother Gobardhan 500 rupees. Harshavardhan, you every Wednesday and, Gobardhan, you every Saturday. You will remember, won't you?'

'What nonsense are you talking?' Harshavardhan looked completely confused. 'I don't follow a thing.'

'Well it is simple. For a while I have been thinking that I want to get over with this matter. Hence, this request. I see no reason why I should continue to stand between the two of you.'

thirteen

The Birth of a New God*

'DEBOTAR JANMYA' IS ONE OF THE best short stories I have read in any language. I am not in a position to judge the writings of Shibram Chakraborty as literature, but he was certainly one of the cleverest writers of the twentieth century. As the narrative in the last chapter illustrates, weaving philosophy into humour, he wrote prose with the sharpness of a trained logician. This short story, which I have translated into English, is a comedy, true; but it is also a criticism of religious obscurantism and bigotry. Then again, it is not just that. It also tells us about human frailty, and raises some deep and troubling questions about the basis of our beliefs and the meaning of faith. And what is wonderful is that it all comes wrapped, first and foremost, in humour.

*This is the author's translation of the original short story 'Debotar Janmya' by Shibram Chakraborty in Bengali. The translation was first published in *The Little Magazine*, vol. 7, 2009.

Stepping out of my house, each day I would stumble on that stone. The other day, I was in no hurry as I opened my front door to go out for a stroll. Yet, thanks to tripping on that stone, I ended up sprinting out of the house and right into the path of an oncoming car. Thank goodness for the driver's alertness. He did a timely swerve and I was saved.

Ever since that day I was determined to do something about it. I had never imagined that a simple stone could acquire the status of a major adversary in the path of my life. Moreover, it was beginning to be a matter of life and death because there was no reason to believe that onrushing vehicles would continue to take a kindly view of my need to exist.

That is why I decided it was time for direct confrontation: it had to be the stone or me. If the stone remained, I would surely not survive for long. And since my survival—at least from my point of view—is the more desirable outcome, one morning I got hold of a crowbar and got to work.

It was a biggish stone with just a sliver jutting out of the ground. It took the better part of the morning and quite a sweat to heave it out. When I did succeed and eventually looked up, I realized there was a small, silent gathering of bystanders who had been watching me intently.

I looked at them, puzzled, and asked, 'Do any of you want this stone?'

There was a slight murmur but no clear answer. So I repeated, 'If you need, you can take it, really. In fact, that would make my hard work worthwhile.'

After a brief pause, one man stepped out and asked a bit awkwardly, 'Why did you dig it out? Was there...was there a dream?'

I looked directly at him and said, 'No. No such thing happened.'

I continued to work, banishing the stone to a far corner, away from my daily path. The man continued to look at me unconvinced. 'You are not telling the truth, are you? Was there really no divine dream asking you to do this?'

'Not at all,' I said irritably and walked back into my house. I asked my mother to make two cups of tea. I needed both after the battle with the stone and my superstitious audience.

After that day, every now and then, when going out of the house or coming in, I would notice the stone, but gradually I began paying no heed to it, now that it had lost its ability to trip me.

But one day, a virtual transformation of the stone caught my attention. It had been washed clean, with all the mud stains gone. I figured it must be one of those Calcutta Corporation sweepers who hose the roads and pavements, who must have noticed the soiled stone and decided to give it a good dousing.

'Do you see what is happening?' I was so absorbed in my thought that the question gave me a start. It was the same man from that day, looking admiringly at the stone.

'Have you been standing guard here since that day?' I asked sarcastically. 'Or did you get a divine dream that brings you here?'

'No, no,' he stuttered, 'I go this way every day.'

He looked uncomfortable for a while, but soon became his usual self. 'The stone seems fine. No one will take it? What do you say?'

He asked in a tone as if this was an object so precious that you would not find a substitute for it in all of India; and as though there were a whole lot of people scheming to abscond with this heavenly gift.

I consoled him, 'Don't worry. The ones who would have been tempted to steal it are by now safely housed in Ranchi[1] by our kind government.'

He smiled a bit unsurely and said, 'You may say what you want. But have you seen some people have offered prayers to the stone?'

---

[1] The town of Ranchi had (and still has) one of the best-known mental asylums in eastern India and 'being sent to Ranchi' had acquired the status of an idiom in Indian writing.

I realized then that he was right. There were marks of fresh vermillion on the stone.

'Good,' I said, 'it looks nice. Now you have someone else that recognizes its divine worth.'

He looked grim. 'That is my fear. That someone else should not take it away.'

The next morning, the stone was gone. I was completely puzzled. Who would take such a useless thing? And where? I could find no answers. All I knew was that that gentleman, who frequented this place, would be very distressed. In fact, I found myself feeling a tinge of sadness for him.

Several days went by. I was coming home, past the enormous peepul tree at the street corner.

Holy cow! Who brought the stone here?

There it was beneath the tree, pushed a little into the soil with the shiny, well-rounded side jutting out like a shiva linga.[2] Strewn around the stone were petals and sacred leaves of bela. I decided it must be one of those God-fearing folks who go that way daily for their holy dip in the Ganges, who made these offerings of flowers and leaves to the stone as a cheap ticket to a good after-life. Anyway, now that the stone had found itself a home, no one at least had to worry about its well-being anymore.

I could not but help feel pride in the stone's elevation from wayside non-entity to an object of veneration. After all, it was I who liberated the stone, and now—bless it—the stone is into liberating human beings.

[2] A symbol of Lord Shiva.

I occasionally wondered if I should tell that man about the whereabouts of his God. I did bump into him a few times but he never raised the matter of the stone. I had thought I'd find him crestfallen at the disappearance of his precious stone but, on the contrary, he looked quite cheerful. Well, if he had managed to overcome the sorrow of this bereavement so well, I had no business to rake up old memories. So I let the subject pass.

Some more time went by. When I occasionally walked past the peepul tree, I noticed that the status of the stone was on a steady upward trajectory. One day, in fact, I saw a group of roving *sanyasi*s gathered around the stone, chanting what seemed to me like gibberish: 'Bom, bom.' And, as expected with such sanyasis around, I could smell ganja from a mile away.

Now that the sanyasis had come—I was certain—there would soon arrive the devotees—ordinary folks in search of blessing. And who knows, a temple might get constructed. And, of course, money would soon be collected from gullible folks visiting the stone God, thereby giving the temple a steady financial foundation.

A few weeks later I learned that I would have to go to Champaran (in northern Bihar) for some work relating to a sugar mill. I would be away from Calcutta for several months; and so, on my way to the station, I thought I should check out how the saga of the stone was unfolding.

It was exactly as I had predicted. The sanyasis had now been joined by several dreamy eyed devotees. I stood for a while eavesdropping. What I could gather from the snippets of conversation I overheard was, in gist, this. The stone is none other than Lord Trilokeshwar Shiva, in other words, God himself. The stone had emerged here from under the ground; in fact, this stone has no ending. One can dig as deep as one wishes, one will not find its root. Accordingly, one sanyasi held forth, to give the stone its due, it is essential to build a temple around it.

I suddenly felt a strong urge to tell all those devotees the true history of this stone and to expose the lie of its bottomlessness. But I did not have a life insurance policy and was fully aware of how violence and devotion can go hand in hand. Moreover, I did not want to miss my train.

As I headed out of Calcutta, I also decided that it was just as well that I did not tell that man about what had happened. He was clearly keen to establish the stone as deity. So the fact that the stone had achieved precisely that status with no effort from him would—human nature being what it is—actually sadden him.

Months went by. When I returned to Calcutta, it was hard to recognize that old street corner. A small, shiny temple had come up. The sound of conch-shells made it hard to hear anything else and the crowds of devotees made it hard to walk. But more mysteriously, right in the middle of the melee, was that man, clad in saffron robes with loud vermillion marks on his forehead.

'What is all this nonsense?' I couldn't help myself asking.

'Sir, this humble servant is the main priest here.'

'I can see that. Nice way to get a free living. Was that the reason why you had your eyes set on the stone from that very day?'

He covered his ears with his palms. 'Don't say such things, please. What do you mean "stone"? This is Vishnu; this is God. This is the great Trilokeshwar Shiva.'

I laughed and said, 'And, it is bottomless it seems.'

He looked hurt and said, 'Well, that is what everybody says.'

'What do you say?' I asked, irritated. 'I know they say that no matter how far you dig, you will find the stone continues like the pipe of a deep tube well. But what do you think?'

'What do I, humble soul, know? Maybe they are right.'

'Well,' I said, 'why don't you dig one day and check for yourself how deep the roots go?'

He bit his tongue. 'Don't say such blasphemous things. The stone God will be angry. He is very powerful.'

'Powerful, my foot. What evidence do you have of his power may I ask?'

'Well, take small pox. As you know there is a lot of small pox raging in Calcutta these days; and vaccination is having no...'

'Are you serious?' I cut him off; I had just returned and did not know there was small pox going around.

'Well, you just have to read the papers to know that people are dying in droves. The city corporation has been conscientious in vaccinating people, yet people are dying everywhere. Everywhere that is, except in this locality. Here not one person has died. Moreover, none of us here have taken the vaccine. We are relying entirely on Lord Trilokeshwar's holy water. If you still have no faith in the stone God's power, you will have faith in nothing.'

I had no time to respond. I had once earlier got small pox and really suffered, and barely survived. 'I am off,' I told him, 'I need to get myself vaccinated immediately. We'll chat another day.' And I set out straight for Calcutta's famous Medical College.

On the way, I ran into a friend. 'Where are you off to in such a huff?' he asked.

'To get myself vaccinated.'

'Well, I am not sure that is of much use. The small pox vaccine is not helping much this time. I would frankly recommend homeopathy. Go straightaway to King & Co. and buy yourself variolinum, strength 200. Have one dose right away, if you want to survive. Next week, one more dose; and, the week after, another. That's it; you will have no further worries. Vaccine failing, we see all around. Variolinum? Never.'

'Really? I didn't know this.'

'How will you know?', my friend said, dismissively, 'Your only faith is in modern medicine, injections and surgery. I have recently started practising homeopathy; so I know what it can do.'

'Well, let me try your advice.'

I went to King & Co., downed a dose of variolinum 200, and began feeling much better.

But just then two or three dead bodies on stretchers went past me. I felt certain they had died of small pox. I got the shivers. There must be hundreds of thousands of viruses in the air. I doubted my variolinum 200 would be able to withstand the onslaught. As I stood there, feeling breathless and weak, I noticed a bill stuck on the roadside wall, advertising an ayurvedic medicine man. I have taken homeopathic medicine, fine; but why not bolster it with ayurveda, I thought.

On arrival at the ayurved's home, I saw several of his helpers grinding some strange substance using an enormous pestle. After I explained to him about my condition, the ayurved signalled to the substance being prepared. 'Roots,' he said. And then added, 'of sacred plants. One dose will fully fortify you against small pox.'

I took the dose, as advised, and got onto a rickshaw to go home. I did not feel well at all. My head felt light and I felt mildly feverish. What made matters worse was that I seemed to recall reading somewhere that these were exactly the symptoms that appeared before the onset of the pox.

On returning home I told my mother I wouldn't eat anything. 'I am not feeling too well.'

Mother looked concerned, 'Why, what's happened?'

'Nothing has happened...yet.... I am...I think...coming down with small pox.'

'Don't even say that. Nothing like that will happen to you. Just tie this amulet on your arm and you will be fine. I have had this for thirty years. And I have been with so many patients and cared for dying human beings. Not only have I never had pox, I don't even get boils. Come wear this,' she said firmly, taking off her amulet.

'Thirty years, with no serious illness? Why didn't you tell me earlier? Let me try it out. Though, given that the disease is quite advanced in me, I'll probably need multiple amulets.'

I tied the holy charm around my arm but did not feel well. My body felt warm and careful inspection in a mirror revealed faint signs of pox on my face. I called my mother and showed her the faint pock marks.

'Don't make such a fuss,' she said. 'It's an ordinary pimple.'

'Not a pimple. This is small pox.'

'Don't use that word,' mother berated me. 'Sitting at home all day, you are imagining all kinds of things. Just go out and take a stroll.'

Strolling with such a worry in the head can be quite unpleasant. That man had said that they were all well by drinking the holy water. I wondered if I should try it as well. Who knows, there may be a perfectly good scientific explanation about that water having some substance in it that destroys virus. But that is unlikely, I thought. Maybe what is true is that mental courage wards off germs. And it is their faith that gives them mental courage. But, in that case, I realized I stood no real chance because I could in no way muster up faith for that piece of stone.

Instead of all this pointless brooding, I should have just gone and got myself vaccinated in the morning. I have read that, once vaccinated, even if one gets small pox, it takes a milder form and is typically not fatal. That was that. I decided to go forthwith to Calcutta Medical College.

A little later, having taken my vaccination, I was returning home, past the peepul tree and the stone temple. And I wondered, maybe it is true, science cannot explain it all. Today I am alive and well, tomorrow...who knows...I may be down with small pox and dying. I remembered Shakespeare's famous words addressed to Horatio. In this vast universe, with stars reaching out into an endless void, how little we really know. No matter how much one swears by science, standing on the brink of our vast ignorance, one cannot but feel humility.

Looking at the temple of Shri Trilokeshwar, I said in my mind, 'You will forgive me for having doubted you, won't you? You will save me from this epidemic, just this one time.'

I felt the little bump on my cheek. Is it a pimple or the start of small pox? There was clearly no time to hesitate any more. I prostrated myself on the ground, head on the stone, and prayed, 'Glory to Lord Trilokeshwar! Lord, please save me.'

Then, lowering my voice, I added, 'Bom, bom.'

I got up and looked all around to see if anyone had seen me.

part five

Dramaturgic Incursions

fourteen

Crossings at Benaras Junction*

Preface

A FELLOW ECONOMIST, ON LEARNING THAT I was writing a play, queried, 'Why?' I ran before he could ask what policy implications I expected the play to have. I feared I would lose all respect for my profession if I heard that. But I must admit that the 'Why' has followed me. The writing of this play was more than mere past-time. At one level, I wrote it because I had to.

I always loved the theatre, but was reconciled to it being an object of vicarious pleasure. I expected to enjoy the theatre, not participate in it. It became even more at arms' length as I took to reading more plays than I watched. Some of my favourite playwrights, such as Tom Stoppard, were too quick, too clever for me to fully appreciate from the rapid-fire dialogue on stage. I needed to mull over his sentences, like one would in taking in mathematics, and reading seemed the right way to do so. The playwright, who perhaps more

---

* This is a play in four acts. Act II is optional. Any person or group wishing to stage this play should do so with the permission of the author. The play was first published in *The Little Magazine*, vol. 6, 2005.

than anyone else got me hooked to the theatre, Tennessee Williams, was too deep, too neurotic for the fleeting experience of watching on stage. Woody Allen wrote somewhere that if he could write tragedies like Williams, he would happily give up all his comedies. Though I think no end of Woody Allen's talent as a writer of farce, I understood what he meant and felt reassured in my need to read, rather than watch, Tennessee Williams, to pause over his sentences, to go back and re-read a sentence I liked, again and again. Let alone the dialogue, Williams' titles are sufficiently lyrical and brooding to give one pause—'The Milk Train Doesn't Stop Here Anymore', 'A Streetcar Named Desire'.

I took to *watching* plays once again when I got interested in the vernacular theatre—Bengali (mother tongue), Marathi (wife's mother tongue), and Hindi (my children were born in Delhi). My reading speed, ranging from slow to zero, in these languages would be the overriding factor in this decision.

The urge to write my own play arose, along with my interest in the vernacular theatre, some time during the years that I lived in Delhi. The only way I could survive the long *mudrika* ride every day, from South Delhi to the Delhi School of Economics and back, was to treat stepping into the bus as stepping into the theatre. And often enough there was no disappointment. One day there would be the theatrical altercation between the bus conductor and some moustachioed man, firmly ensconced in the 'ladies seat' and feigning an unshakable interest in the world outside the bus window, so as to prevent eviction in favour of an elderly lady. Another day there would be the fight, first, between the conductor and the passenger, who needed persuasion that to say that the DTC (Delhi Transport Corporation) is 'our bus system' did not preclude the need for him to buy a ticket, and, then gradually, involving virtually all the passengers in the captivating debate, some of whom would lament while getting down that they would now have to take a bus back one or two stops, to where they were meant to get off.

Somewhere along the line, I do not quite remember when, the urge took hold of me to write my own play. It would be a play about nothing in particular. It would be a play about the quotidian. And indeed I would present this as the 'theatre of the quotidian', if I were pressed to classify. Though it was about the mundane, about everyday life that I wanted to write, the need to write has been compulsive. For a long time I stole little bits and pieces of time from my professional life as an economist to write down notes for a possible play, secreted away conversations I overheard in trains, omnibuses, and people's homes, and made mental jottings of everyday human follies and foibles.

Then in the summer of 2000 I wrote compulsively, late into the nights and pushing aside deadlines for papers in economics. The play that took hold of me from the large amount of material I had gathered is the one in your hands—'Crossings at Benaras Junction'. Tennessee Williams will have to take a couple of spins in his grave, I know, and I am sorry for that.

When I say that this is a play about nothing very much, I really mean it. At least that is the way my conscious self views it. Yet I will be dishonest if I say that that is all there is to it. Living the life of a research economist, writing papers for journals with peer reviewing, one cannot but be aware of the bruises left by the professional shackles one wears at all times. You cannot put something into print unless you have 'proved' it. An observation is not valid unless it is drawn from a random sample. Every claim must be precise, built up from axioms, and established as theorems. What the professional expert often forgets is that the most important human ideas are ones that cannot be made fully precise, that our knowledge owes much more to imprecision than to precision. You do not teach a child what 'pigeon' means by defining it, but by pointing to pigeons and talking about pigeons.

I suppose—and I am trying a bit of self-psychoanalysis here—the reason why I felt that I had to write the play is that I had things to say which could only be said indirectly, which the audience could only pick up from between the lines, from the sub-text. The theatre is the perfect medium for that. And facetious though 'Benaras Junction' is, it does say things, tucked away in conversations and in little sub-tales that are meant to make one ponder and perhaps even persuade. There are also, I am embarrassed to admit, moral messages—of openness and tolerance—in this play.

One may wonder about the need for a theatre of the quotidian. We all, by definition, live our everyday lives. What use is it to see it portrayed on stage? One of the grouses I have had with the vernacular theatre, even the very best, be it Habib Tanvir's plays from Chhattisgarh, the late Ajitesh Bandyopadhyay's memorable reconstruction of Pirandello's 'Enrico Quatro', or Vijay Tendulkar and Jabbar Patel's 'Ghasiram Kotwal', is that they are too theatrical. I am of course not complaining about these unforgettable plays but what I mean is that there is too little of anything but the theatrical on the Indian stage. But everyday life, carefully sliced out and held up in front of us, can be a mirror where we see ourselves, where we realize things that are in us, unrecognized. Even a farce, like 'Benaras Junction', can help us see our own follies and the minor tragedies of our lives.

One may get the impression that, unlike the theatre of the absurd or the progressive theatre, the drama you are about to read can allow the audience to sit back dormant, and take it in quietly. One may think of this kind of a play as the polar opposite of Augusto Boal's celebrated theatre of the oppressed. It has been said (by, no doubt, someone unfussy about the aesthetics of words) that the spectators for Boal's plays should be thought of as 'spect-actors'. I like to believe that something similar is true also of the theatre of the quotidian. This is because a slice of everyday life, witnessed on stage, is open to interpretations. One is compelled to participate and fill the outlines of the sketches with one's own imagination, drawn from the web of one's own experience.

I am not sure it is a good idea to spell out what it is that one has tried to convey in a play. And even less sure about the merits of making a case for a particular kind of theatre. If I have done so, it is because I needed to do it for my own sake and also because of the firm belief that very few people will ever read this, for plays are typically watched, not read. And the few who do read it will be people like me, and, with them, I would be happy to share these few, hesitant, and inchoate thoughts.

As waiters in American restaurants, flouting the rules of transitivity, say, 'Enjoy.'

Cast

SIDDHARTH CHATTERJEE   39 years old; charming; shock of unkempt hair, though the director should be prepared to trade hair quantity for acting talent.

MELBA IYENGAR   Late 20s; pretty; stylishly attired.

PROFESSOR CHAUDHURI   50s; has a pompous style and speaks the Queen's English, or nearly so.

JUNE CHAUDHURI   Late 40s; pleasing looking.

PROFESSOR SRIVASTAVA, THE VICE-CHANCELLOR   60ish; grey hair; always in dhoti kurta.

SURESH GUPTA   Thin, small built; speaks English with a desi accent; like with a lot of thin people, difficult to tell his age, could be in the early 40s.

MR SHARMA   Mid-30s; has the style of an unabashed entrepreneur, which he is.

LACHHU   Has the style of a street ruffian, which he may or may not be.

MADHU   Mr Sharma's new secretary; vaudeville.

MR GHOSH   Avuncular; in his 40s.

MR TREHAN   Delhi middle class; late 40s.

MRS TREHAN   Delhi middle-class housewife, or home-maker, if you wish; mid-40s.

GAUTAM   12 or so years old.

JENNIFER (JENNY)   Sweet hippie-ish American girl; early 20s.

MR BENTLEY   Grumpy and arrogant foreign tourist.

KAVITA SHARMA   Early 30s. Good looking and, more importantly, has sex appeal; sari-clad.

Ticket collector and miscellaneous others on the train and platform.

Act I

Siddharth's drawing room. Inexpensively but stylishly done up. Plenty of books. Some nice, well-chosen furniture; modern but not abstract art on the wall. The room has at least two doors—one which is the main entrance and another leading to the interior of the house.

It is evening. Siddharth is reclining on a couch. A cassette recorder is on; it is playing 'Mai zindagi ka saath nibhata chala gaya'. The bell rings. Siddharth opens the door; Melba enters.

MELBA   Congratulations! Such fantastic news.

SIDDHARTH   Thank you. It does feel good. Where did you hear about it?

MELBA   The Vice-Chancellor announced it earlier this evening at the Director of Courses Meeting. ... But what's all this whining music? You should have something more grand to celebrate.

SIDDHARTH   Whining music? Old Hindi film music is the best music on earth. (*Quietly listens for a while, looking at Melba, as if urging her to appreciate.*) In comparison Mozart sounds pedantic.

MELBA   Mozart pedantic? Don't say that in public. I am sure the IPA will want to take back the prize if they hear you speak like such an ignoramus.

(*Siddharth turns off the music.*)

The prize must have come as a total surprise?

SIDDHARTH   That's a nice put down.

MELBA   (*giggling*) Come on, don't be so cynical. I mean it is not the most natural thing to happen—being based in India, as young as only 40, and getting the annual IPA prize.

SIDDHARTH   Melba, you have come to congratulate without checking on your facts. I am 39.

MELBA   Oops, what a huge mistake, describing a 39-year-old man as 40. I am sure you will justify the concern as part of your general fastidiousness for accuracy and perfection.

(*Changing the tone of her voice.*)

This really gives me great pleasure. As a lecturer in philosophy, struggling away with so little success but with an ability to admire talent that rivals Salieri's, I can only look at you with awe. As a matter of fact, I did that even before I got news of the prize this evening. And I look at myself with pity and wonder if trying to be a philosopher was the right thing for me at all.

SIDDHARTH   Don't be so modest Melba. You are much more than a lecturer in philosophy. You are an activist, which I am not. Each of your documentaries probably has much more effect on society than all my rigmarole papers on reason and cognition put together.

MELBA   Isn't it unfair that we are probably the only profession where we can't say what we do without sounding pompous? A person who teaches economics can say he is an economist, the professor of physics can say he is a physicist. But only we are doomed to say 'I *teach* philosophy or even I do research in philosophy.' But not 'I am a philosopher' without sounding false. … Well I suppose you can, I can't.

SIDDHARTH   You are so self-deprecating. I wish I had half the many talents you have.

MELBA   You are so kind.

(*She has picked up a book and is browsing through it. Then without closing the book…*)

The trouble is I find kindness in men sexy.

(*Pause.*)

SIDDHARTH   (*smiles uneasily*) Well I find women who find kindness in men sexy charming.

MELBA   That response took too long to sound authentic. It is the response of a nervous philosopher trying to get out of a tight spot by saying something clever.

SIDDHARTH   Nonsense. Why should I be nervous?

(*Ruffles her hair and switches on a bright light.*)

MELBA   Bright lights make for safer neighbourhoods.

SIDDHARTH   You are impossible. ...
Why should I be nervous? I am in fact almost in love with you.

MELBA   With no behavioural manifestation of that whatsoever.
You are not in love with anyone, dear Siddharth. You are in search of that perfect woman, the 10, Bo Derek, just as you search for that perfect idea to craft into the perfect paper.
You should be proud. A good Hindu girl—arguably somewhat Westernized—telling you in advance that the answer will be yes. (*Laughs. Not clear if she is saying this in jest or seriously.*)
And mind you I am not hard up. There are lots of eligible bachelors who would offer their hands at the drop of a hat. Zafar, Arun, and, admittedly with a little bit of work on my part, Aslam. So look at the sacrifice I am willing to make, waiting for you.

SIDDHARTH   You are really in a modest mood today. I don't think you would have to work on it at all to get poor old Aslam.
Secondly, I would any day propose to you if I knew you would say yes. But I know you won't and I will not be able to bear that.

MELBA   (*giggling*) Okay, I defy you. Go ahead and try.

SIDDHARTH   No I refuse to fall into the trap of the big humiliation you are planning for me.
Incidentally, this talk of huge sacrifice is crap. It involves what an economist friend of mine from JNU calls 'double counting'—

just that in this case it is worse—it involves triple counting. You are counting three bachelors who would be sacrificed in the event of our getting married. But look at it this way. If you married Zafar, you would have missed out on Aslam and Ashok—or was it Arun? In fact, no matter whom you chose to marry among the three, you would miss out on the other two. So if you are waiting for me, which I don't believe for a moment, what you are sacrificing is not Zafar, Aslam, *and* Arun, but only one of them. Presumably you would pick the best of them. So what you are sacrificing is the best of Zafar, Alam, and Arun. This is what I believe economists describe as 'opportunity cost', though for the life of me I cannot see why you need a special name for something as obvious as that.

MELBA   What's all this economics suddenly?

SIDDHARTH   ... Actually the sacrifice is even less, because with two-thirds of your potential marriage partners you would have the Janambhoomi Party goons disrupting the wedding ceremony. You would have to deduct the expected cost of that from the benefit.

(*The door bell rings.*)

MELBA   (*referring to the bell*) And now you are saved from this nerve-wracking talk of having to go in for an unwanted marriage.

(*Siddharth walks up to the door and holds it open.*)

SIDDHARTH   Ah, the eminent Professor Chaudhuri, and the charming Mrs Chaudhuri. (*Looks over them.*) And the Vice-Chancellor himself.

VC   I took note that there were no adjectives used to describe me. (*Laughs.*)

(*All of them shake hands, rub shoulders, etc., amidst remarks like 'Great news! Congratulations!'*)

It makes me proud to be VC of New Delhi University, when I hear such news. This World Philosophy Society award is one of the most important philosophy prizes in the world ... and for it to come to someone in NDU ... What could be better?

SIDDHARTH   Let us not get it out of proportion. There are many prizes in philosophy and this is just one of them. And even this is given each year to one philosopher. Since a philosopher of any worth appears no more than once every 30 or 40 years (*pauses trying to calculate, gives up*), a large percentage of recipients do not deserve the prize.

MELBA   Couldn't calculate the percentage? (*Laughs.*)

SIDDHARTH   (*looking at the VC and turning to Melba*) By the way, you do know her? She is ...

VC   Of course, I do. I interviewed her when she joined NDU. I'll tell you ... Isn't your name Peach?

MELBA   It's actually Melba.

SIDDHARTH   He's got the essence of it.

PROF. CHAUDHURI   (*putting his arm around Siddharth's shoulders*) Well done, my boy. It must be quite something to have got the prize of an organization as famous as the World Philosophical ... , the Global Association ...

SIDDHARTH   International Philosophy Association.

PROF. CHAUDHURI   Yes, ... that is what I meant—International Philosophy Association. It must be a time of contemplation for you. I remember when the University of Newcastle Upon Tyne conferred on me the prize for political studies on Mongolia since the dissolution of the Soviet Union, it plunged me into a kind of self-revaluation ...

(*The door bell rings. Siddharth opens the door. Mr Gupta at the door with a huge garland. Puts the garland on Siddharth's neck and embraces him, crushing the flowers.*)

SIDDHARTH   Gupta, so good to see you. But you should not have wasted money on such a fat garland; and having done so, you must not crush the flowers by embracing me so hard.

GUPTA   (*laughing and speaking to everybody*) He is always joking with me ... .

SIDDHARTH   Let me introduce you. This is my old friend, Mr Suresh Gupta ...

GUPTA   Dr Suresh Gupta. It is not so important but since I am taking nine years to do my PhD ...

SIDDHARTH   I am sorry. Dr Suresh Gupta. He takes adult education classes in Rajiv Gandhi University, but deep down he is a philosopher. The world's greatest philosophers were not professors of philosophy, the way I am, but they did other things. Spinoza lived off polishing and grinding lenses in Amsterdam and The Hague, Nietzsche was a professor of philology when he was not mad, Leibnitz was a civil servant and a librarian. Gupta is a true philosopher like these people; not a sham like us professors of philosophy.

(*To Gupta*) And you probably do not know these people. This is ...

GUPTA   You don't have to tell me. Everybody is knowing Professor Srivastava, VC of New Delhi University. This is not as important as VC of Delhi University; but sir, I should say, you have almost equally challenging job.

By the way, we are both hailing from the same place, Benaras. I have been telling Professor (*referring to Siddharth*) he must visit Benaras once. It is India's heritage city.

SIDDHARTH   I was actually tempted to do a stopover in Benaras this coming January, when I go to Calcutta. You know the new Delhi–Calcutta express stops at Benaras ...

GUPTA   Coming January? You mean two months from now? I will be in Benaras at that time. You must come to my home. It is just by the side of the station ... hardly five minutes. I stay all alone, you will have no noise problem. Full room for the great philosopher. And food from the Happy Lodge Canteen, next to my house. Really, it will be a great honour for me.

SIDDHARTH   You are really very kind. I feel tempted.

GUPTA   And if by then some lady is foolish enough to marry me, you will have hot, home-cooked food.

SIDDHARTH   You are taking her cooking skills for granted. ... Gupta, realistically, I don't think it will work out ... not this time. Besides, I have already bought my ticket. Next time. *(Beginning to turn towards the Chaudhuris)* And this is ...

GUPTA   Calcutta? I forgot you are going to the World Philosophy Congress.

SIDDHARTH   Yes, I have to give a lecture there.

GUPTA   Yes, I know. You are giving a plenary lecture. I actually submitted a paper for the conference. But they rejected it— basically saying politely ... not too politely ... that my English is not good enough. I wrote to them that this is a conference in philosophy, not spoken English, but they did not reply. ... I am told the conference will be a big mela, with speakers from all over the world.

SIDDHARTH   Yes, I believe so. ... I should introduce you to others. This is ...

GUPTA   Professor Chaudhuri, Chairman of Political Science Department. *(Laughing)* I am telling you I know everybody in Delhi. Chaudhuri I used to see at the ballroom dancing class for beginners at the YMCA. And last year you win the prize from the chhota British university—New Castle River.

SIDDHARTH   University of Newcastle upon Tyne is not chhota at all and, by some rankings, quite close to Oxford.

GUPTA   But nothing compared to the International Philosophy Association with its headquarters at ... at ... Harvard.

MELBA   No, Stanford.

GUPTA   Chalo. That is not too bad.

SIDDHARTH   And these two ladies are June Chaudhuri, wife of ...

GUPTA   (*doing namaste*) I am knowing her.

SIDDHARTH   And Melba Iyengar.

GUPTA   Melba? Iyengar? Christian–Hindu mixture. Chalo good for Indian unity. But the Janambhoomi Party people will be confused, not knowing whether to do namaste to you or to beat you.

VC   No, no, no, that is not right, Guptaji. The JBP does not beat up anybody.

GUPTA   What are you telling? Only yesterday JBP cadres do danga at Dainik Khabar office, stopping newspaper from coming out, beating editor Shekhar …

VC   That was totally different. Shekhar's editorial day before yesterday was just slander. He wrote that the JBP believes in violence, without being able to produce a shred of evidence.

GUPTA   But with due respect sir, that is no justification for using the strong-arm tactics.

VC   Well if someone wrote an editorial full of lies about me, I would be tempted to use a little force and stop the editorial.

SIDDHARTH   But once they used violence to stop the newspaper from coming out, the editorial ceased to be a lie. And so they had no reason for stopping the newspaper from coming out.

VC   You jolly well have the right to stop an editorial from seeing the light of day if it tells a lie.

GUPTA   But sir light of day is irrelevant here because this is evening newspaper.

SIDDHARTH   (*ignoring Gupta*) But *in retrospect* it was not a lie what the editorial said. The JBP's use of violence proved that they use violence. Even if Shekhar's criticism was false, as soon as they used violence, it ceased to be false; so their violence occurred even when there was no false criticism of their party.

So this proves not only that the JBP uses violence but that it does so even when there is no false criticism of the party.

MELBA   Not quite a flawless philosophical argument, but all for a good cause.

GUPTA   (*turning to Melba*) I have seen you before. Did you go to India International Centre discussion on foreign policy one month ago?

MELBA   Yes, I did.

GUPTA   Now, I remember. You were sitting next to Dr Zafar Khan. ... Very good man. Even more handsome than good.

(*Siddharth is controlling a smile. Melba blushes. June listens in. The VC and Prof. Chaudhuri are paying no attention.*)

Then you are also knowing my friend Arun Kapoor, I think.

SIDDHARTH   That leaves out only Aslam.

GUPTA   What?

MELBA   (*to Siddharth*) Shut up.

(*Gupta looks confused.*)

GUPTA   (*to Siddharth*) Professor, there is one more good news. I am starting a new institute. It will be an institute for social science and practical philosophy—fully multidisciplinary but no faaltu mathematics and abstract logic.

SIDDHARTH   I like that. Never waste time being diplomatic.

GUPTA   Diplomat? Diplomat? Oh (*without understanding*) ha ha (*quick forced laugh to brush aside the interruption*)... So this institute ... this institute... (*has lost the thread of his thought*).

SIDDHARTH   I hope it will be fully multidisciplinary?

GUPTA   Certainly. Fully multidisciplinary. Oh yes, I was saying that this institute will have economists, political scientists, who know Indian reality. People like you, Professor Srivastava, ... Professor Chaudhuri.

You cannot be an economist or a political scientist without knowing ground reality.

Can you make shirt without cloth? Can you make soap without … without …

SIDDHARTH   I cannot help you with this one.

GUPTA   Without what soap is made of?

SIDDHARTH   Even if the answer to the shirt question is 'Yes', I suppose to the soap question it can only be 'No'.

GUPTA   (*to others*) He is always talking difficult things. Like true philosopher. But with me he is just a friend. (*Shakes Siddharth's hand.*)

But I want advice from you high-achievement people. How can I run a good institute?

PROF. CHAUDHURI   I do not know if you can ever run a good institute, but Mr Vice-Chancellor, I am sure you will second me on this, the secret of a good institute or department can be put in one word, 'involvement'. You know what I had to do to bring our Political Science Department to world class?

I was a young man then, and I dare say somewhat callow (*laughs*). The chairman was none other than the formidable Prof. C.B. Das. He was up to tricks trying to drive a wedge between the theorists and the empiricists. I would have none of that; so I decided to confront the formidable man himself. So I went straight to C.B. Das.

GUPTA   Excuse me, sir. Who is B. Das?

PROF. CHAUDHURI   I have no idea. I went to C.B. Das.

GUPTA   Very funny. You don't know B. Das but you go to see B. Das?

PROF. CHAUDHURI   In principle, I see nothing funny in this. We do often go to see people whom we do not know. Indeed without such adventures our circle of friends would remain forever stationary.

Be that as it may. In this case I went to see C.B. Das not only because I knew who he was but I knew what he was up to. I must say the man was quite magnanimous. He said, 'Why don't you organize a seminar to bring the two fractious groups together?'

Ever since that day I have kept the great man's challenge in mind and even now, as department chairman myself, I try to keep everybody involved. I have made a rule that every week one faculty member has to initiate a discussion. He or she can choose any topic. I have no objections to that. But he … that is, he or she … has to be prepared to take questions from the floor.

GUPTA   How many ladies are you having in your department?

PROF. CHAUDHURI   Ah … none. All our faculty members are, as a matter of fact, male.

GUPTA   No, because you are saying 'he or she', I am thinking there are many ladies in your department.

PROF. CHAUDHURI   Well one says he or she because it is shameful to presume that all our references are to men. It is a political correctness with which I am in full agreement.

GUPTA   I think this is very good idea. In my institute I will also employ men as professors and refer to each professor as he or she. Sir, if you have other such fine ideas for my new institute, please kindly let me know.

(*The VC gets up. The back of his dhoti [the part that is tucked in at waist level] has come off.*)

VC   I will take your leave now, especially given that you have the company of your good friend Gupta.

GUPTA   Sir, your dhoti is open.

(*The VC coolly gathers the loose end and tucks it into the back of his dhoti.*)

VC   It is true that everything is not translatable from one language to another. And this frequent lapse on the part of the rear end of the dhoti is difficult to describe in English. Perhaps one can say 'Your dhoti has come loose.' That is not quite right but conveys the general sense. But to say 'Your dhoti is open' is plain wrong. In addition, it causes undue alarm in the listener.

(*The VC exits.*)

GUPTA I think he is angry with me because my English is faulty.

SIDDHARTH Of course not. He is ... Your English is just fine. And why do you need fancy English?

GUPTA No, English is important. I did not tell you earlier, just last month I again wrote to the organizers of the World Philosophy Congress that I am very keen to participate in the conference, so if someone whose paper is accepted is unable to attend, I can come to Calcutta at my own expense and read out his ... (*looks at Professor Chaudhuri*) his or her paper. Prompt reply. Such a contingency is unlikely, but if it arises, they will need someone with good spoken English. I think they were still angry about my previous letter.
And now the VC is angry with me.

SIDDHARTH Don't be silly. He is angry with me because I won a prize. He just took a little bit of that anger out on you. He is a political appointment and detests any criticism of government. Perhaps he just gets nervous about his own job security. Did you know that he censored one of my articles from the university newsletter? He does not belong to any party himself, too unimaginative to have a proper line on anything. He is a professor of English but is really a hack.

JUNE I did not know the VC tried to muzzle your voice. He seems such a soft-spoken, decent person.

SIDDHARTH Human beings are such complex characters, June. At one level he is decent. ... Tennessee Williams once wrote how each person weaves a web around himself, a web based on his own private history, that dooms him to be lonely and incomprehensible to others. He said it much more elegantly but it was something to this effect.

A soft-spoken, decent person he seems. It also seems he does not dance. But who knows? Perhaps when he is alone he puts a hat on his head and dances and gyrates wildly to music. It is frightening how little we really know one another.

PROF. CHAUDHURI   Well, well, ... It is time to go.

MELBA   So must I.

GUPTA   And Gupta also has to take leave of the great professor.

SIDDHARTH   You can't all abandon me at the same time. My life is lonely enough. Professor Chaudhuri, June, you live on campus, what is your hurry?

PROF. CHAUDHURI   I am expecting a phone call from Paris. There is a UNESCO project on transition economies and they have been phoning me repeatedly to recommend someone to be based in Paris for two months.

SIDDHARTH   So whom will you recommend?

PROF. CHAUDHURI   Well they insist it has to be someone mature, so ... I figured ... I had a duty to offer myself. So they will phone me a little later to discuss the details.

JUNE   Well I can stay on a little while so that you don't have to cope with the sudden exodus. (to Prof. Chaudhuri) Leave the front door open, I'll be there very soon.

(The others bid goodbye and leave. Siddharth sees them to the door. June makes herself comfortable on a couch.)

SIDDHARTH   Thank you for staying.

(He walks up to the music shelf and puts on 'Abhi na jaayo chorkar. Yeh dil abhi bhara nahi', listens for a few seconds, smiles at her.)

SIDDHARTH   If one has a decent Hindi film music collection, one can pretty much do without speaking.

(Brief pause.)

JUNE Instead of talking about Tennessee Williams, uplifting songs, and loneliness, why don't you fall in love and get yourself a nice wife?

SIDDHARTH I have fallen in love many times, but the only time I wanted to get married, the person in question dumped me for a much older person.

JUNE She was nearly 10 years older than you and did the right thing. But you must find someone now and build a home. Through all this mirth and laughter, I feel you carry with you a burden of pain. (*Siddharth laughs.*)

SIDDHARTH You know what Aristotle said about marrying? He said he would recommend it to every man, because if he gets a good wife, he will be happy, and if he gets a nagging wife, he will be a philosopher. Since I am already a philosopher and Aristotle cannot be wrong, whomever I marry must be a nag. Since I do not knowingly want to marry a nag, my only option is not to marry.

JUNE Well, whether you marry or not, I am so glad you got the prize. You are so passionately committed to philosophy, you deserve it.

In fact, when about a month ago, when someone mentioned that you may get the prize, I prayed that you would. See how God listens to me?

SIDDHARTH Well this is no hard evidence of God listening to you, because when I heard about the possibility, I also prayed.

JUNE What? An atheist who does not believe in prizes, praying to God to give him a prize?

SIDDHARTH I don't not believe in prizes as much as I don't not believe in God.

JUNE Whatever that means. ... Since when have you taken to praying?

SIDDHARTH   Actually I didn't quite pray. I said, 'God if you exist
and if it is true that I am in the running for this prize, go ahead,
give it to me. I need it because it will upset my department
chair. If I get it, I will immediately go to a temple and pray.'
So you see it was a conditional prayer.

Actually I did not want to make even such a vow. But,
you know, it was one of those familiar situations, where you keep
telling yourself, 'Don't make such a promise, don't make such a
promise', but nevertheless the promise flits through your mind and
you are stuck with it.

JUNE   And have you, may I ask, been to the temple?

SIDDHARTH   No, because God cannot now take away the prize.
It has been announced. And even if he does, my chairman has
already heard about it and suffered, so the ultimate objective
has been fulfilled.

JUNE   But God is all-powerful.

SIDDHARTH   (*thinks for a while*) So you mean he can turn back
time, like Christopher Reeves did in Superman. ... But on
the other hand, he is all-merciful. So I am sure he will not
want to hurt me.

JUNE   You seem to be presuming that his mercy does not extend
to your department chair.

SIDDHARTH   But if he wanted to show mercy to the department
chair, he should not have given me the prize anyway, whether
or not I prayed.

Look June, an all-merciful, all-powerful being and the world as
it is constitute a logical impossibility. So don't make me go out on
into the dark night.

(*June stands up, readying to leave.*)

JUNE   Put on your sandals and just walk over to Plaza Gardens,
if for no other reason than because promises are meant to be
kept. And I have to go now, because otherwise I will have

to deal with an irate professor, especially if by now there has
been a theft in my home.

Remember there is nothing wrong in fearing God.

(*June is at the door.*)

SIDDHARTH   But Swami Vivekananda, a man of God himself, said,
'There is no sin bigger than fear.'

(*Siddharth kisses her hand in an exaggerated Western style; June exits.*)

SIDDHARTH   (*Stands at the door vacillating*) I am not a coward.

(*Turns on the cassette, it begins to play from where he had stopped, 'Abhi
na jayo chorkar …'. He sits down on a sofa for a short while. He gets
up abruptly, puts on sandals, and walks out of the front door. Lights fade.
Curtain.*)

Act II

*The interior of the VC's house. The drawing room. There is a biggish couch,
with a high back, at the back of the stage and facing the audience. The
sound of a key in the keyhole. Eventually the door opens. The VC, in the
same attire as in Act I, enters.*

VC   Shobha … Shobha … . Is anyone there?

(*Gives up on her. Goes up to the music system and switches it on and sits
down. The tail end of a song plays. Then begins Manna De's 'Jhanana,
jhanana tore baje payaliya'. The VC gets up and begins to dance to it.
Somewhat comical, but not without skill. It is evident that he is a closet
dancer. His dancing gets increasingly vigorous as the song progresses. He
gyrates, mimics going down the staircase, behind the couch (rather like
Austin Powers or Mr Bean). He does not wear a hat, as Siddharth had
said might happen. Music ends and he flops down on the couch. Lights
off. Curtain.*)

Act III

Mr Sharma's drawing room-cum-office. Quite gaudily done up. Evidence of money. On the wall, travel posters, girlie posters. Mr Sharma is sitting on a swivelling chair; Lachhu is leaning on a chair, and Madhu, Mr Sharma's new secretary, in short skirt, sitting self-consciously on a chair.

SHARMA (*to Madhu*) In this office, dearie, there are two rules. The work hours have to be long and the skirt short. You have fulfilled one of these requirements; I will have to see how you do on the other. Remember these two principles and you will do very well in this job. Ask Lachhu and he will tell you. Of course, I have exempted him from the short skirt requirement, but he has to work long hours. I am close to making my first million and want to make it within this year.

LACHHU Boss's last business make big loss.

SHARMA O shut up. My last business did make a loss but through no fault of mine.

MADHU What business was it?

SHARMA There is only one kind of business in the world—the business of making money. (*Laughs loudly.*)
  It was based on some stupid theory Kavita had read in some psychology book that people cannot judge their own future fears. They consistently underestimate it. I immediately converted it into a good business plan.

LACHHU Boss bought roller-coaster for joy-ride.

SHARMA I did not buy it. I leased it with a loan from a friend.

LACHHU Friend now not talking to boss.

SHARMA The novelty of my idea was that there would be no charge for getting on the roller-coaster. Each rider would just have to show that he has at least Rs 500 in his pocket.
  Then half-way through the ride, when they are very frightened, the roller-coaster will be stopped and people will be given the option

to leave if they pay Rs 200. Otherwise they will have to complete the full ride.

LACHHU   Boss has very good idea how to cheat the people.

SHARMA   Arre chup kar. There was no cheating involved. People were told all the rules in advance. It followed from the theory of some Ainslee fellow and some economists that most people would be sure that they would not get off half way and so they would get to have the joy-ride free. So lots of people will want to take the ride. But then, when they actually start the ride, they will realize that they are more scared than they had anticipated, and they will be willing to pay Rs 500 just to get off.

LACHHU   Boss is birlliant.

MADHU   Then what happened?

SHARMA   Kavita did not tell me that all these theories were about Americans. Indians are such kanjoos. They would rather fall from the roller-coaster and die than part with Rs 500. I lost a lot of money. Don't remind me about that.

LACHHU   Another birlliant business boss did. He leased Mercedes car and keep it …

SHARMA   I did not lease it. I bought it.

LACHHU   Same thing, boss. He keep car outside gate of five-star hotel. Any lafda person coming to five-star hotel by bus or auto can get into Mercedes for Rs 50 and I drive him into the hotel.

MADHU   What a clever idea. I would pay Rs 50 just to get out of a Mercedes anywhere. And to get out of a Mercedes in front of a five-star hotel, I would any day pay Rs 100. The nasty looks those gatekeepers give when one gets off from autos.

LACHHU   Ask boss what happened to business?

SHARMA   The hotel gatekeepers soon got to know the car and this idiot Lachhu and would laugh at any passenger who would get down from my car.

LACHHU   And in business once repootation is spoilt, business is no good.

SHARMA   I made a huge profit all the same. The profit was from the car. It was actually a raddi Mercedes, with an Ambassador engine inside ... I had bought it for nothing.

LACHHU   Boss sold it to his best friend at full price of Mercedes. Friend now not talking to boss anymore.

SHARMA   History is history. Let us now concentrate on my new business.

LACHHU   Ganga Travel and Tours—G-A-T-T.

SHARMA   Yes, that is my new tourism business. I had a much grander name earlier: World Travel Operators—W-T-O. But someone wrote to me from Geneva saying that I would get into trouble with some other organization called WTO. I tell you these Westerners treat the names of their organizations like their wives. Anyway, I did not want unnecessary trouble. That's why I have named it GATT—Ganga Travel and Tours.

This is basically for up-market tourists from all over the world—Europe, America, Japan, Australia. Please excuse me for not including Third World countries. If this one fails, dearie (*puts his arm around her*), you and Lachhu will have some explaining to do. So please do your best to make this business a success. In fact we are starting with a crisis. Next week, on 6 January, the first group of tourists will arrive, and two days later they will leave for Benaras by the Delhi–Calcutta express. The trouble is, my guide has run away. So I am training Lachhu to take his place.

MADHU   But he does not seem to know anything. How will he be a guide?

SHARMA   Don't worry. He is very good at speaking so that no one can understand what he is saying. Lachhu, tell Madhu madam about Biswanath temple in Benaras.

(*Here, as a couple of times later, Lachhu will have to speak gibberish and the gibberish that I write, here and later, does not have to be it. It is meant to be merely indicative. But one must avoid the pitfall of thinking that nonsense can be extemporized. Lachhu needs to practise the gibberish, keeping in mind that it must sound like English but not be intelligible, and every now and then he should return to the subject on which he is allegedly speaking, articulating the subject clearly.*)

LACHHU   Biswanath temple. Ther Biswanath temple is very important temple in India. Ther Biswanath Temple ees to vary grilt, venthe istry cumthe ton temple. Ter grant ood colact id and distreebis the stag elnashon is langvand steed ice Biswanath temple. Ven till king condrast hadnot hill berry shin tiklen. That vry is Biswanath temple.

SHARMA   What did you follow?

MADHU   Nothing.

SHARMA   That is exactly it. There is no question on which anybody can say that Lachhu has given a wrong answer. He can answer any question that an American or German or Australian may ask.

LACHHU   Or Japanese. Whenher roosen where contilda hooren end is goseep.

SHARMA   Shut up Lachhu, there are no foreigners here.
    My main problem is I have no tour boss to go with Lachhu and the tourists. Lachhu can't keep accounts and cannot speak to the hotel reception and do a variety of other jobs that have to be done during a tour. I myself cannot leave office and go since I have my other business to look after.

MADHU   I can go as tour manager.

SHARMA   I want you here to look after my office ... and me. With Lachhu gone, you will have a lot to do. ... I have a brilliant idea. My wife can do it. She is very intelligent ... the trouble is when she hears the kind of tour Lachhu will give, she will not want to be a party to it. Silly morals.

MADHU   You mean she will not listen to you?

SHARMA She jolly well will. Lachhu, Kavita madam ko bulake la.

(*Lachhu exits, and promptly returns, following Kavita. She comes in on her crutches, with her limp visible to the audience.*)

Kavita, on 8 January, you are going to Benaras with my first tour group.

KAVITA Why don't you keep me out of this? Besides, I am not very good with people.

SHARMA Treat this as your wifely duty. Anyway you will have to do nothing but keep the money and the day-to-day accounts.

KAVITA What about my teaching?

SHARMA You are not teaching at Harvard. The slum children can do without their teacher for one week. When you come back, you can give them a first-hand account of Benaras.

(*Laughs flamboyantly.*)

By the way, the professor of philosophy you used to talk about, has won some prize. It was in the papers.

KAVITA I know. I read about it.

SHARMA But the prize money is a joke. It is what I make in two months.

LACHHU That means, boss, professor's prize is what I will earn in next 20 years. Madam, where I can learn philosophy?

(*Curtain.*)

Act IV

Bustling platform at New Delhi railway station. Familiar sounds: 'chai garam, chai garam, …'; 'badhia amrood'; …. In the background is the train, with two compartments in view—the right one (which I will call compartment 1) is in full view and the left one (compartment 2) is partial. Once the train starts, the platform scene will vanish, and the two compartments is the view that the audience will see. Then on, the action will shift between the two compartments and the director may like to have some arrangement for shifting the two compartments slightly, so as to bring more centre-stage the compartment which is in focus.

Eventually the following people will enter the train and occupy the seats in the train as follows: Compartment 1, right to left: Bentley, Jenny, Ghosh, Mrs Trehan, Mr Trehan, Siddharth. Compartment 2, right to left: Siddharth (after the TC asks him to move), Kavita. Gautam will be initially on the bunk in compartment 1 but will move later to the bunk in compartment 2.

People are jostling on the platform; coolies are getting in and out of the train. Lachhu comes into view with a huge placard, which reads G A T T, and below it, in parentheses, (formerly W T O). He looks around and then goes off stage from the left. Kavita enters, self-conscious about her crutches. Lachhu is with her and helps her to her seat. Mr Ghosh, Gautam, and Jenny have also entered the platform, entered the train, and taken their seats. Gautam climbs onto the bunk.

GHOSH   Good evening.

JENNY   (smiles) Good evening.

GHOSH   Am I right in presuming that your good-self is a tourist going to Benaras?

JENNY   You guessed right.

GHOSH   You are very young. Are you travelling alone or with mother father?

JENNY   (giggles) I am not alone. We are a large group of Americans and Europeans, taking this wonderful tour organized by Ganga Travel and Tours.

GHOSH   You are, I should say, keenly interested in Indian history?

JENNY   I am. But even apart from history, India is such a wonderful country, full of lovely people. It gives one a sense of peace that one cannot find anywhere else, certainly not in New York. ... I suppose I have come to India to discover myself.

GHOSH   (*laughs appreciatively*) Discover Mysore? You are interested in Tippoo Sultan's life? But then you have to go to South India. The best way is to go to Bangalore and take a bus.

JENNY   What I mean is I want to find my soul. In America you have your body, even your mind, but all too often we forget about our soul. They say you can always find your soul in Benaras.

(*From the left side of the platform enter Mr and Mrs Trehan, coolies in tow [there can also be some young relatives who have come to help them board the train and will leave before the train starts]. [Mr] Trehan is limping and Mrs Trehan seems to be finding this funny.*)

TREHAN   Arre baba you may laugh as much as you want. The first thing I will search for on reaching Benaras is for sole.

(*Takes off his left shoe and examines the sole, or rather its absence.*)

They charge so much money for shoes these days and the sole comes off on the first day. Laugh, laugh. You have never walked with shoe with no sole.

(*They clamber into the train and are settling into their seats. The earlier conversation occurred at a distance where Jenny could not have heard him.*)

JENNY   (*to Ghosh*) In the West people behave as if the soul does not matter.

(*The word 'soul' catches Trehan's attention.*)

TREHAN   They are fools I tell you. Total nincompoops. Sole is the most important thing.

JENNY   (*nods sweetly*) This is what I like about you Indians, you realize what is truly important in life.

TREHAN   For smooth transportation through life, I tell you, there is nothing as important as a good sole.

JENNY   Exactly. I was telling this gentleman …

GHOSH   Ghosh. My name is Ghosh.

JENNY   I was telling Mr Gosh that I am going to Benaras to find my soul.

TREHAN   (*shakes hands with Jenny in appreciation*) I will not go so far as to say I am going to Benaras with the only purpose of finding a sole; but on reaching Benaras the first thing I will do is certainly to buy a sole.

JENNY   (*laughs*) You will buy a sole?

TREHAN   Yes. Some mochi may give it to you free but I would not trust the quality. Too many people are doing the shoddy work in India.

MRS TREHAN   Kamaal kar diya. Ek to atman ke baare me baat kar rahi hai, ek joota ke.

(*Mr Robert Bentley comes rushing in.*)

BENTLEY   (*to Jenny*) Thank God I have found at least one of us. This is the most mismanaged tour I have been on. Where are the others?

JENNY   I don't know. But sit down. We are in a compartment with the most lovely set of people. This is Gosh, Mr Treehang, and this is, I presume, Mrs Treehang ...

(*Mrs Trehan ignores the introduction. The others shake hands. From the upper bunk Gautam leans forward.*)

GAUTAM   (*loudly*) And my name is Gautam.

GHOSH   Gautam is my neighbour's son. I am his guardian for this journey to Calcutta.

JENNY & BENTLEY   Hi, Gautam.

(*They all settle in. Awkward silence for a while.*)

BENTLEY   Beautiful weather.

TREHAN   Rather I should say the finest weather.

(*Silence.*)

BENTLEY   Clear blue skies. One rarely gets such weather in Europe and we have had this now for three days without a break.

TREHAN   You are 100 per cent right.

(*Silence. Bentley feeling awkward.*)

BENTLEY   Hardly any clouds, cool but not cold …

TREHAN   May I ask you sir, why you are taking too much interest in the weather? Are you working in the weather forecasting bureau?

BENTLEY   O no no! I work for an investment bank.

GHOSH   (*laughing*) I also used to think like that before I went to England. Then I learnt that English people are taking very much interest in the weather.

(*Commotion. Siddharth enters from the right, rushes in. He is late. Lachhu also comes in. Siddharth sits down, takes out some books and papers. Lachhu turns to Jenny and Bentley.*)

LACHHU   Here you are, number 5 and number 7. (*Looks at a sheet in his hand and ticks off.*) All GATT people are now in the train.

BENTLEY   (*irritated*) You said all those taking the Varanasi tour with you will be together. Where are the others?

LACHHU   Sir, please to understand. Train is very full so travellers get separated.

BENTLEY   I don't remember the condition that we would be together if the train was not full.

LACHHU   In Benaras we will all be together. Let me now say 'Welcome to the tour. Next seven days you will be guest of Ganga Travel and Tours. You will see the ancient cities of Benaras and Allahabad.'

JENNY   Which one is the older of the two?

LACHHU   Older? … Older?

JENNY   I was wondering, between Varanasi and Allahabad, which is the older city?

LACHHU   Oh (*as if he has at last understood the question*). Valder city? Vich is valder city? Ther Allahabad ees thutty thaned the king is ther baltineder. Ven ther king madden city, ganga river had the ventilenil. Benaras and Allahabad is ther menthe reddin valder city, time ven world westhen laden. Ther Benaras and Allahabad.

(*Jenny nods unsurely. Of the others, some feign understanding, some look puzzled.*)

SIDDHARTH   What he means is that Benaras is the older city.

LACHHU   Now please to make yourself comfortable. I will attend to other travellers and see you later.

(*The train starts with a jerk. People on the platform slide away. The stage goes dark. The sound of the train in full speed can be heard, suggesting the passage of time—perhaps two hours. The lights come back and a crackling sound system announces in a marked Bengali accent:*)

'Hum-e khed hai ki kooch majboori ke karan hamari Dilli–Kalkatta Express apne nischit samay se lag bhag tees minute der se chal rahi hai. Is waqat hum Etawah station se guzar rahe hai.'

'Ladies and gentleman, due to some un…abhoidable reason our Dilli–Calcutta Express is running 30 minute late. At this time we are passing Etawah station.'

(*Passengers in different states of repose. Ghosh takes out a black, cloth eye-cover, examines it with affection, tries it on, and takes it off.*)

GHOSH   I never go for any long journey without this.

GAUTAM   What is it, uncle?

GHOSH   This was given to me by British Airways when I went to Toronto for a meeting. I find this eye cover very useful, because God has made our eyelids too thin (*laughs*). So the English people, who are always trying to improve on what God has done, produced this. It is very good for relaxing or sleeping.

GAUTAM   Can I try it, uncle?

GHOSH   Wait. I will give you another one. (*Shows the one in his hand and says*) Calcutta–London. (*Takes another one out of his bag, holds it up, and says*) London–Toronto. I am very lucky British Airways does not fly non-stop from Calcutta to Toronto.

(*He gives the second one to Gautam. The lights fade out, the sound of the train becomes louder. Lights come back on. Siddharth is reading. Jenny is looking out of the window. Bentley is staring blankly. Ghosh's face is turned towards him, though Ghosh does not seem aware of that since he has his eye cover on. Gautam is sitting straight with his eye cover on. Mr and Mrs Trehan also have eye covers, clearly from Ghosh's return journey collection.*)

GHOSH   (*with his eyes still covered, reaches into his pocket and takes out something*) If anybody is being disturbed by the sound of the train, you can use these ear plugs.

GAUTAM   (*whips off his eye cover, looks at the ear plugs*) Where did you get these, uncle?

GHOSH   British Airways.

(*Lights fade. Sound of train becomes louder. Lights come on, there is animated conversation going on in compartment 1.*)

GHOSH   Okay, now I will ask you an even harder question …

(*Lachhu comes in running, goes straight to Siddharth.*)

LACHHU   Sir, is Benaras older or Calcutta?

SIDDHARTH   Benaras.

(*Lachhu runs out.*)

GHOSH   My question is harder than that. Tell me the name of India's national bard?

(*Gautam leans over to Jenny. Evidently he is finding out what 'bard' means.*)

GAUTAM   I know the answer. Rabindranath Tagore.

GHOSH   Wrong …

GAUTAM   Wait …wait … Don't tell me.

(*Mrs Trehan whispers something to Mr Trehan.*)

GHOSH   What is she saying?

GAUTAM   She said Kaifi Azmi.

GHOSH   Wrong again. Just because he writes good poetry does not mean he can fly.

(*Mrs Trehan whispers again to Mr Trehan.*)

TREHAN   Arre, you keep quiet.

GHOSH   No, no. You must not stop her. Nowadays ladies are doing very well in GK. What is Mrs Trehan's second guess?

TREHAN   She is telling Thiru … Thiru …

MRS TREHAN   (*loudly*) Thiruvalluvar.

GHOSH   Wrong again.

SIDDHARTH   I think I have got the answer. Could it be peacock by any chance?

GHOSH   Brilliant, you have got it bang right. You must be a great philosopher.

GAUTAM   I don't understand. How is it peacock? …

(*Lachhu charges in. Goes straight to Siddharth.*)

LACHHU   Are we going east from Delhi, or west?

MRS TREHAN   Buddhu, does he think this is the train to Pakistan?

LACHHU   Madam, please don't waste my time. Which way are we going?

SIDDHARTH   East. You should allow Mrs Trehan or me to take over your job.

(*Lachhu races out, while Gautam leans towards Siddharth to find out how the answer could be peacock. Lights fade. Sound of train becomes louder. Lights come back.*)

GHOSH *(to Gautam)* ... Then one day a real wolf came and the boy started shouting, 'Wolf, Wolf.' But this time no one came because they thought he was bluffing again and the wolf killed the boy. So you see, you must never bluff.

GAUTAM   Yes, I know. I heard that story many years ago.

SIDDHARTH   Now let me tell you another story. There was a boy who was a fisherman. One day, when he finished his morning prayer, God appeared and told him that since he was so good, God would give him a gift. Four days later, he would find a bag of gold in the river. The gold would be his to keep, but on one condition. He would have to tell all the villagers that he had found gold and only if no one went and took it, it would be his. Knowing how greedy people are, the boy realized that the chance of his actually being able to keep the gold was very small. But he was a very intelligent kid and soon he worked out a scheme. The next day when he came back from fishing, he started shouting and jumping that he had found gold in the river. All the villagers rushed to the river. But they found no gold and returned disappointed. The boy did the same thing the next day and once again the villagers rushed out and were disappointed. Again the third day the same thing was repeated. Then on the fourth day, when the boy found the actual gold, he came back shouting and jumping that he had found gold. But the villagers had by now learned their lesson. They laughed at him and no one stirred. The boy went and collected the gold and got to keep it.
So what is the lesson of the story?

GAUTAM   That bluffing is good.

SIDDHARTH   That is what this story says. But coupled with the story that Ghosh Uncle just told you, the lesson is that there are no simple rules in life.

MRS TREHAN   Kahani sahi hai, par ladka to confuse ho jayega.

(Mr Trehan, who was reading Jenny's palm, turns to Bentley. Jenny begins to chat with Ghosh.)

TREHAN Okay, now it is your turn. I will tell you your future. *(Takes his hand and turns it, palm up.)* But first, sir, you will have to tell me when is your happy birthday.

(Train comes to a halt at some station. Familiar station sounds rent the air. People get in and out of the train. Trehan lets go of Bentley's hand.)

BENTLEY Thank God for little mercies.

(A new entrant throws some garbage on the floor.)

GHOSH *(interrupting his conversation with Jenny)* Please be civilized, don't throw garbage here. Garbage must always be thrown out of the window.

(Trehan and Gautam go out of the compartment. A beggar comes on crutches. Goes into compartment 2, asking for money. Kavita gives. This may not be seen, since it is possible to have so little of compartment 2 seen that Kavita may remain unseen most of the time—of course, that changes once the action shifts to her compartment. The beggar walks into compartment 1.)

GHOSH Chalo, chalo yahan se. Kuch nahin hai hamara paas.

SIDDHARTH Fortunately, I do have some small change.

(Reaches into his pocket and gives the beggar a note. So does Jenny.)

BENTLEY God knows I have seen more beggars on this trip than in my previous years on earth. I don't think we should encourage them by giving them money. *(Turning to Siddharth)* If I were you, I would not give them any money at all.

SIDDHARTH If you were me, you would give money, because I gave.

BENTLEY You are wrong. I would not. You just saw me. I did not.

SIDDHARTH But that is because you are you. If you were me, you would do exactly what I did, which means that you would give … .

GHOSH   One animal that I like a lot is the sambar. You know sambar?

JENNY   (*loudly, to Ghosh*) O Mr Ghosh, I feel exactly the same way. I love all animals, but the sambar is special. It is such a beautiful animal, with sad eyes. I think hunting all animals should be banned.

(*Trehan and Gautam, conversing, are on their way to the compartment, slowly, with stops.*)

TREHAN   All human beings are same. Hindu, Muslim, Christian, we are all brothers. You must love everybody.

(*Gautam says something.*) What? (*He bends down to hear.*)

Yes, even Bentley. ... I agree that is a little difficult. But you must. Actually, Indian climate is little harsh. But gradually he will get used to it and then he will be fine person.

You see Gautam, in India we have so many kinds of people. I tell you that is what is so good about India. We must learn to appreciate different kinds of people, different culture. I am North Indian, but I like South Indian people very much. Mrs Trehan and I lived in Madras for one year. Since then, I am even liking South Indian food—idli, dosa, sambar ... . Actually I am liking sambar more than dal.

GHOSH   I also like spotted deer and bisons.

JENNY   (*as Trehan and Gautam enter the compartment*) I do also, but the sambar is really special to me.

TREHAN   Arre vah, I am saying as North Indian I like sambar, but this young lady is even more daring than me. She is from North America and she is having the courage to say she is also liking sambar.

JENNY   I sure do. With its brown-beige colour it looks so lovely.

TREHAN   The colour is nice, I agree. But, more importantly, I tell you, it is full of protein. I give full credit to South Indians for this great discovery.

JENNY But I thought you can find sambar in North India as well.

TREHAN Nowadays you can find it everywhere. Even in Washington, my friends in the Indian embassy are telling me. Wherever there is Udipi restaurant, there is sambar.

MRS TREHAN Kamaal kardiya, ek to janwar ke bareme …

(*The ticket collector comes into the compartment.*)

TC Ticket, ticket.

(*The passengers show their tickets and the TC ticks off names from his chart.*)

BENTLEY Can you explain to me why this train is running two hours late?

TC (*rudely, in case you did not know how TCs speak*) No. This train normally runs three hours late. I cannot tell you why it is travelling so fast today.

BENTLEY That's very funny. Surely someone knows why this train is running late.

TC For a satisfactory answer to that, you have to know Indian history and sociology, and maybe economics.

GHOSH And why leave out zoology? Some poor animal may have come out on the track and slowed down the train. (*Laughs. Mr Trehan and he shake hands over the joke.*)

But I think Bentley is right. Many times the train was completely stopped with no reason.

In fact, half an hour ago, it was so still, with everybody sleeping, I thought for one moment that the whole world has come to a complete halt.

(*The TC looks at the papers in his hand and turns to Siddharth.*)

You are in the wrong seat. You should be in the next compartment (*points to compartment 2*) in 8C. Please shift because there will be a passenger coming to this seat at the next station. (*And to Gautam*)

And you also have your seat on the bunk in that compartment, but no one will come here I think. But if someone comes, please move there to uncle's compartment.

(*TC exits.*)

MRS TREHAN   You know, Ghosh, if everything stops, how can we be travelling again?

TREHAN   (*laughing*) Ghosh is not saying everything is permanently stopped. Ghosh's theory is that the world had stopped, but has restarted. (*Laughs and shakes hand with Ghosh.*)

SIDDHARTH   I think Mrs Trehan's unease about the possibility of the world restarting after a total halt is reasonable. If everything in the world really ever came to total halt, it is not clear that things could restart.

GHOSH   No no, Professor Chatterjee, I think you are maligning the Indian train drivers unnecessarily. Just because they take a short break, it is unfair to say they will never get up again.

TREHAN   Ghosh is 100 per cent right. I sleep at night, but I get up every morning.

SIDDHARTH   That is because there are processes that keep in motion inside you all through the night. If everything came to a halt …

MRS TREHAN   Ram, ram ….

SIDDHARTH   In that case she would have reason to be concerned. But don't worry. Fortunately, we are all hale and hearty. I feel very bad leaving this compartment since we are having such nice conversation, but I have to go. (*He starts collecting his belongings.*)

JENNY   Why don't you forget Calcutta, and join us for the Benaras trip?

SIDDHARTH   That's very sweet of you. I wish I could, really … . But I am not a free man, Jenny.

TREHAN   Yes, that will be very nice. My nephew is having a large bungalow. You can stay with us.

JENNY   Be a sport. Be adventurous. Just change your plans. I have done it so many times ... set out for one place and end up somewhere else. ... Is it because of that lecture you have to give in Calcutta?

SIDDHARTH   I'd merrily give that lecture a miss. But you know I am carrying the paper of a famous British professor, who could not come and has sent me his lecture. And I have agreed to read it out. He will be very upset if his lecture is not presented at the conference.

TREHAN   Then tell us one more philosophy puzzle before you go. It is good for thought.

GHOSH   Yes, puzzle-solving is good way to pass time on train. In British Airways they were giving all little children a puzzle book. I tell you these English people really know how to awaken young minds.

SIDDHARTH   Well, okay. I will give you a partly physical puzzle. This is called the Indian Rope Trick and is meant to help foreigners get close to Indians. Does any one have two pieces of string? About this long (*he stretches his arms wide*).

GHOSH   No problem. I have one string but you can cut it. (*He rummages in his bag, and pulls out a string.*)

GAUTAM   British Airways, uncle?

GHOSH   No, Mrs Ghosh ... aunty.

TREHAN   (*laughs, turning to Mrs Trehan*) Ghosh is really funny. Now he is calling the little boy aunty.

(*The string is cut into two with Mrs Trehan's scissors.*)

SIDDHARTH   Okay. Now, Mr Bentley, will you please step forward here.

BENTLEY   No, let someone else.

TREHAN   No, no, this is your turn. I am sure this will not hurt
    you.

JENNY   Come on Mr Bentley, be a sport.

(*Bentley steps forward, reluctantly.*)

SIDDHARTH   And I need one more volunteer ...

(*Ghosh is up on his feet, before Siddharth can finish.*)

You see philosophical thought has to be supple. You need
abstract reasoning, logic, mathematics. But it is more. It needs
you to view things unusually, from angles that most people, even
trained scientists, may not think of doing. This is what made Socrates
who he was. This is what marked the originality of the Buddha.
So, here is a little puzzle to test your philosophical acumen. ... And,
in this case, also a little of your physical flexibility.

(*He ties a knot around Bentley's right wrist and then another knot around
his left wrist. [This is explained in Figure 1.] He pulls and tugs at the
string to show that Bentley's arms and the string now constitute an unbroken
loop, somewhat like a huge rubber band or a hoola-hoop.*)

Okay? Now Ghosh come here.

(*With the second string he ties a knot around Ghosh's left wrist, passes the
string through Bentley's loop, and ties a knot around Ghosh's right wrist
(see Figure 1). This show should be properly visible to the audience, since
it offers some of the pleasures of a magic show.*)

I hope you are all convinced that these two persons are tied
inseparably. There seems to be no way for them to separate from
each other without opening up one of the knots. But that is
what they must do, free themselves without opening a knot. You
have 3 minutes.

GHOSH   Are we allowed to cut the strings?

SIDDHARTH   Good question. No. ... Now don't waste time, get
    started.

GHOSH   I know ... it's easy. ... Bentley, just stay there.

(He puts one foot into Bentley's loop, contemplates the situation and puts the other foot in. They are almost in an embrace. But now Bentley has got involved. He mutters, 'Wait, wait. I have to come over your shoulder.' During the next few minutes there are acrobatics. The following conversation is interspersed with the action.)

BENTLEY   I think it will work if I come down from one of the bunks through your string.

(He climbs onto a bunk and tries to go head down into Ghosh's loop.)

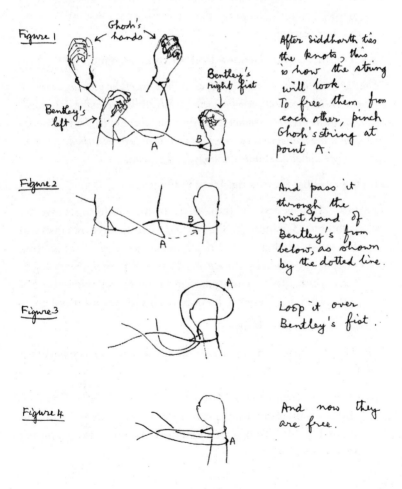

Figure 1

Ghosh's hands

Bentley's right fist

Bentley's left

A   B

After Siddharth ties the knots, this is how the string will look. To free them from each other, pinch Ghosh's string at point A.

Figure 2

B

A

And pass it through the wrist band of Bentley's from below, as shown by the dotted line.

Figure 3

A

Loop it over Bentley's fist.

Figure 4

A

And now they are free.

MRS TREHAN   But if climbing the bunk is necessary, then this puzzle can only be solved in Indian trains.

TREHAN   True, very true. But perhaps the puzzle can be solved only in Indian trains.

GHOSH   But Socrates had never been in an Indian train.

(*Mrs Trehan is now involved, trying to manoeuvre Bentley's hand and twist Ghosh's arm, asking one of them to step back, the other forward, and so on.*)

SIDDHARTH   I should clarify that this puzzle has nothing to do with Socrates, excepting that it requires a form of Socratic contemplation.

MRS TREHAN   Wait, Bentley. Both of you, just stand.

(*They stand with their hands apart, as in the start of the puzzle, as shown in Figure 1. She looks at them for a few seconds, walks up, and in 10 seconds or so has them free [see Figures 2 to 4 for how this can be done]. Bentley and Ghosh are now separated, standing with their arms stretched, the knots intact. They are quite stunned at how this happened.*)

BENTLEY   That is amazing. How did you do it?

TREHAN   That is easy. In India there is one Goddess, ... we are calling her Chamundi. She has eight hands and three eyes and has great—rather I should say, amazing—power for getting people out of tricky situation. My wife is praying everyday to Chamundi. And Chamundi is listening to her whenever my wife is praying to her. Chamundi can solve every problem.

GHOSH   But that is cheating.

(*The TC passes down the corridor. Is clearly displeased that Siddharth is still there.*)

SIDDHARTH   I had better not incur the wrath of the Indian Railways anymore. I suggest you play the same game again, but disqualify Mrs Trehan or Goddess Chamundi from coming to anybody's aid.

(As he speaks, he has picked up his belongings and moves over to compartment 2. There is only Kavita there. The partition between the compartments should be shifted right, so that compartment 2 now occupies centre stage with only a fraction of compartment 1 visible.)

SIDDHARTH   I am sorry to encroach on your nice private domain, but I can't help it. It is by order of the Indian Railways.

KAVITA   I don't own the property. Make yourself comfortable. It is so rare to find a compartment in an Indian train with so few people, isn't it?

(Silence, while Siddharth settles in.)

SIDDHARTH   You are right. This room is like a Buddhist meditation room in comparison to that compartment. That is like a juvenile detention centre. It was fun though ...

KAVITA   I was enjoying the conversation as well ... what little I could hear.

SIDDHARTH   What was the most interesting thing you heard?

KAVITA   Well, I could not really hear that much. But I liked the bit about whether, if everything came to a halt, things could restart. That is an interesting question.

SIDDHARTH   And did you agree with me?

KAVITA   I could not hear that much.

SIDDHARTH   I felt no. Things could not restart.

KAVITA   I guess that is right. Though I don't quite know why I agree.

SIDDHARTH   I have not thought through it to know the answer myself. But see if everything stops, the earth, you, the protons and atoms inside you and inside me ... and everything. It does seem obvious, right? That things cannot restart?
One way to reason is this. Whatever happens at any time is caused by the state of the world just before that. Now if the world is motionless for some time, no matter how brief, there is a time

when the world is motionless and just before that the world was motionless. Hence, motionlessness causes motionlessness. Hence, once there is no motion, there cannot be any motion.

This has lots of interesting implications. It means we can never invent a TV that can switch itself on. If it does, it is because we have programmed that in and there are small actions occurring inside it throughout. (*Pause.*)

What I wonder is if we are reaching this conclusion purely by deduction or whether this is just a fact of life that motion cannot come out of motionlessness.

KAVITA The fact that you reach this conclusion without ever having experienced the stoppage of everything suggests, doesn't it, that you are reaching this conclusion by deduction.

(*Siddharth stares at her in disbelief.*)

SIDDHARTH Are you a philosopher? I am sorry to inflict this trivia on you ...

KAVITA No, but I was taught philosophy. In fact, by you—at NDU.

SIDDHARTH Really?

KAVITA You taught us epistemology.

SIDDHARTH You were one of the students in that crazily large epistemology class? Which batch?

KAVITA Ten years ago.

SIDDHARTH What is your name?

KAVITA Kavita Sharma. But I was Kavita ...

SIDDHARTH Puri?

KAVITA Professor Chatterjee! I can't believe it. You remember me?

SIDDHARTH If it wasn't for the low-voltage lighting, I would have recognized you earlier.

KAVITA   That is impressive.

SIDDHARTH   It is not that impressive. I never forget pretty faces. Besides, I was charmed by you (*smiles teasingly*).

KAVITA   (*blushes, though I am clueless how that can be shown to the audience*) You certainly gave no evidence of that.

SIDDHARTH   I see you took your Gilbert Ryle very seriously. Emotions do not always have to be hung from balconies ...

KAVITA   But some little evidence, no?

SIDDHARTH   I was the professor. How could I?

(*Longish pause.*)

I remember you because, when I lectured, you looked troubled ... puzzled the way a good philosophy student ought to be.

KAVITA   Thank you so much for clarifying. No one should be under any misconception.

(*Siddharth laughs.*)

SIDDHARTH   There can be two reasons for remembering someone.

KAVITA   Yes, there *can* be, but I doubt if there were.
But in *our* case I can tell you, the majority of us—your students—were in love with you.

SIDDHARTH   Now you tell me that? And that too with a ring on your finger and a bindi on your forehead. You should have told me that at that time—I would have been a happier being. But wait ... you are not telling the truth. Half the class was boys.

KAVITA   Well since all of us girls certainly were; so if one boy was in love with you, that would make it a majority of us. And in such a large class, I am sure (*giggles*), there was at least one boy in love with you.

SIDDHARTH   (*laughs*) But you really should have told me that.

KAVITA   About the boy who was in love with you? (*Kavita laughs.*)

But you never told me you found me charming. I could have done with that confidence booster.

SIDDHARTH You were my student. I did not want you to feel uncomfortable.

KAVITA How come you don't mind making lone female train travellers feel uncomfortable?

SIDDHARTH My God, this is like a conversation with Sherlock Holmes. ... I just remembered you were quite an all-rounder. Didn't you play basketball for the university and win some inter-university match?

KAVITA That was such a long time ago...

By the way, Professor Chatterjee, congratulations! ... for the prize, I mean. You must be very happy.

SIDDHARTH Thank you. I was pleased but not as much as most people think. You appreciated philosophy, so you will understand ... one does not do philosophy to get anything out of it—for recognitions from people in no position to recognize. One does it because it involves reasoning so beautiful, so arresting that you cannot get away from it. And partly also because it is such a wonderful way to get away from reality.

KAVITA Do you need to?

(*From the wings, Trehan appears, wearing Ghosh's eye cover, trying to walk very straight, down the train corridor. Gautam comes charging out, behind him, followed closely by Ghosh.*)

GAUTAM Out, out. I just saw you touch the left wall and then the right wall. The rule is all the way till the end with maximum one touch.

TREHAN One touch on each wall. I am not out.

GHOSH Gautam is right. You are out. The rule was maximum one touch ...which wall does not matter.

(*Lights fade. The sound of the train becomes louder. The lights come back. Kavita and Siddharth are comfortably seated and in mid-conversation.*)

KAVITA   And gradually one gets used to it. So Siddharth … . Are you sure?

SIDDHARTH   Yes, absolutely.

KAVITA   Well it does sound nice … so Siddharth it has not been that bad, … at least no longer. The last year, with the involvement in the school, it has, in fact, been quite nice, Siddharth.

SIDDHARTH   Don't overdo it now …

KAVITA   (laughs) I will, Siddharth. Now that you have given me permission, it is my prerogative.

(Siddharth laughs. Then, after a pause, thoughtfully …)

SIDDHARTH   I don't know. Your tamely giving in to your parents and agreeing to marry someone, whose—pardon me for saying this—only interest in life seems to be to make money, does not fit in with what little I know of you.

KAVITA   You are getting my parents wrong. They love me ….

SIDDHARTH   I know you will resist this. When one has decided on a particular course of life for oneself, one no longer wants to admit to the unpalatable aspects of what one has accepted.
But you know Kavita, it does not still all fall into place. It is as if there is a piece of missing information. Why did you accept the life you have for yourself? It does not fit in with your adventurous self. How could you accept being such a non-entity…? Well not being such a nonentity, at one level we all are nonentities, but accepting a life where you are treated as such.

KAVITA   That is not so difficult. I am a very resilient woman. Did you know, tomorrow is Simone de Beauvoir's birthday?

SIDDHARTH   You are really a nerd. Imagine knowing Simone de Beauvoir's birthday. Is it really her birthday or you are just relying on the certainty of my ignorance?

KAVITA   I know that only because it is also my birthday. … During my weaker moments I try to learn from her … to be strong like her. But it is difficult.

On those dreadful days that I was telling you about, I would tell myself what philosophers have repeatedly reminded us ... of ... of the insignificance of man in relation to the universe ...

SIDDHARTH Bertrand Russell called it the 'cosmic insignificance of man ...'. Carry on, I'll tell you later why Russell had got it all wrong.

KAVITA In fact at my lowest times, I made it a point to sit for a while on the terrace late into the nights and look at the stars. With much of the city lights having gone off by then, the sky would be studded with stars, twinkling, literally twinkling the way fairy tales tell you stars do. I would think of the enormous size of the stars, the great distances between the stars, of our galaxy, of the many other galaxies. I would feel infinitely small, insignificant, and for that very reason peaceful.

SIDDHARTH That is so interesting. I used to do the same thing to cope with adversity. But in my case it did not work for too long.

KAVITA Why, what happened?

SIDDHARTH One evening, after contemplating about the cosmic insignificance of man, as I stepped into my bedroom, I saw a trail of ants. They were tiny, almost miniscule. And I felt large, huge. And I thought of bacteria and molecules and atoms ... all busy going about their daily chores and I started feeling as large as a galaxy itself. After all, an atom does resemble a planetary system with a sun in the middle and planets going around it, like electrons. Now blow up that atomic planetary system sufficiently and perhaps you may be able to see civilization on one of the electrons, just like there is civilization on earth, and in that miniscule civilization there could be someone like me, who is in turn made up of atoms many times smaller than the atoms that make me. And soon I realized that just as largeness is endless, so is smallness. You can enter into a labyrinthine endlessness inside a single atom. And then ... and then ... I realized that Russell was wrong.

In a cosmic sense we are neither small nor large. Either claim is meaningless. Do I make sense?

KAVITA   Not only do you make sense but I should thank you for having destroyed the one talisman I had.

(*Lights fade. The sound of the train becomes louder. Lights come back on. Siddharth faces Kavita, his hand touching the edge of her sari. She is not uncomfortable.*)

KAVITA   And I don't think it was just infatuation. I really was in love with you.

SIDDHARTH   I see you choose your tense very carefully. But thank you. I have a great suggestion. Come away with me to Calcutta. Just hide in the train when Benaras comes.

KAVITA   I should not have said so much and put you in a tight spot. But anyway, you have nothing to worry. I am sure my bindi and ring are a source of great comfort.

SIDDHARTH   No, Kavita, I mean it.

(*In compartment 1, everybody is sleeping, except Gautam, who is fidgeting about, unable to sleep.*)

GHOSH   (*in a very sleepy voice*) Gautam, why don't you go to Chatterjee uncle and tell him to tell you a story? I am sure he can tell you a nice children's story.

(*Gautam walks over to compartment 2. The door is shut. He fidgets with it and opens it.*)

GAUTAM   Uncle, you are awake?

(*Siddharth and Kavita are both taken aback by this sudden intrusion. Siddharth takes a moment to recover.*)

SIDDHARTH   Aah Gautam. You have come at a very good time.

GAUTAM   (*puzzled by that remark*) What uncle?

KAVITA   (*giggling*) Uncle is saying that you have come at a very good time. You have saved uncle (*pause*) ... from getting bored.

GAUTAM   Uncle, everybody is sleeping in that compartment. Can you tell me a story?

SIDDHARTH   (*hesitates for a moment and then*) Okay, come up here. (*Helps him onto the bunk.*) I will tell both of you a nice story.

(*Kavita settles in snugly on her seat to listen to the story.*)

SIDDHARTH   There were two good friends, Ritu and ... and Anu. They used to live in a lovely little barsaati in Defence Colony. No. No. They lived in an apartment on Kasturba Gandhi Marg.

GAUTAM   You first thought they lived in Defence Colony and then remembered that they lived in a house on Kasturba Gandhi Marg?

SIDDHARTH   That's right. I forgot for a moment.

For some time Ritu had been a little worried about Anu. Anu seemed distracted, a little depressed ... And on many weekends she would go off somewhere without telling Ritu where she was going. This was not normal, Ritu felt. You see, they had known each other from college. ... No ..., from school, when they were 15 years old.

GAUTAM   Uncle, it is difficult to remember everything, isn't it?

(*Kavita laughs.*)

SIDDHARTH   Yes, especially at my age.

KAVITA   You have a very very nice uncle, Gautam.

GAUTAM   Yes, I know.

SIDDHARTH   And you have a lovely lovely aunt.

GAUTAM   What is happening to the story?

SIDDHARTH   Now, 10 years later, they were not girls any more, they were working women. For all these years they told each other everything. Between them there were no secrets. So naturally Ritu was puzzled and also a little hurt about Anu's recent behaviour. She wondered how she could help Anu.

Ritu remembered how supportive Anu had been when ... when that stalking affair started. This chap called Ravi, to whom Ritu had once been introduced at a party, had started following Ritu everywhere. He sent her letters professing undying love for her. But Ritu disliked him and was actually quite terrified of him.

Once Ritu, Anu, and their friends went for a picnic to Faridabad.

GAUTAM   Uncle, picnics are great fun, na?

SIDDHARTH   They are. But this time it was not much fun, because suddenly near Badkhal Lake Ritu realized that a pair of eyes was watching her all the time.

GAUTAM   Uncle, is this a horror story?

(*Kavita laughs.*)

SIDDHARTH   No, my dear Gautam, don't worry. (*Gautam nods.*) The eyes, Ritu soon realized, were those of Ravi. Clearly, he had begun stalking her even when she was travelling outside Delhi.

GAUTAM   Uncle, 'stalking' is the same thing as following someone?

SIDDHARTH   Yes, following someone all the time.

KAVITA   What useful words uncle is teaching you.

SIDDHARTH   Ritu was scared but Anu told her not to worry, that she would in fact speak to Ravi, telling him not to do this. Actually Anu was not scared of Ravi at all. In fact, in an odd way, she was quite attracted to him.

KAVITA   Gosh, this is becoming a psycho thriller. Gautam, you have a very nice uncle, (*giggling*) who, however, has no idea what children's bed-time stories are all about.

GAUTAM   But the story is very interesting.

SIDDHARTH   (*turning to Kavita*) See?

Some months went by and Ritu could take it no more. So she lodged a complaint with the Delhi police. And the police immediately served a restraining order on Ravi.

KAVITA   Now we know this is a story.

SIDDHARTH   He was not to go within a mile of where Ritu was.

That seemed to work. Weeks, months, went by, no sight of Ravi. In the beginning whenever she was alone in the streets, she would look back over her shoulders obsessively. But gradually her fear went away, she felt liberated, and put Ravi out of her mind. In fact, now her only worry was for Anu's welfare.

What could it be? Suddenly Ritu knew what she would have to do. She would have to follow her one Saturday or Sunday and see where she went. It was not nice to follow a friend, but she was doing this for the sake of the friend; so she did not feel bad.

So one morning, when around 10 o'clock she heard Anu leave the house, she quickly put on her sneakers and got out behind her. She could see Anu in a beautiful mauve sari, walking briskly towards CP. Within minutes she had reached the inner circle of CP. Anu walked along the inner circle in a clockwise direction. Ritu decided to keep the maximum possible distance without losing sight of her quarry. She calculated that that would be about one-third the circumference of the circle. So when Anu was near Jain Book Depot, Ritu was somewhere near Art Today.

Suddenly Ritu felt worried that her worst fears may be right. CP had recently become a den of addicts and traffickers. Perhaps Anu was headed to some dealer. Ritu was so absorbed in these thoughts that she did not realize that she was going past Jain Book Depot a second time. What was Anu up to? Ritu smiled to herself. Anu was probably just out window-shopping. CP was always such a feast for the eyes, with those Rajasthani art works being sold on the pavement and beautiful paintings outside Dhoomimal Art Gallery. The December nip made walking a pleasure. So much so that Ritu did not realize that she was coming up to Jain Book Depot for the third time. She suddenly felt worried and tired. She could not keep up with this anymore. Outside Galgotia's she saw some empty chairs and plonked herself down on one. She was reconciled to the fact that she will now lose sight of Anu. But so be it. She could not keep up with this madness anymore.

But then, miraculously, Anu slowed down and stopped.

After 10 minutes, feeling a little rested, Ritu got up and began walking slowly. And soon, almost like magic, Anu was also up, walking once again.

It was then that the more chilling thought struck Ritu. Was Anu going mad? This was utterly irrational—going round and round one circle. Ritu smiled, for it struck her that if someone was watching Ritu, that person would think the same. But of course Ritu was not mad or irrational. She was doing this on purpose; she was following someone. ... But if her seemingly odd behaviour was rational, why could not Anu's seemingly odd behaviour be rational?

And suddenly she froze. For she realized in one blinding flash that Anu was not aimlessly going round CP. She was going around for the same reason that Ritu herself was going around. And that is when she realized with a shiver that she herself was not out of danger from Ravi.

(*Long pause. Kavita's gaze is fixed on him, and his on her.*)

KAVITA   Gautam's fast asleep. I don't know if it was your lullaby or the fact that it is close to four in the morning. Why don't you also try to catch some sleep? I wonder when we will reach Benaras. The train is running so late ...

SIDDHARTH   Come with me to Calcutta. I mean it. Come, Kavita.

KAVITA   Are you off your head? What about these tourists? Leave them with Lachhu?

SIDDHARTH   Why not? That way they will have a trip so memorable, they will never ever forget.

KAVITA   You are crazy, Siddharth. You hardly know me.

SIDDHARTH   I knew you many years ago.

KAVITA   But you don't know the person I am now. ... And what will happen after Calcutta? I will be left to fend for myself.

SIDDHARTH   No, we will live together.

KAVITA   I thought you did not believe in the institution of traditional marriage.

SIDDHARTH   We do not have to marry. And even if we do, since you are already married, ours will not be a traditional marriage. Moreover, in case this was not clear from my lectures, I should clarify that what I have been against is the *institution* of marriage. Society, I believe, would be better off without it. But if the institution is there and everybody gets married, I see no compelling reason for a single pair of persons not to marry.
Don't tell me you are wedded to the middle-class value of once wedded, wedded for ever.

KAVITA   I am not, but I have a feeling you don't know what you are trying to commit yourself to.

SIDDHARTH   You talk in riddles Kavita. I am a simple philosopher, I don't understand the householder's riddle. Come away with me, Kavita.

KAVITA   I would love to; I would love to throw everything aside, every little thing I own, ... and go away with you ... wherever you take me.

SIDDHARTH   ... And we will vanish in the milling crowds of Calcutta. We will live in an overcrowded part of North Calcutta, in a sultry bylane where balconies rub shoulders with balconies ...

KAVITA   ... in an old house with tinted windows and wrought iron grills. And with so many people living in that neighbourhood it will be easy to vanish ... to go shopping in the local bazaar, to the fish market where all the local Bengalis go, and be unnoticed ... to be just the two persons who came from nowhere, who have no history.
But I can't ... I can't. I don't even know you want to ... I am scared, Siddharth.

SIDDHARTH   If I were not saddled with this damn lecture by this blessed British philosopher, I would have got off in Benaras.

I would have no qualms missing my own lecture but I don't think I can do this to him.

(*Pause.*)

KAVITA   I need to be excused. Can you please help me? Get me my crutches from under the seat.

(*Siddharth looks hesitant, puzzled.*)

SIDDHARTH   Crutches? (*Gets her the crutches.*)
How did this happen? Did you hurt yourself recently?

KAVITA   This happened the year I left college—nine years and two months ago. ... I had an accident ... DTC. ... I'll be back.

(*She goes out of the cabin door towards the bathroom. The light focus shifts from this compartment to compartment 1, which is in virtual darkness. Bentley has got up and is nudging Ghosh, who is fast asleep. Ghosh opens his eyes, screams, pulls the sheet over his head, turns the other way, and tries to sleep. Bentley nudges again, Ghosh peeps, screams, and again covers his head.*)

TREHAN   (*from his bunk*) Ghosh, what has happened? Why you shouting?

(*In this scene, there is no need to show the full breadth of compartment 1. It could be only Ghosh's bunk that can be seen. Trehan could be outside the audience's view. In that case, the sleepiness in his voice should make it clear that he is in bed.*)

GHOSH   Nothing. I occasionally have nightmares in which I see the same man with a dark face. He comes and calls me. Today, I was little extra frightened because the face looked white.

TREHAN   Ghosh, you are not seeing the dream. Mr Bentley is trying to call you.

BENTLEY   (*softly*) Mr Ghosh, I am awfully sorry to trouble you. But can you please give me one of your British Airways eye cover? I am not being able to sleep, and I feel that will help.

(*Ghosh props himself up and starts rummaging in his bag and speaking simultaneously.*)

GHOSH   This will certainly help. It is better than Calmpose.

TREHAN   I am thinking it may also be better than Valium.

GHOSH   I don't need it. Here, please use this.

(*Bentley takes it ….*)

Actually I would advise you to keep second one. Soon the sun will come out and I think if you are not used to the Indian sun, one cover may not be enough. (*He thrusts a second one into his hand.*)

TREHAN   I do not think British Airways is designing this for use in Indian Railway. British people are occasionally mean. What do you think, Ghosh?

MRS TREHAN   (*disembodied voice in the semi-darkness*) Kindly sone ki koshish kijiye.

(*Complete silence for a few seconds. Lights fade out and the sound of the train becomes louder. The train's sound system crackles into life:*)

'Ladies and gentleman. Our Dilli–Calcutta express is about to reach Benaras Station. In the night our driver drove the train very fast … above the speed limit set by the Japanese expert. We are therefore lucky to have arrived in Benaras (*pause*) with only one-hour delay. The train will stop here for 45 minutes. Passengers getting down here kindly make sure to take your belongings … otherwise other people are taking them.'

(*Sitar music, typically All India Radio, comes on. There is pandemonium. People moving about, taking their luggage down. Mr Trehan, Mrs Trehan are getting down. We catch a glimpse of Lachhu helping Kavita. Siddharth keeps sitting. The passengers spill out onto the platform.*

The focus shifts to the platform. On the right hand side of the stage, Lachhu comes in, holding up the hoarding that says 'GATT, formerly WTO'. Foreigners, including Bentley and Jenny, mill around him. Some distance away there is a pile of suitcases, amidst which Kavita is sitting, looking forlorn. Suddenly, causing a bit of a flutter, Gupta charges in, with a garland, looking for Siddharth. As they see each other, Siddharth gets up, and is promptly garlanded.)

SIDDHARTH What a pleasant surprise, Gupta. What are you doing here?

GUPTA I came to see you only.

SIDDHARTH You came all the way to the station to see me?

GUPTA I stay only two minutes from the station.

SIDDHARTH I am really happy to see you, but you must not waste money buying garlands for me every few months.

GUPTA You are going to give such an important lecture. I think mala is fully deserving.

SIDDHARTH Gupta, do you think you can read a philosophy paper?

GUPTA Sure. It will be my pleasure to read what you write. But I cannot say I will be able to understand it.

SIDDHARTH The understanding is not important. I am actually not talking of my lecture but that of another philosopher. And I am not talking of your reading it for yourself but to the conference audience in Calcutta.

GUPTA But, Professor, I am not going to Calcutta conference.

SIDDHARTH I know that. But can you go to Calcutta? Can you take my place in the train? I will then get off here in Benaras. I need to very badly. I'll tell you about that later. (*Beginning to speak very quickly.*) But tell me, can you board this train in the next half an hour or so, go to Calcutta, and read out the paper I will give you? (*He rummages in his bag and pulls out a paper and gives it to Gupta.*)

GUPTA That will be a great honour. But won't conference organizers object?

SIDDHARTH Of course, not. This is my decision. I shall give them a letter about my not being well and appointing you to read the paper on my behalf.

GUPTA But my English is not so good.

SIDDHARTH   Your English is just fine. It is high time we learnt that content matters more than the accent. Besides, English is not our native language anyway.

Look, there is no time. You come with me and I will give you a few important documents. (*They start moving towards the compartment where Siddharth's luggage is kept.*) Then you run home as fast as you can. Pick up some clothes and come back and take my ticket and be off. Actually, if you are going, you may as well read two papers ...

(*They go into the compartment, talking, and then Gupta is seen running out.*)

LACHHU   (*gesticulating at the tourists*) Please be patient. Mini-van will be here soon to take us to hotel.

BENTLEY   (*quite friendly now*) We don't mind waiting. Why don't you tell us a little history of Benaras in the meantime, as you had promised?

LACHHU   What? ... What?

BENTLEY   You told us in Delhi you will tell us a little history of each city before we get there. But you forgot to tell us about Benaras.

LACHHU   What? ... What you telling?

JENNY   Lachhu, Mr Bentley is saying, you should tell us a little about the history of Benaras that you were beginning to tell us in Delhi. Remember? When you had to suddenly go away because you remembered you had to meet your son's class teacher. So tell us some of the history now, while we wait. Please.

LACHHU   Oh ... history? Benaras history? Benaras is valdest citty. Very valdest citty. Wayne the tame cum the river Ganga the people catlest the centium dreem. Then teem the city keltum needem ees the Benaras. Porter eshsquare ven the lesteeng isleting dam. Motherater is thel tenny ven the Benaras history.

(The foreigners nod, unsurely.)

Gem kalidusten gest come. Ven the mandrin kartejenna vel ten lethen is Agra, Jaipur, Patna, ... Agra ... and the Benaras history ...

(Siddharth furrows through the crowd, with his suitcase, unwittingly carrying the garland in the other hand. Sets the suitcase down. Shoulders Lachhu aside.)

JENNY *(genuinely pleased)* Professor Chatterjee, what a lovely surprise.

(Siddharth whispers something to Jenny.)

SIDDHARTH Benaras is one of the oldest cities of India, in fact, of the world. It was originally called Kashi. What is amazing about this city is that it has been continuously settled and a centre of commerce, trade, and religion from as far back as the sixth century BC. The Buddha delivered his famous sermon just a few miles outside the city, at Sarnath. In the sixth century AD, the famous Chinese scholar and traveller, Huan Tsang, came to this city. By some yardsticks, the interaction between India and China in those days was more than it is today, in this so-called age of globalization. It was a remarkable relationship, based not on domination and commerce, but the interchange of culture and literature.

Ladies and gentleman, I wish I could be with you throughout this entire trip of yours, but I cannot, as I just explained to Jenny. There are many reasons for that but one of the most compelling is that the sum total of what I know about Benaras I have already told you.

I think there is no getting away from the fact that you will not get your money's worth on this trip. The owner of Ganga Travel and Tours, Mr Sharma, has taken you for a ride. But don't feel too bad. People have been duped before. Whole civilizations have been destroyed by the greed and expansionism of some nations and people.

Moreover, while you may have lost a little bit of your money to Mr Sharma, you may be comforted to know that Mr Sharma is about to lose his wife to me.

(Kavita has walked up to him; she touches his arm and then clings to it. Siddharth does not notice Gupta, who is seen running on to the platform, wearing a tie and an oversized suit, shiny suitcase in tow.)

Today, as you all no doubt know, is Simone de Beauvoir's birthday. As such, this is an auspicious time for Kavita to reclaim her own life.

(Gupta boards the train, waving good bye, and shouts out …)

GUPTA Professor, I highly recommend that you request her to wait one more day only to reclaim her life, because tomorrow is even more auspicious. *(Pauses, and then speaks louder, to counter the noise of the train starting up.)* It is Hrittik Roshan's birthday.

(Complete silence. All actors freeze, except Gupta, who glides out of the platform, still waving. Music starts up: 'Ankhon hi ankhon me ishara ho gaya.' Kavita breaks into a dance (no limping), Bentley joins in, Siddharth, Jenny, Trehan, Mrs Trehan—everybody on the stage begins to dance, free-hand, simply celebrating life. The others enter dancing from the two wings. The Vice-Chancellor comes in dancing more vigorously, skilfully, and acrobatically than anybody else. As the song fades out, the actors are in a row, bowing and accepting ovation, if there be any. Curtain.)

part six

End of Alliterations

fifteen

Duidoku and Ultimate Duidoku*

D UIDOKU AND ULTIMATE DUIDOKU, THE TWO two-player games that I am about to describe, are games that I developed some time ago. I created these games purely as a diversion from everyday work—for me to play with friends and students. But the games have come to acquire lives of their own, with some electronic versions now available. A user-friendly electronic version of Duidoku, though for a 4-by-4 board (which is less challenging than the original 9-by-9 version), was developed by Michael Rudd Zwolinski and is available on the web (see: http://www. duidoku.com/).

Duidoku can be played anywhere, on an ordinary sheet of paper or, more conveniently, on a regular board, if someone, someday produces the board to play it. I have played Duidoku numerous times and used Duidoku and Ultimate Duidoku in my game theory lectures to illustrate arguments. Ultimate Duidoku requires

---

* The author has made both these games available from his website. Anybody wishing to develop software or to produce these games in some other form for commercial use should acknowledge the source and seek the author's permission.

software to play and is best viewed as an electronic game. To insert a note on etymology, 'dui' denotes 'two' in Bengali and Sanskrit, and so Duidoku connotes a two-player version of the well-known Sudoku.

To play either of these games, you need a board with 9-by-9 squares, with every cluster of 3-by-3 squares demarcated by a separate colour, as in the standard Sudoku board and as illustrated in Figure 12.1. Hence, the board consists of 81 squares and 9 clusters. You also need 81 counters, nine of each marked 1, 2, ..., 9.

As will be evident, if the game is being played on ordinary paper, instead of using counters, players can simply write in the numbers on the board and discard the board after the game is over.

FIGURE 12.1   DUIDOKU AND ULTIMATE DUIDOKU BOARD

Kaushik Basu

Duidoku

Duidoku is played as follows. First, one player (call her player one) chooses a counter (that is, a counter marked either 1 or 2 or ... or 9) and places it in a square on the board. Then player two chooses a counter and places it in an empty square of his choice; and then again player one does the same; and so on.

To describe what constitutes a win, and also to enable me to describe Ultimate Duidoku more easily, let me define an 'illegal move'. If a player places a number in a square, such that the same number is already there in the same row or column or cluster, then the action of the player is an 'illegal move'. The first player who makes an illegal move loses; and in that case the other player wins. If neither player makes an illegal move and the entire board is covered with counters, then the game is declared a draw.

Ultimate Duidoku

Ultimate Duidoku is now easy to describe using the language developed above. It is a two player game in which players make moves just as in Duidoku. The loser is the first person who makes a move that is illegal or it is such that it is impossible to, then on, play the game without making an illegal move. In other words, the first person who makes a move such that it is illegal or it is inevitable that someone will have to make an illegal move thereafter is the loser; and the other player is the winner. If the game has no winner or loser, in other words, it is played till the board is covered with counters and no illegal moves have occurred, the game is declared a draw.

It must be evident that in Ultimate Duidoku one will typically need a computer on hand to recognize when a person makes a losing move. It is, therefore, best played as an electronic game.

A Note for the Game Theorist

These games can also be fun for the theorist who does not want to play them but simply analyse them. Game theorists like to ask what the 'solution' of a game is or, more colloquially, if perfect players were to play this game what will the outcome be? We know from a theorem proved by the German mathematician Ernst Zermelo in 1912 that for any game of this kind the outcome will be the same each time the game is played by perfect players. But which one? For some games we know what the answer is, for others, such as chess, we do not. What I will show is that, in the case of Ultimate Duidoku, perfect players will always end up with a draw. There is no first mover advantage or disadvantage. Since the strategy of ensuring a draw is complex (indeed I do not know what that strategy is), as a parlor game this continues to be interesting, despite the solution being known.

The proof is as follows. Note that no one can lose the game in the first move. No matter which number is placed where, we can always fill the board with the other numbers so that no move is considered illegal. Assume that there exists an nth move where the player who makes that move loses. We have just shown that this n must be greater than 1. This must mean that, no matter how the player makes the nth move, the game thereafter cannot be taken to a closure with no illegal moves. Remember these are perfect players. But this, in turn, must mean that the $(n-1)$th move that was made was such that the player who made that move lost. But that is a contradiction. Therefore, there is no nth move which results in the player losing. Hence, the game must end in a draw.

If perfect players play Duidoku what is the outcome? The answer is not as easy as in the case of Ultimate Duidoku and nor do I know the answer.

Name Index

Carlyle, Thomas, 56
Carroll, Lewis, 116
Cavafy, Constantine Peter, 82
Chakraborty, Shibram, 239, 244
Chakravarty, Sukhamoy, 104,
    115, 117–18
Chelliah, Raja, 119
Chidambaram, P., 23
Chowdhury, Jogen, 130
Clay, Risha, 104
Clinton, Bill, 15, 17
Cohen, Stephen, 20, 46
Condorcet, Marquis de, 116
Corbett, Jim, 17
Cournot, Antoine Augustin J.,
    215, 228, 231
Crowe, Russell, 113
Curie, Marie, 63

d'Agliano, Luca, 90
Dalai Lama, 15–16, 161
Dante, 88
Dasgupta, Partha, 115
Dasgupta, Utteeyo, 191
Dasho Karma Ura, 77
Datta Chaudhuri, Mrinal, 104
Demuth, Helene, 101
Deng, Xiaoping, 138
Dixit, Avinash, 115
Dobbs, Lou, 24
Dodiya, Anju, 128
Dodiya, Atul, 128
Duhring, Eugen, 100
Dutt, Barkha, 125
Dutta, Bhaskar, 99

Einstein, Albert, 104
Emerson, Patrick, 70

Empiricus, Sextus, 10, 106
Engels, Friedrich, 100–2, 126, 218
Erdoğan, Recep, 161

Fanzhi, Zeng, 129
Faumuina, Tiatia Faaolatane
    Liuga, 73
Fleming, Alexander, 94
Fox, Megan, 131
Freeman, Richard, 210
Freud, Sigmund, 234

Galileo, 88
Gandhi, Indira, 28, 121, 139, 157,
    187, 265, 304
Gangadharan, Lata, 191
Gaud, Laxma, 128
Gauguin, Paul, 72, 74
Goh, Gillian, 16
Gordhan, Pravin, 67
Goswami, Omkar, 16
Gramsci, Antonio, 90

Harsanyi, John, 113
Hassett, Kevin, 161
Hazlewood, Charles, 138
Herodotus, 51
Hess, Moses, 100, 226, 320
Hicks, John, 109
Himanshu, 31, 47
Hitchcock, Alfred, 234
Hockett, Robert, 214
Hon, Vivian, 79
Hughes, Chris, 44–5
Hunt, Tristram, 100–2, 126
Hussain, M.F., 127, 130

Intan, 79

Subject Index

200–11, 213, 217, 220, 223–5, 234–5, 313

Christianity, 84

CIA, 107

CNN, 24, 118

CO_2 emissions, 112

Columbia University, 108, 121–2

communism, 171, 176, 216, 232

Communist Party, 125, 137, 138, 234

Communist Party, 19th National Congress, 137

Confucian values, 136

Consumer Protection Act, 144

Cornell University, 6, 8, 69, 112, 161, 239

corporate social responsibility, CSR, 131

Credit Suisse, 204

crony capitalism, 30, 316

culture, 26, 36, 49, 50–1, 53, 58, 80, 84, 118, 127, 129, 130–2, 135, 154, 156, 169, 185–7, 196, 225, 232, 290, 313

Debt Recovery Tribunal, DRT, 153–4

Delhi School of Economics, 98, 104, 117, 239, 256

Delhi University, 128, 263, 265

demonetization, 139, 180–5, 194

dictatorship, 108, 139

Die Brucke, 56

Diepsloot, 49, 67, 69–70

Dodd-Frank, 144

Doing Business, 142, 152, 163, 166, 185

Dow Jones, 143

Duidoku/Ultimate Duidoku, 318–20

Economic and Political Weekly, 46–7, 119

Economic Survey, 28–9, 33, 222

efficiency wage, 122

Emergency, 28, 30, 139, 168–9, 187

environment/climate change/pollution, 18, 42, 45, 50, 75, 77–8, 175, 206

Eurozone, 68, 71, 78, 196, 211

evidence-based policy, 142, 161, 163

Federal Reserve, 123

Filix School, 85–6

Financial Product Safety Commission, 144

financial scam, 142, 146

Financial Stability Development Council, FSDC, 144

Financial Times, 20

Food and Drugs Administration, 144

Forbes, 24

foreign exchange, 16, 23–4, 32–3, 37, 172, 196

full employment, 123

fundamentalism, 96, 105, 235

game theory/ games, 4, 90, 111–12, 149, 191, 228, 231, 318–20

Ganga, 82, 191, 278, 281, 284–5, 312–13

Gary, Indiana, 102

global constitution, 220, 228–9